IMAGES
of America

WEBSTER PARISH

IMAGES
of America

WEBSTER PARISH

John Agan

ARCADIA
PUBLISHING

ISBN 978-0-7385-0604-3

Published by Arcadia Publishing
Charleston, South Carolina

Printed in the United States of America

Library of Congress Catalog Card Number: 00-104880

For all general information contact Arcadia Publishing at:
Telephone 843-853-2070
Fax 843-853-0044
E-Mail sales@arcadiapublishing.com
For customer service and orders:
Toll-Free 1-888-313-2665

Visit us on the Internet at www.arcadiapublishing.com

Contents

INTRODUCTION

Although Webster Parish was not created as a political unit until February 1871, the history of settlement in the parish goes back more than 50 years before that date. Located in the northwestern corner of Louisiana and sharing a border with Arkansas, Webster Parish is very much a part of the piney hill, Anglo-Saxon, Protestant culture of North Louisiana. The first settlers in what is today Webster Parish had already arrived in the region by 1820. By 1835, Minden, the largest town and the parish seat, had already been founded as a community and soon became the largest town in old Claiborne Parish. Thus, the story of the people of Webster Parish must begin years before the parish could be found on any map.

The early settlement in the parish centered along the eastern bank of Bayou Dorcheat. In those years, it was possible for smaller steamboats to come from the Red River through Lake Bistineau into Bayou Dorcheat. The first significant community in the territory covered by modern Webster Parish, Overton, had a brief and tragic history. Settlement in the area of Overton along Bayou Dorcheat (south of modern Minden) had begun in the 1820s. By 1836, Overton had become the parish seat of Claiborne Parish. However, it was located in a low area, subject to outbreaks of disease. A Yellow Fever epidemic in the 1840s turned Overton into a ghost town, and today the site of the town has disappeared under gravel pits. All that remains is a small portion of the town cemetery.

Later communities were more successful. Minden built a booming trade through its port on Dorcheat, although the town was located on a hill several miles from the Dorcheat, a more healthy site than Overton. Soon other communities sprang up in the southern section of the parish and further north on the east side of the Bayou. Dubberly, south of Minden, was settled in the 1840s, and at the same time, settlers were coming into the area of modern Heflin, particularly in the area of Lake Bistineau. In the 1850s, Lanesville, later to be know as Sibley, was settled. Shongaloo, in the northern half of Webster, emerged on the east side of Dorcheat near an existing Native-American village. The bayou was the lifeline of the parish in those days, and is still a unifying factor today as it runs the length of the parish.

By the time of the Civil War, the southern and eastern sections of what is now Webster Parish had achieved a fairly high level of civilization and were emerging from a frontier era. Minden was home to a successful female college and located on the main stagecoach route across North Louisiana. While the fighting of the Civil War did not affect this area of the state, the aftermath of the war brought profound change. Minden was briefly occupied by federal troops during 1865, and local white citizens were forced to adjust to the newly freed slaves gaining citizenship and voting rights. The black citizens were equally unaccustomed to exercising their newly earned rights. Fortunately, while there were some violent episodes in the Webster Parish area, the violence was not as severe as in many other locations. Perhaps one reason for this was the absence of significant numbers of outsiders coming to the parish after the war. Webster Parish was created as a political maneuver to increase Republican voting strength in North Louisiana, so the parish does owe its existence to the political strife of Reconstruction.

In the 1880s, the railroad came to Webster Parish as the east-to-west line of the Vicksburg, Shreveport and Pacific Railroad came through extreme southern Webster Parish. Minden would connect to this line with a small north-to-south railroad, but by 1898 the Louisiana and Arkansas Railroad had constructed tracks covering the length of the parish from north to south. The coming of the railroad coincided with the development of the timber industry in the northern end of the parish on the western side of Bayou Dorcheat. By 1891, the forerunner of the town of Springhill had been founded, based on the harvesting of timber. Soon the small settlement of Cotton Valley, which had been depending on the cotton industry, began to reap benefits from the timber trade. Sarepta also emerged as a thriving community as the timber industry grew. In Minden and southern Webster Parish the effects of the timber industry were also felt. In 1900, Minden became home to the Minden Lumber Mill, which was the fourth largest mill in the world when it was constructed. Further south, the boom town of Yellow Pine grew around the operations of the Globe Lumber Company.

Through the early years of the 20th century the timber boom continued, until the mill at Yellow Pine went out of business and the Minden Mill burned. However, in 1922, the Cotton Valley oil field, which would become the most productive in the state, was discovered and newfound prosperity came to the northern half of Webster. Although the parish did suffer hard times along with the rest of the nation during the Great Depression, both ends of the parish received tremendous economic boosts as the Depression era drew to a close.

In 1937, Springhill was selected as the site for a huge International Paper Mill. This plant would become the major economic power in North Webster for more than 40 years and, even though its presence has been reduced in recent years, it still employs many workers in the Springhill and Cullen area. In the summer of 1941, a huge shell loading plant, the Louisiana Ordnance Plant, was constructed west of Minden. Later renamed the Louisiana Army Ammunition Plant, this plant would operate for nearly 50 years. At its peak it employed more than 8,000 workers and became the main driving force in the economy of South Webster.

Today, both sections of Webster Parish are adapting to new economic realities. Minden/South Webster is attempting to use its proximity to Shreveport to attract retirees, service industries, and Shreveport workers seeking a small-town lifestyle. Springhill has been able to attract several industries with its solid history as an industrial town and is leading North Webster into the 21st century. Enjoy these pages as you see glimpses of the people, places, and events that have made Webster Parish, LA, one of the best places in our nation to call home.

One

North Webster

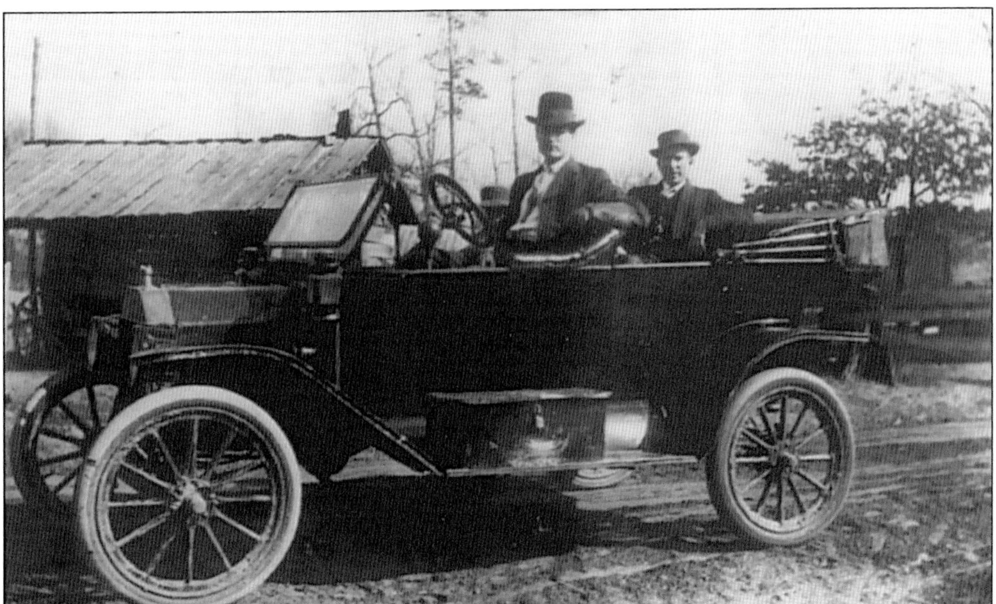

The first car in Springhill is pictured about 1913. The community was less than 20 years old when this picture was taken as it was founded in the early 1890s by the establishment of a mill by the Bodcau Lumber Company. The town was first known as Piney Woods, and then Barefoot before acquiring its present name. (Courtesy of Major DePingre.)

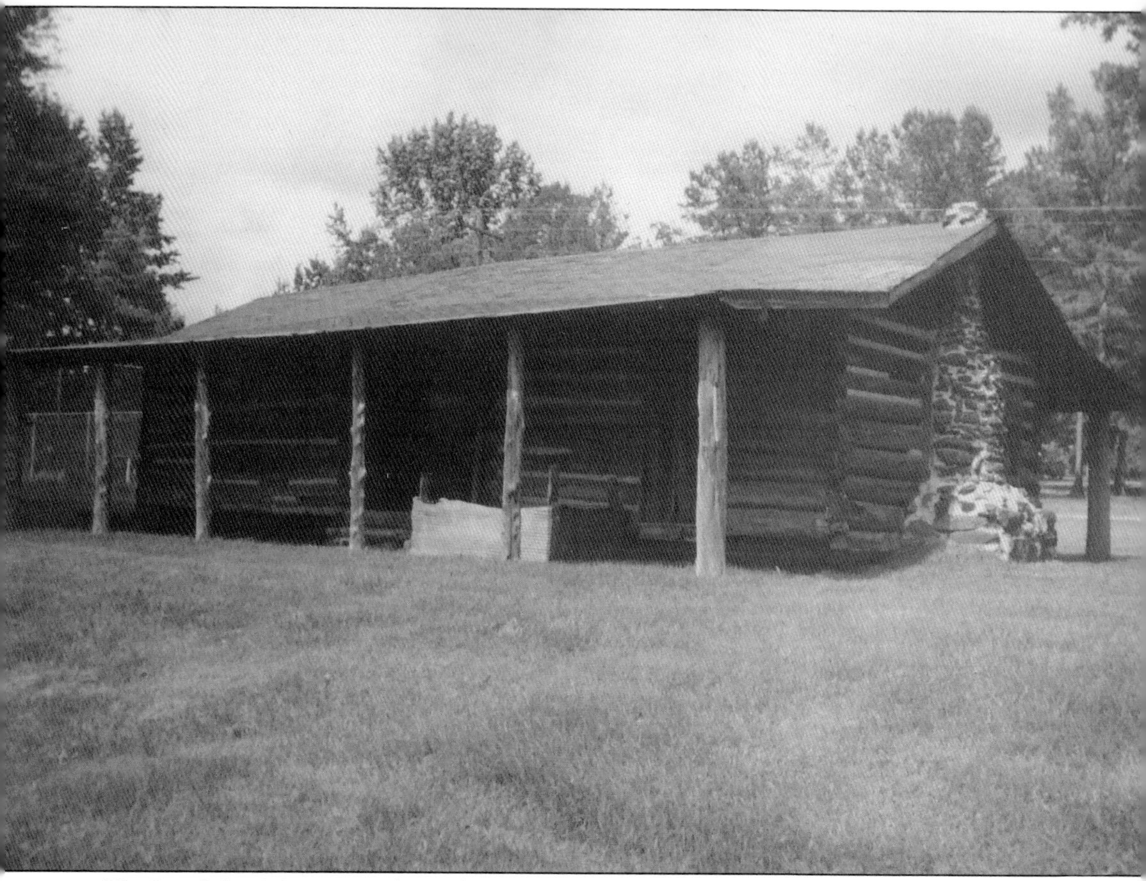

The Log Cabin Museum in Shongaloo is pictured here. This structure is believed to have been the home of Dr. G.J. Wise, a pioneer settler and physician in the community. The settlement where he lived was known as Wiseville because it was settled by seven Wise brothers. It was located south of a Native-American village in the region. The community north of the village was called Shongaloo. Eventually Shongaloo absorbed the Native-American village and Wiseville to form modern Shongaloo, and the original settlement is today called Old Shongaloo. Dr. G.J. Wise served as a surgeon in the Confederate Army during the Civil War. One traditional story from the area is that the chief of the Native-American village attempted to negotiate a swap of wives with Dr. Wise since the chief believed Mrs. Wise was prettier than his squaw.

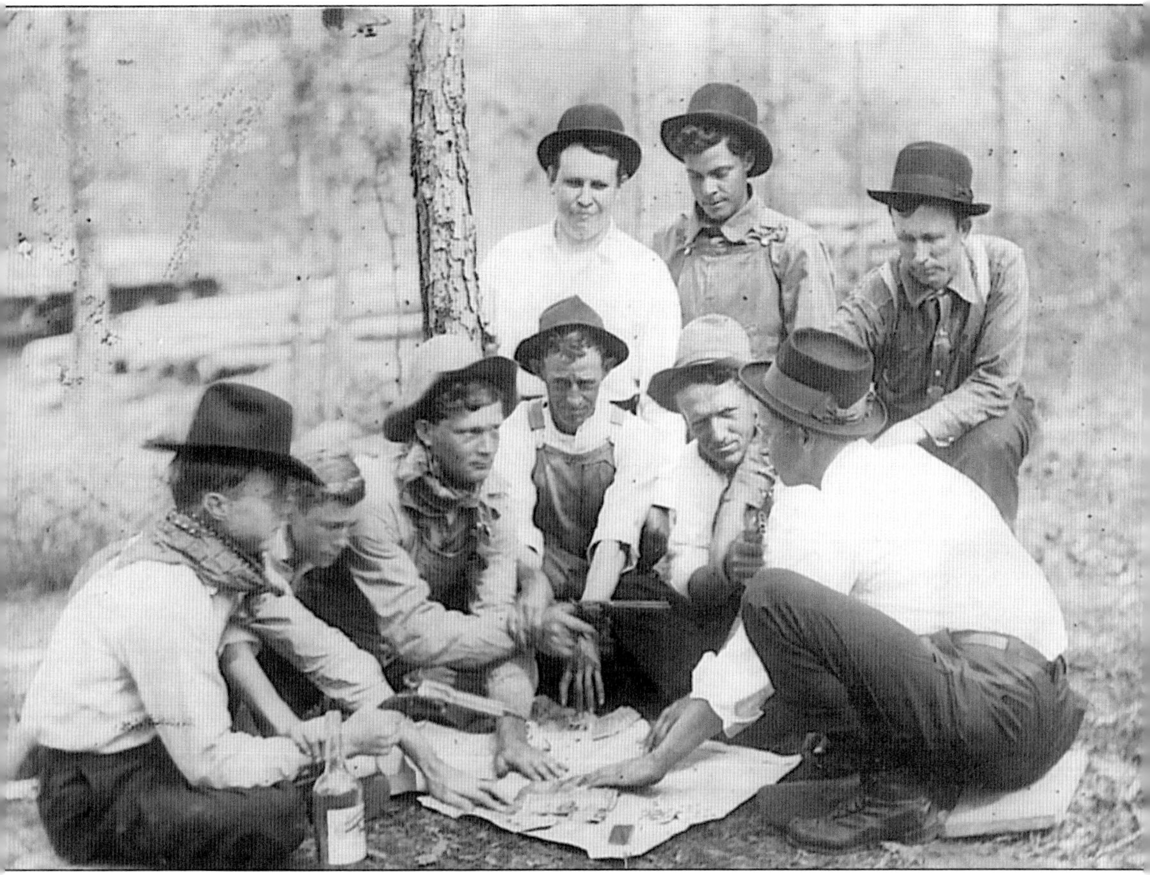

This group of young men from the Evergreen or Shongaloo area attempted to portray all the evils associated with gambling in this prank picture, *c.* 1880. Notice the two drawn guns, the desperado-like bandannas ready to be pulled up to conceal the face, and the prominent display of the liquor bottle. It appears that the "bandits" are in the process of robbing the winner of the card game as he reaches to pull in his winnings. This picture was probably intended to shock the parents of the young men in the image, and was probably a great success. (Courtesy of R.O. Machen Jr.)

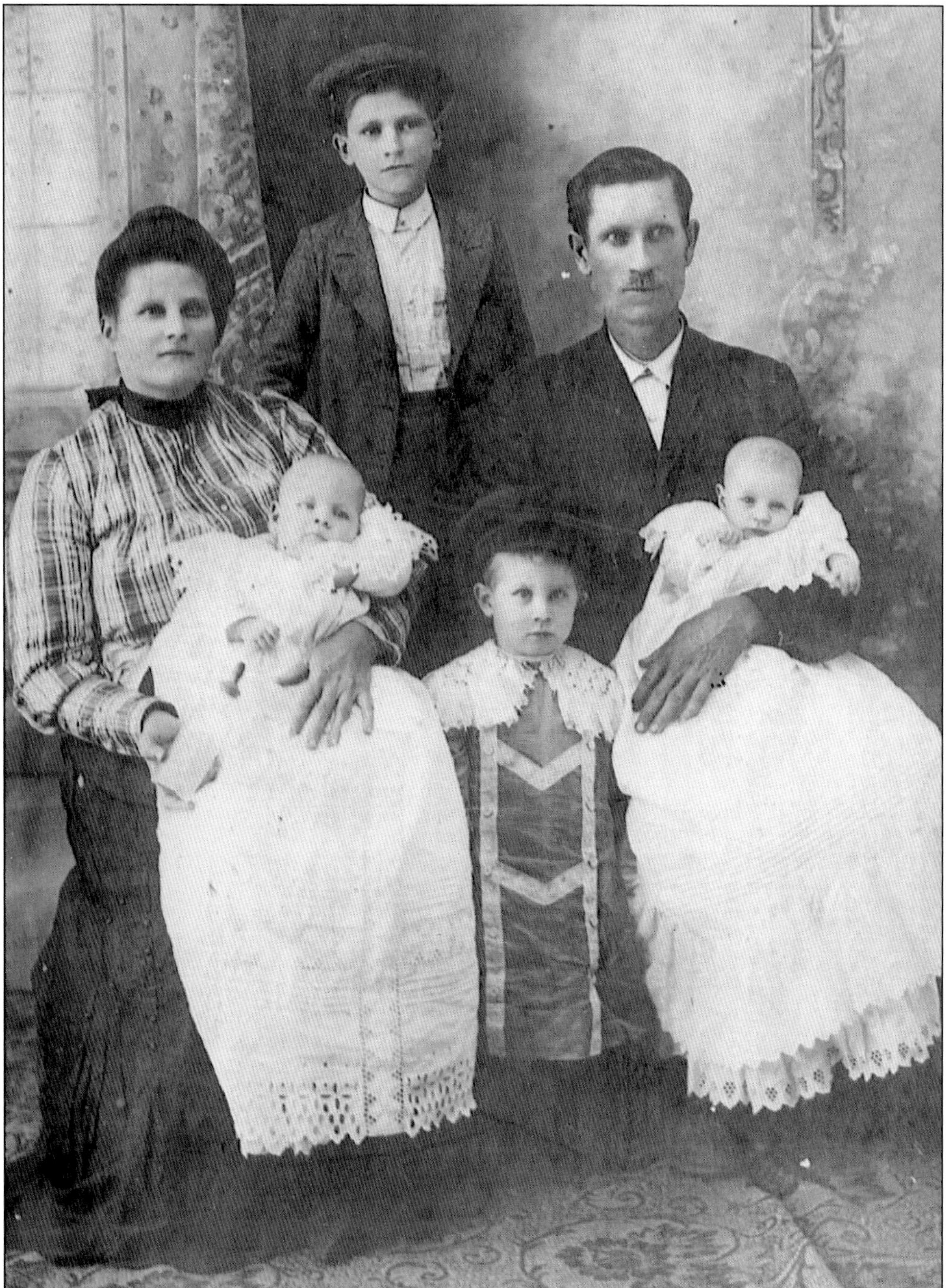

The John Kirkley family is pictured in the 1890s. Seated are Love Lewis Kirkley (holding her infant son, Bernice), and her husband, John Kirkley (holding their infant daughter, Beulah). Bernice and Beulah were twins. The small child standing between the parents is Alton, with his brother Johnny standing in the rear. Johnny Kirkley, the young boy in this picture, would later be very prominent in public affairs in Webster Parish and played a key role in the building of the Caney Lakes near Minden in the late 1930s. (Courtesy of R.O. Machen Jr.)

Pictured here is W.S. Martin of Evergreen in 1880. His daughter Lela would marry R.O. Machen, who became a teacher, coach, principal, and superintendent of schools of Webster Parish. Their son, R.O. Machen Jr., has been prominent in banking and public service in the parish. W.S. Martin's grandson, Matt Martin, also became prominent in education in the parish, serving as a teacher, coach, principal, and retiring as assistant superintendent of schools. (Courtesy of R.O. Machen Jr.)

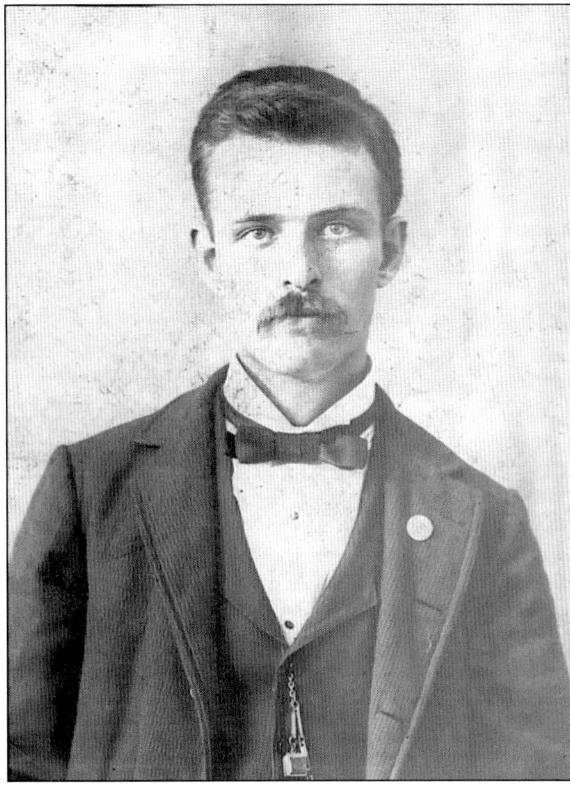

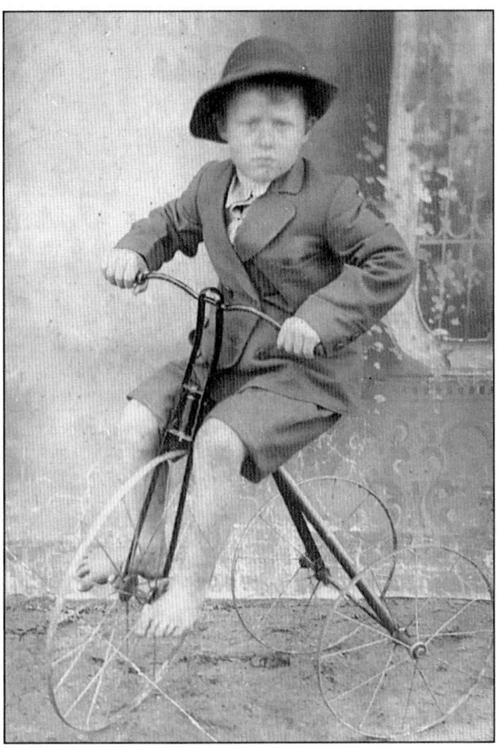

William "Bill" Martin was the son of W.S. Martin and father of Matt Martin. He is pictured here c. 1910. Mr. Martin was a successful cattleman and farmer in North Webster for many years. (Courtesy of R.O. Machen Jr.)

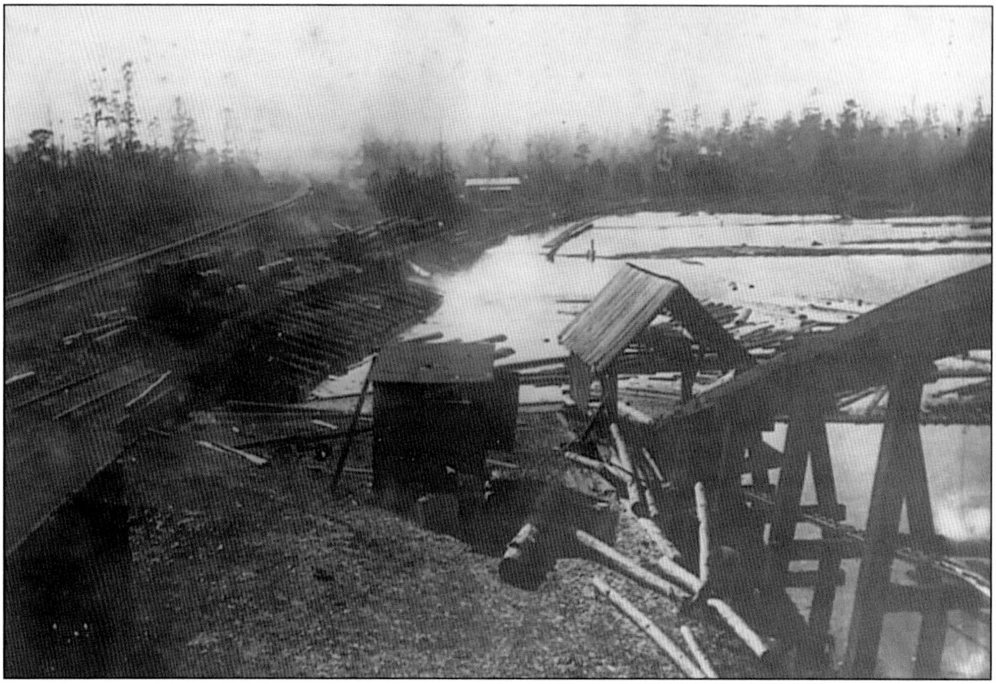

Seen here is a log sluice at one of the many lumber and sawmills in the area of northern Webster Parish. The timber industry was responsible for much of the growth on the west side of Dorcheat Bayou in the Springhill area. (Courtesy of Major DePingre.)

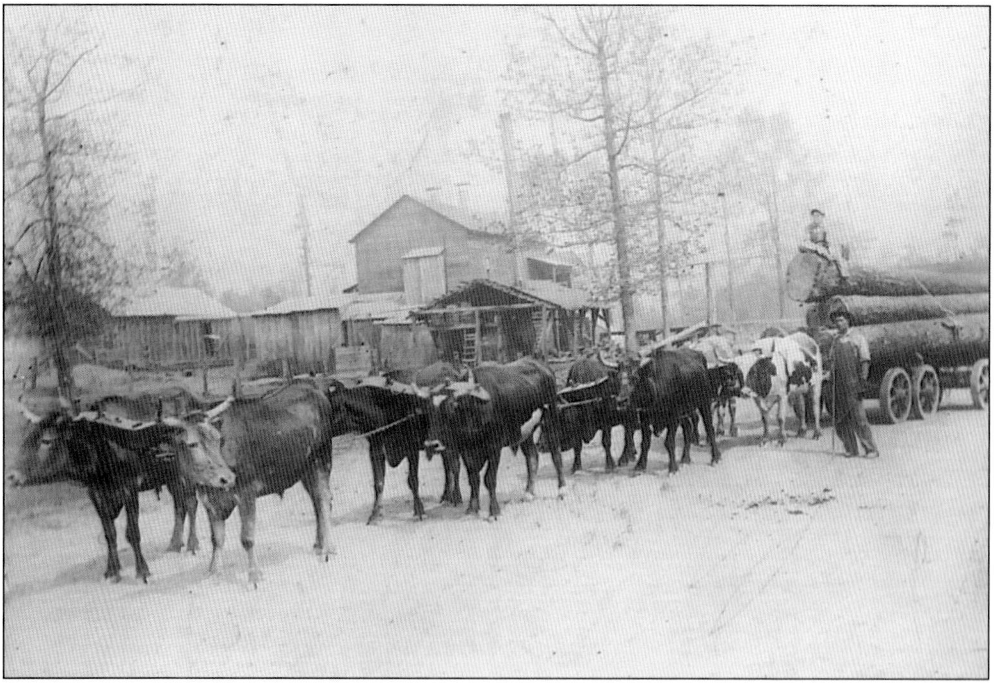

An ox team pulls a log wagon in Springhill in 1914. The wagon is passing by the Springhill Gin on Spring Branch Road. Sitting on top of the logs is "Tap" Machen. (Courtesy of R.O. Machen Jr.)

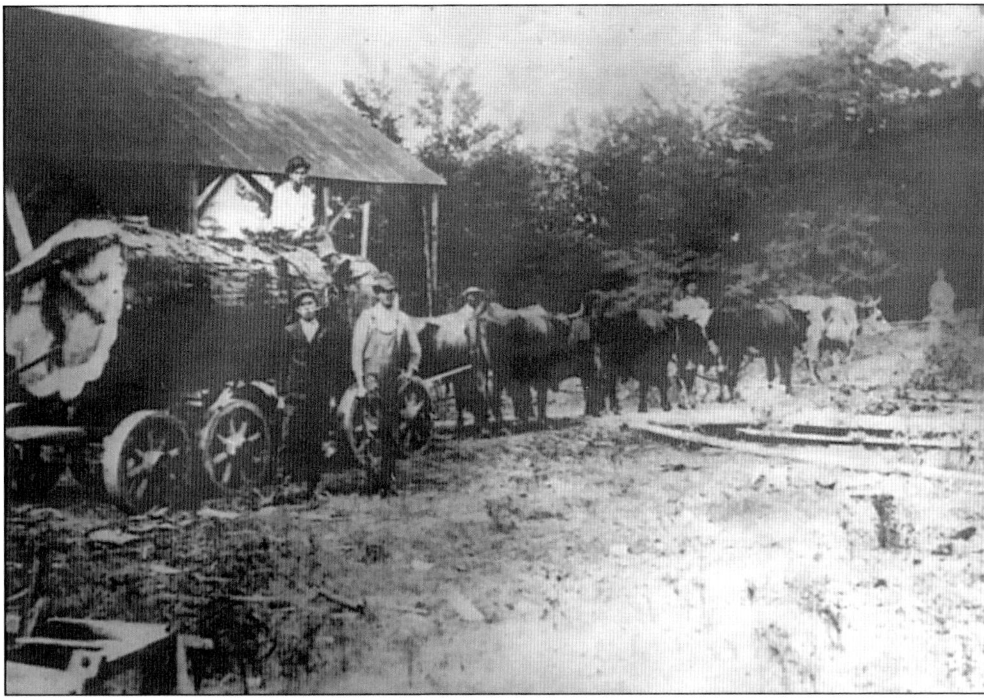

Several loggers and a team are pictured as they haul away a large tree in the Sarepta area in the first few years of the 20th century. (Courtesy of R.O. Machen Jr.)

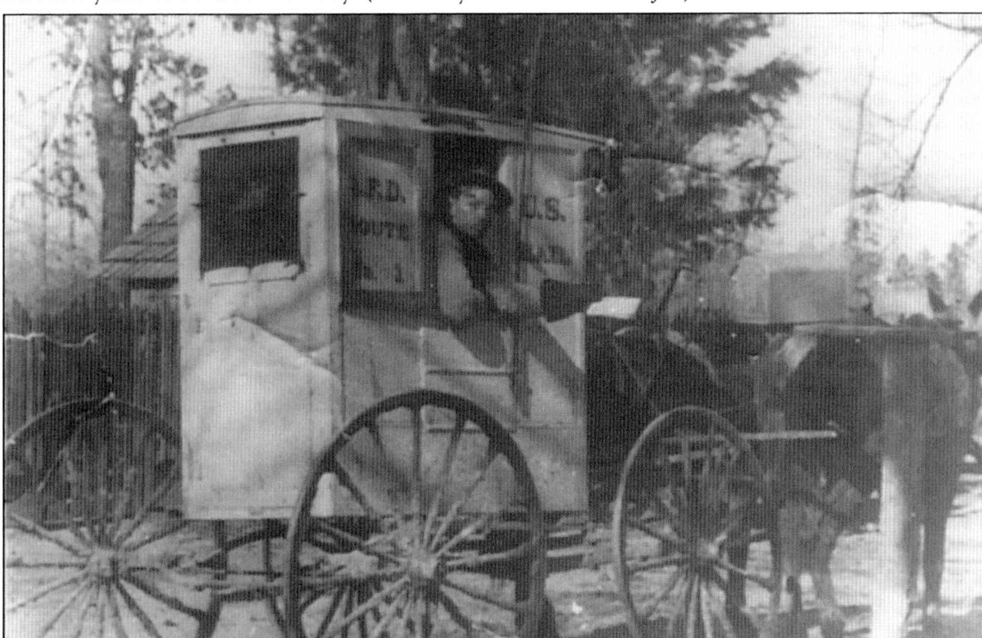

This is the U.S. Mail delivery wagon in Sarepta some time after 1907. You can see the inscription "RFD" on the side of the wagon. The first rural free delivery in Webster Parish was not established until 1907. Before then, rural residents had to come into town to pick up their mail. (Courtesy of Major DePingre.)

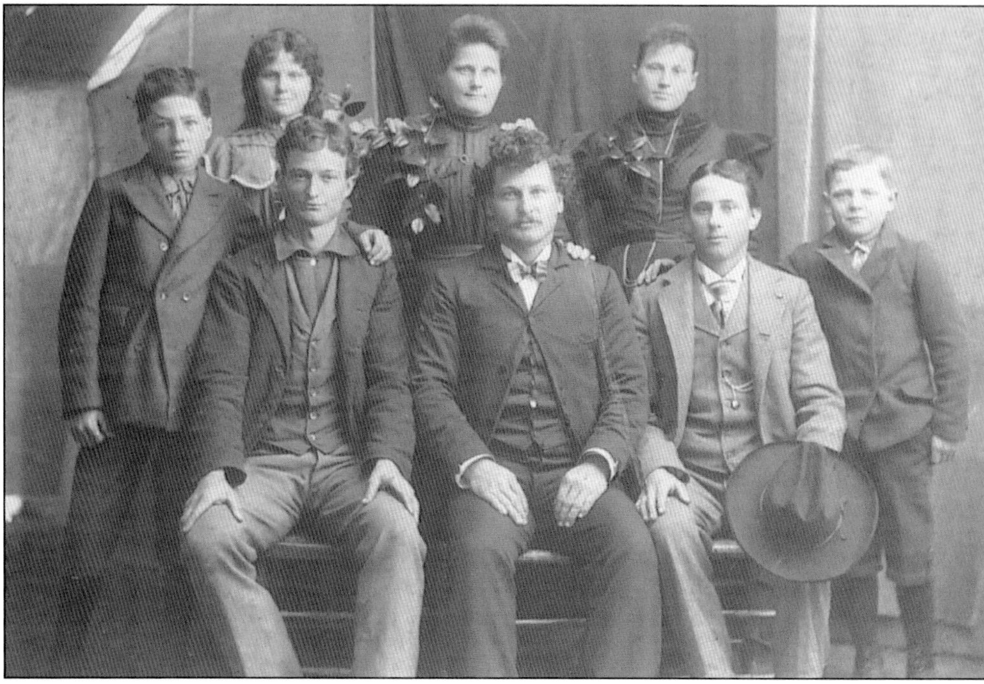

Pictured above is the Lewis family around 1875. Love Lewis, second from left on the back row, was pictured earlier in this book as Mrs. John Kirkley. Seen from left to right are as follows: (front row) Will Lewis, Jake Lewis, Mack Lewis, and Nolan Lewis; (back row) Rose Lewis, Love Lewis, Mary Elizabeth Lewis, and June Lewis. (Courtesy of R.O. Machen Jr.)

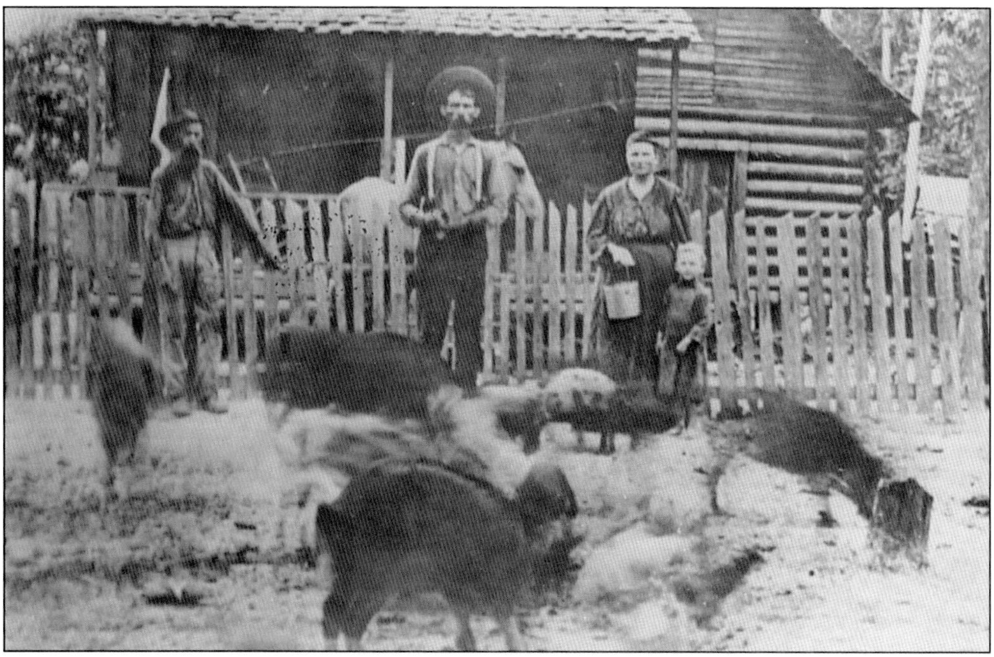

The James Pruitt family is pictured in front of their Evergreen home in 1908. The Pruitts have been leaders in the farming community in the parish for many years. Various family members have held key positions of leadership in organizations such as the Farm Bureau.

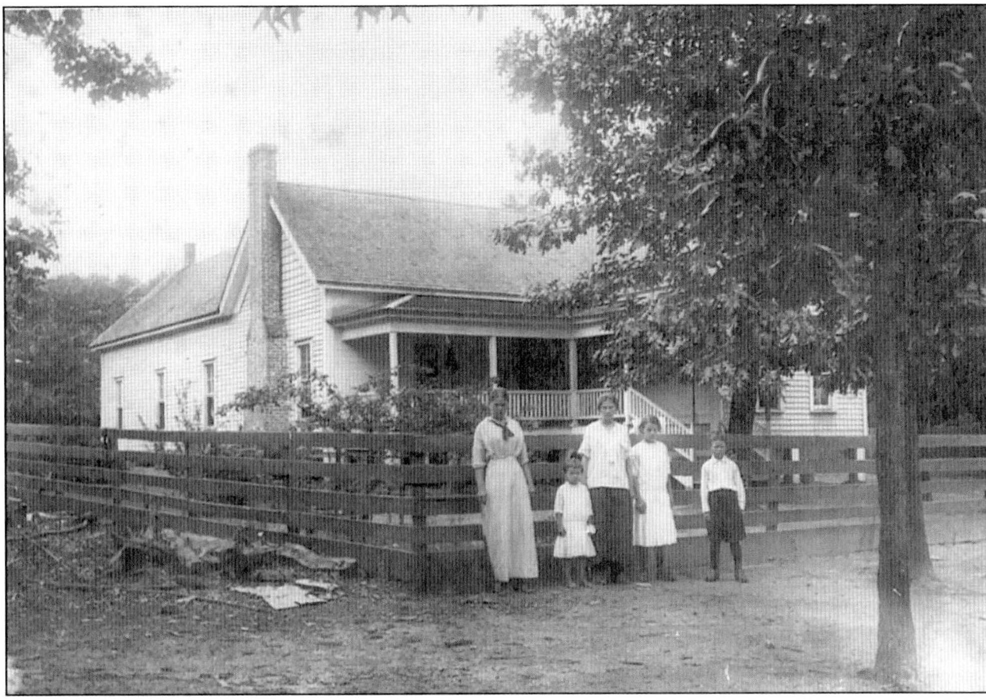

The children of W.S. Martin are pictured in front of the family home in about 1915. From left to right they are Emma Martin, Lela Martin (later Mrs. R.O. Machen), Winnie Martin, Sally Martin, and William "Bill" Martin. (Courtesy of R.O. Machen Jr.)

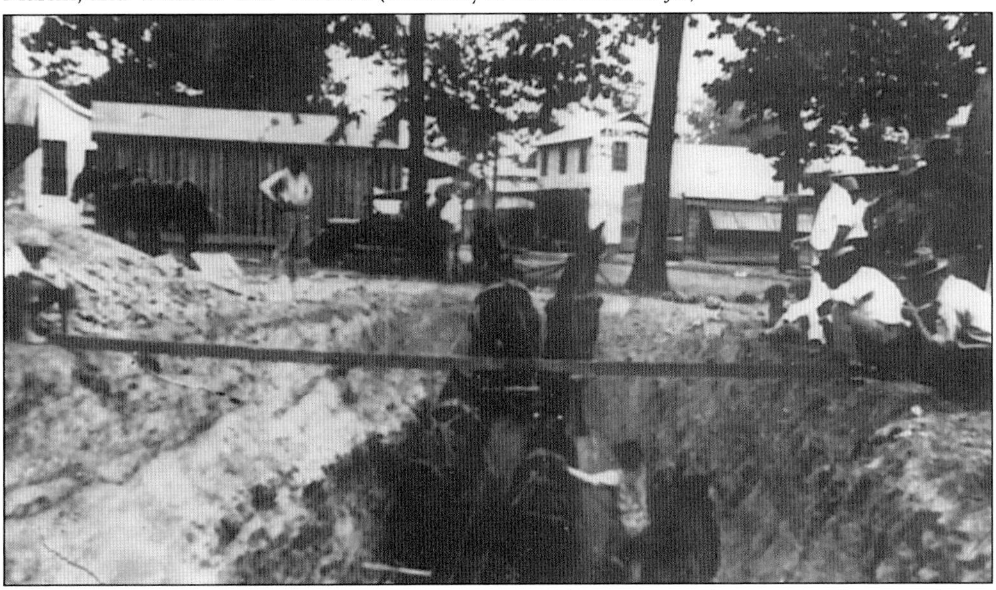

Street construction on Cox's Station in Cotton Valley is pictured in 1924. This was during the years when Cotton Valley was one of the fastest growing communities in Louisiana. After the discovery of the Cotton Valley Oil Field in 1922, the population swelled and all sorts of businesses and industries relocated to the tiny community, which had previously depended on timber and its namesake, cotton, as an economic base. The oil and gas industry is still a key employer in Cotton Valley today. (Courtesy of Major DePingre.)

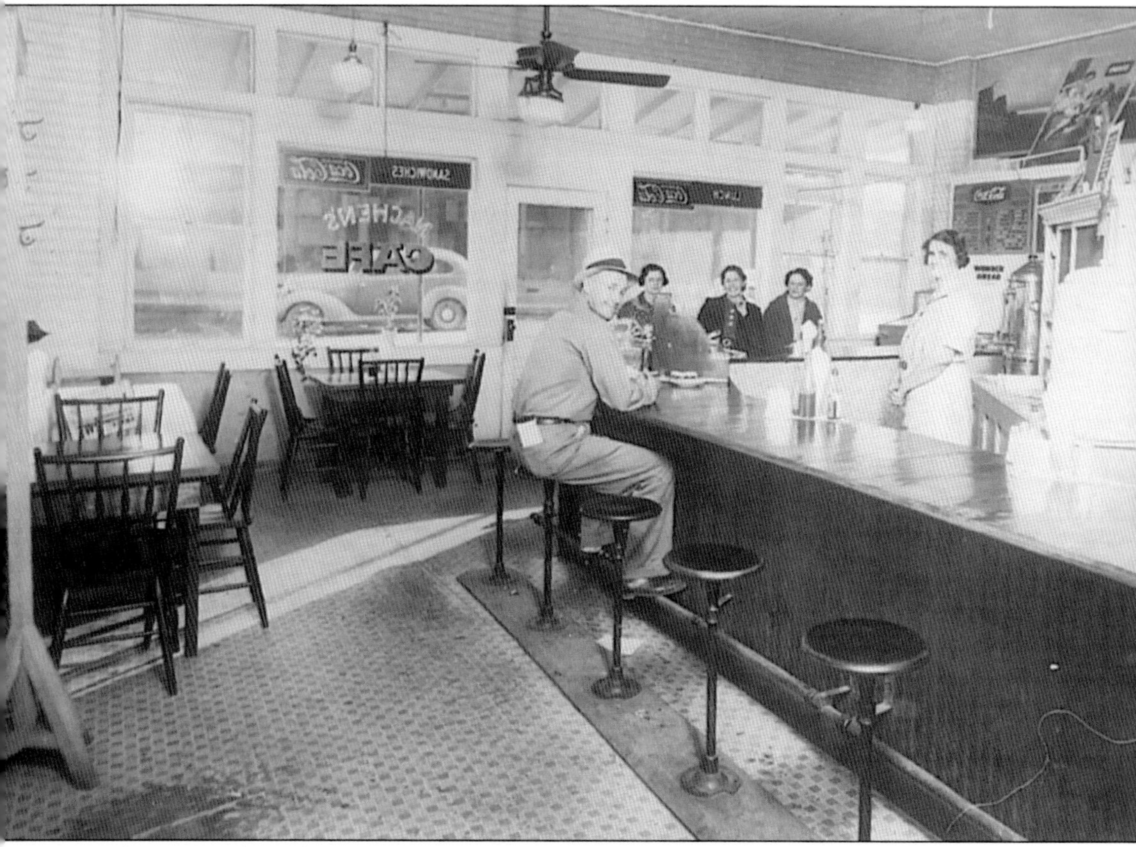

The Ritz Cafe in downtown Springhill is pictured about 1937. Standing behind the counter is Mrs. Ella Machen, owner of the cafe. Her son, T.O. Machen, is seated at the counter. The ladies in the background, from left to right, are Mrs. Sam Jernigan, Mrs. Malock, and Mrs. Sally Mitchell. (Courtesy of R.O. Machen Jr.)

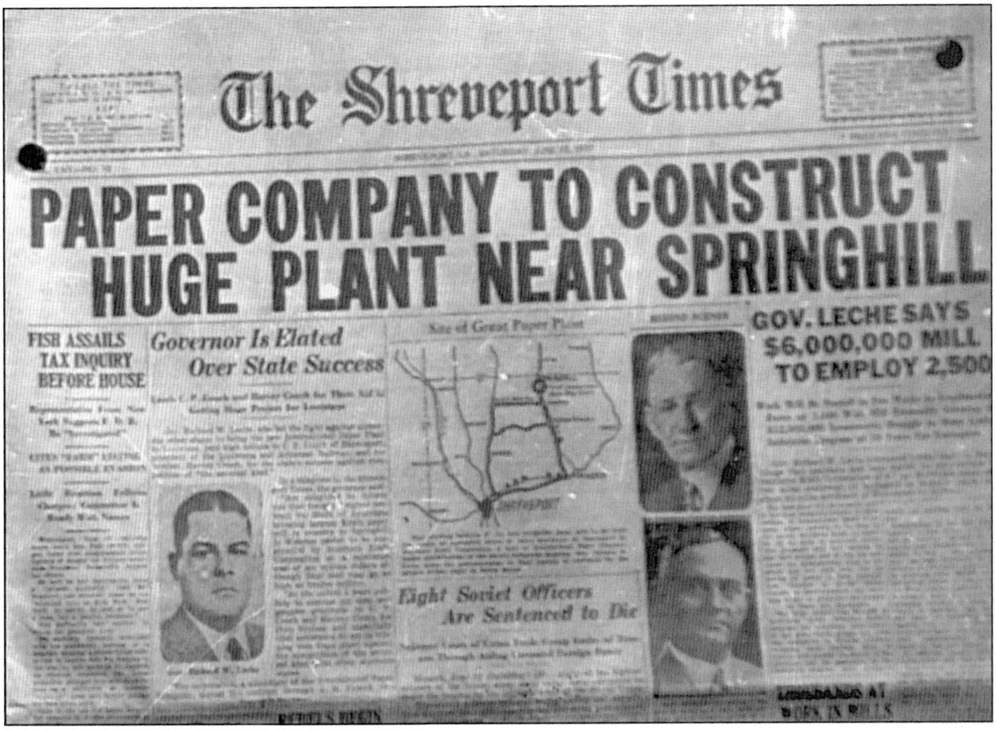

The Shreveport Times

PAPER COMPANY TO CONSTRUCT HUGE PLANT NEAR SPRINGHILL

FISH ASSAILS TAX INQUIRY BEFORE HOUSE

Governor Is Elated Over State Success

GOV. LECHE SAYS $6,000,000 MILL TO EMPLOY 2,500

Eight Soviet Officers Are Sentenced to Die

A newspaper headline from the *Shreveport Times* of June 12, 1937, announces the most significant economic event in the history of Springhill and North Webster Parish—the construction of the International Paper Mill in Springhill. For most of the last half of the century, International Paper would be the most significant industry and driving force behind the economy of North Webster. (Courtesy of Dr. A.C. Higginbotham.)

Even with its now scaled-back presence, International Paper is still a key element in economic life in the parish. Pictured is one of the buildings at the Springhill plant in 2000.

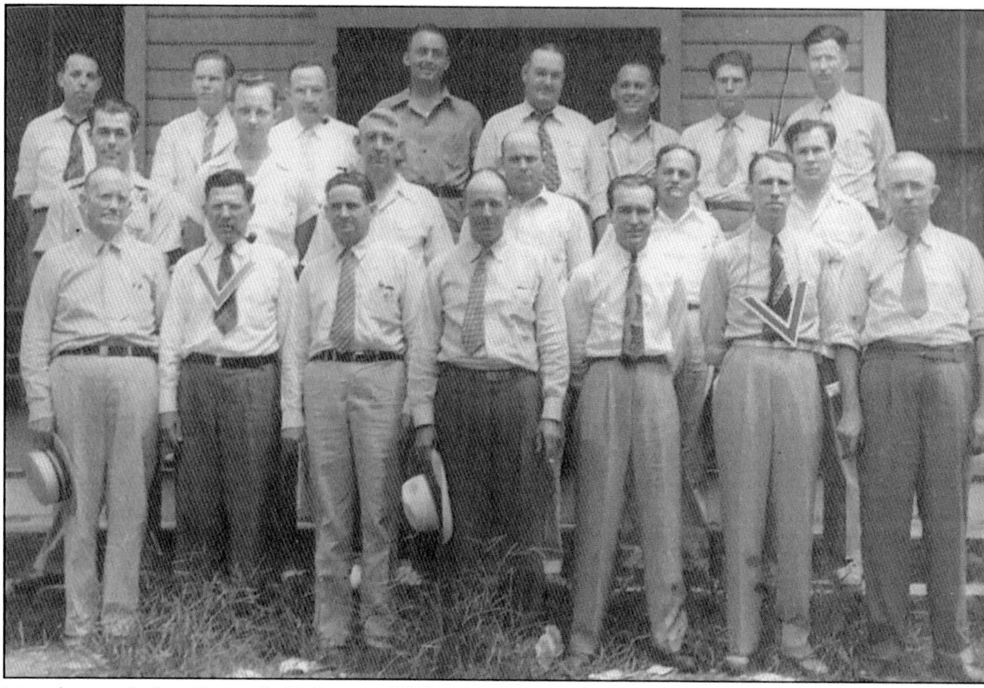

Members of the Springhill Lions Club are pictured above in 1941. (Courtesy of R.O. Machen Jr.)

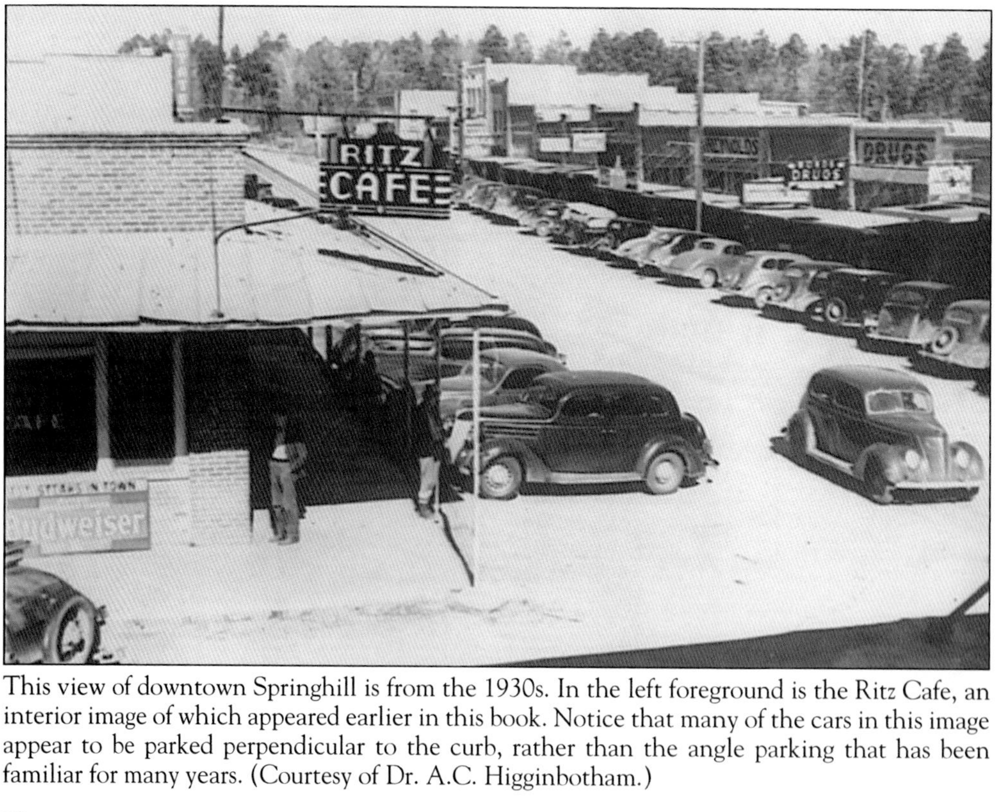

This view of downtown Springhill is from the 1930s. In the left foreground is the Ritz Cafe, an interior image of which appeared earlier in this book. Notice that many of the cars in this image appear to be parked perpendicular to the curb, rather than the angle parking that has been familiar for many years. (Courtesy of Dr. A.C. Higginbotham.)

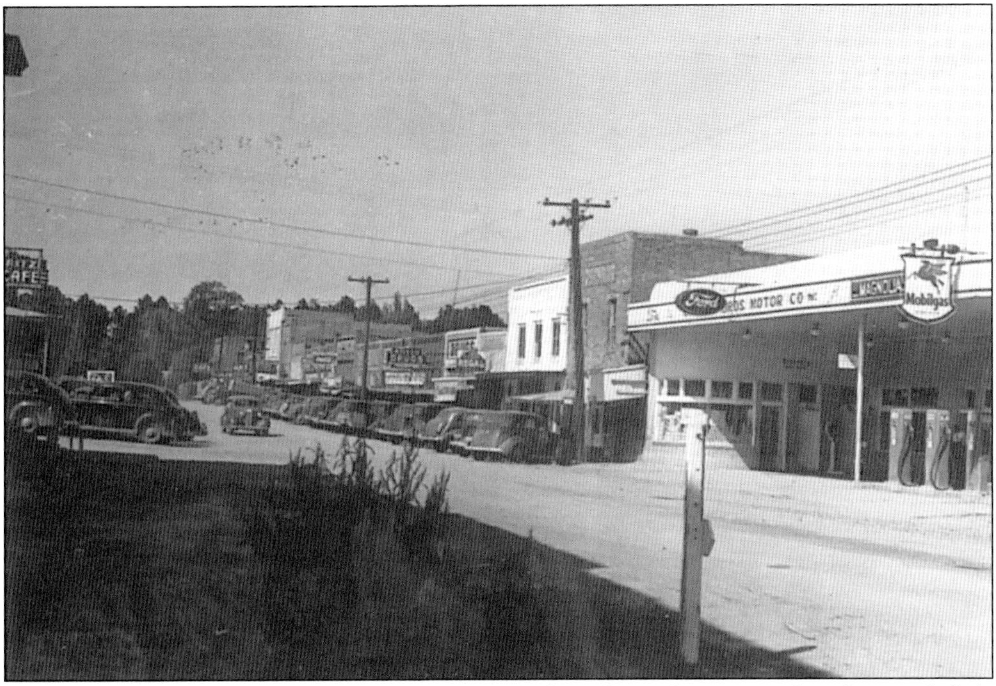

Seen here is another image of downtown Springhill in the early 1940s, taken from a slightly different angle. The Ritz Cafe is again shown at the left, with Branch Brothers, the longtime Ford Dealer for Springhill, located at the building in the right foreground. This picture was taken shortly after Magnolia Gasoline become Mobil. Notice the projecting sign above the pumps reads "Mobil," while the sign on the building reads "Magnolia." (Courtesy of Dr. A.C. Higginbotham.)

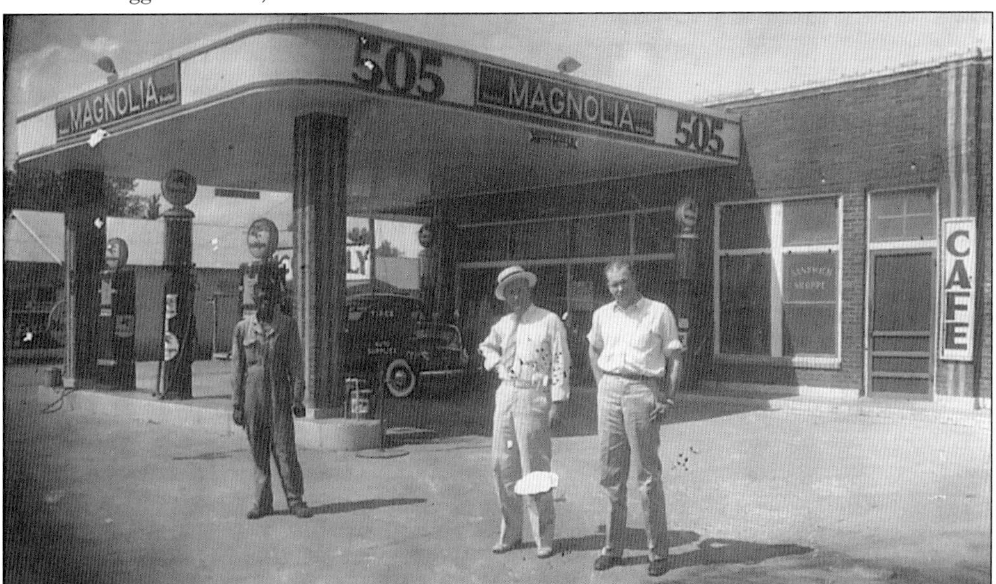

The 505 Service Station in Springhill was owned and operated by T.O. Machen, shown earlier in his mother's Ritz Cafe. Notice that this was also a Magnolia station—the picture was taken in 1940, before the gasoline brand was renamed Mobil. (Courtesy of R.O. Machen.)

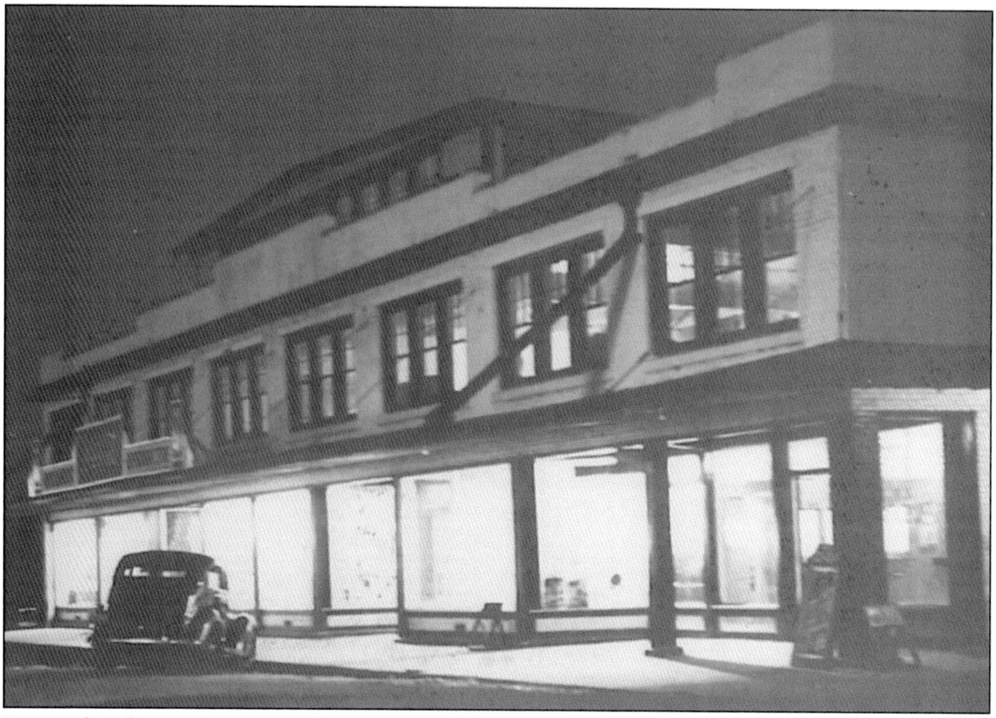

Pictured is the commissary of the Frost Lumber Company in Springhill in 1940. This building was destroyed by fire in 1943. (Courtesy of Dr. A.C. Higginbotham.)

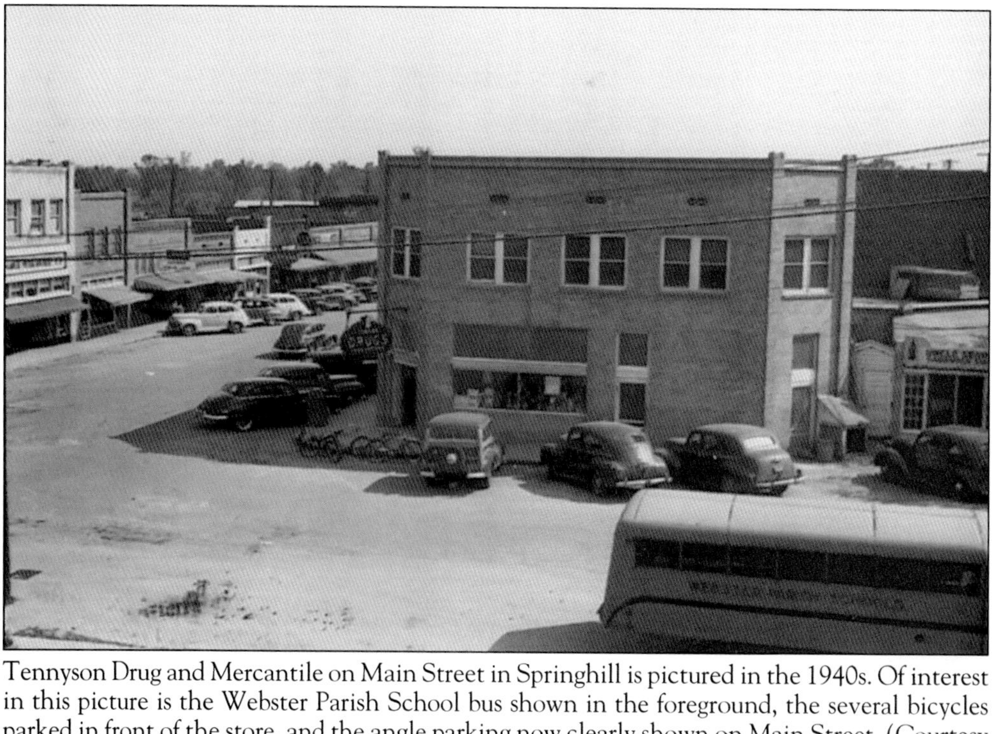

Tennyson Drug and Mercantile on Main Street in Springhill is pictured in the 1940s. Of interest in this picture is the Webster Parish School bus shown in the foreground, the several bicycles parked in front of the store, and the angle parking now clearly shown on Main Street. (Courtesy of Dr. A.C. Higginbotham.)

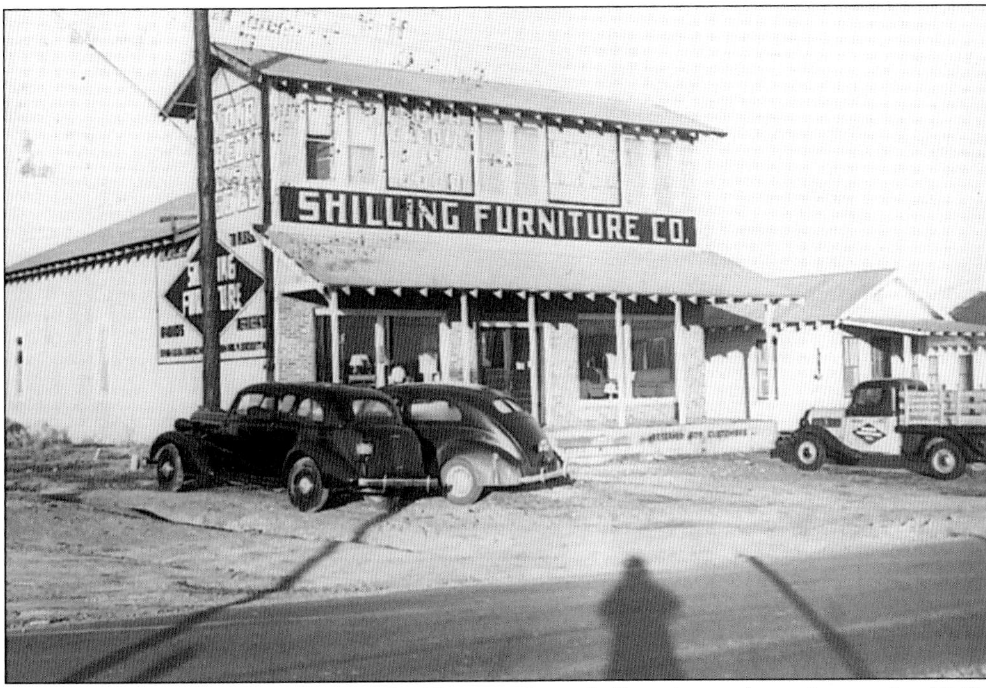

The Schilling Furniture Company building in Springhill is shown here during the 1940s. (Courtesy of Dr. A.C. Higginbotham.)

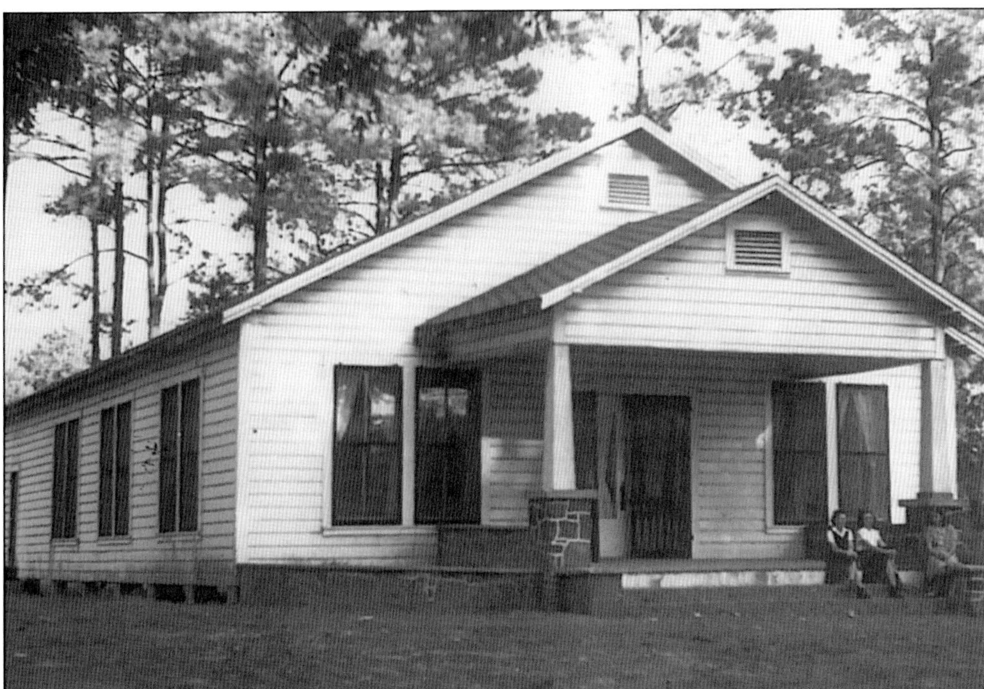

This image of the Springhill Community House was taken in 1943. (Courtesy of Dr. A.C. Higginbotham.)

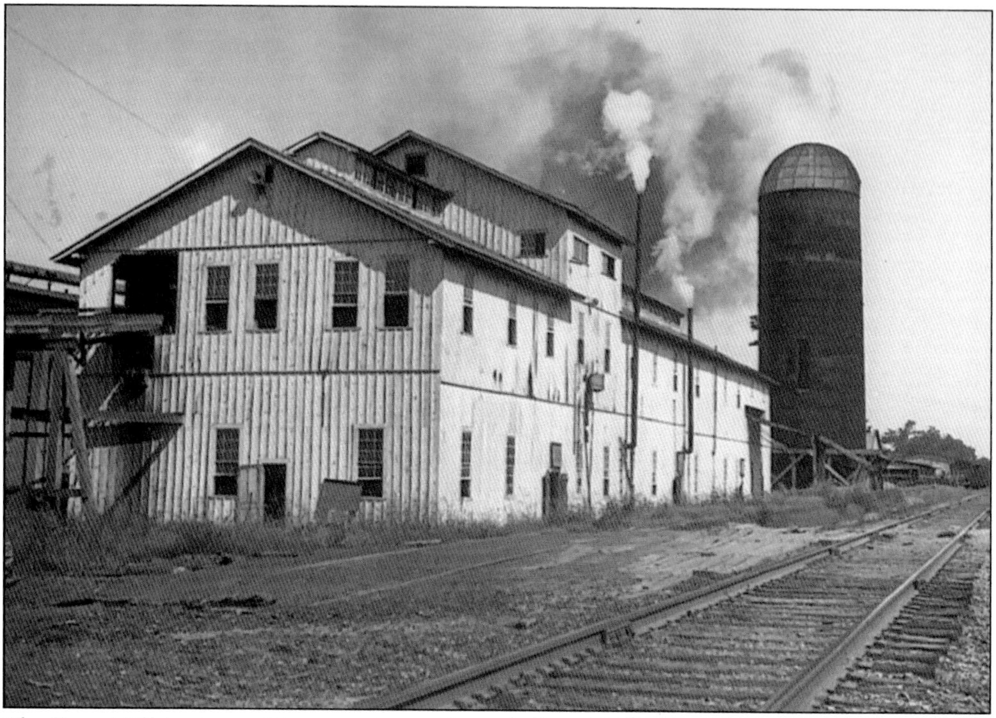

The Frost Mill is pictured in operation at Springhill in 1945. An earlier image was of the mill commissary, which burned in 1943. (Courtesy of Dr. A.C. Higginbotham.)

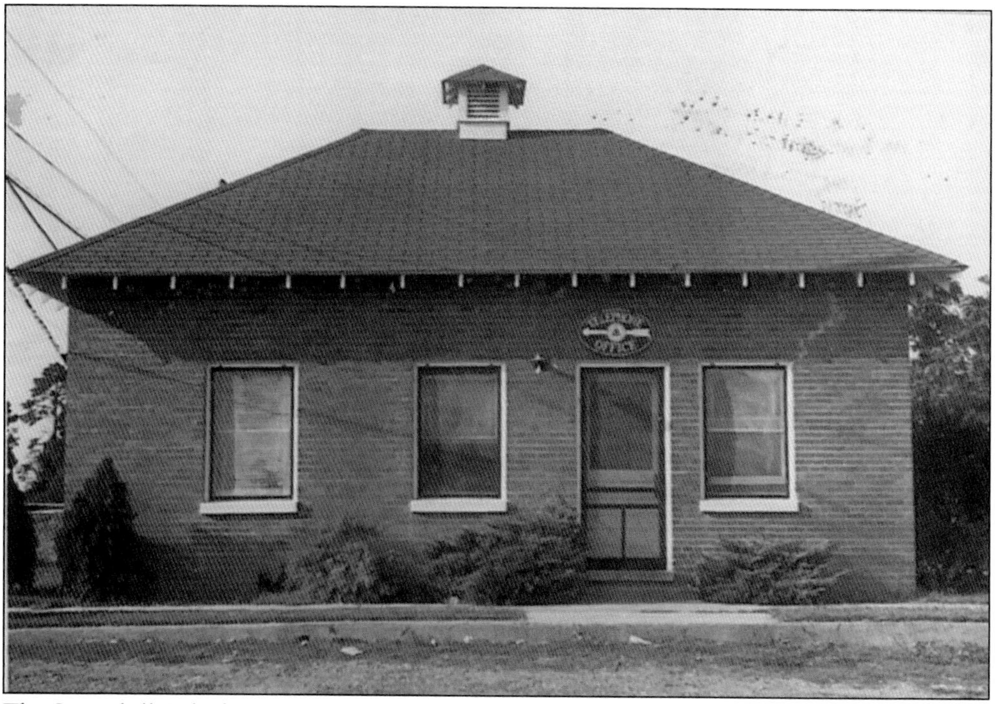

The Springhill Telephone Company office is shown here in September 1945. (Courtesy of Dr. A.C. Higginbotham.)

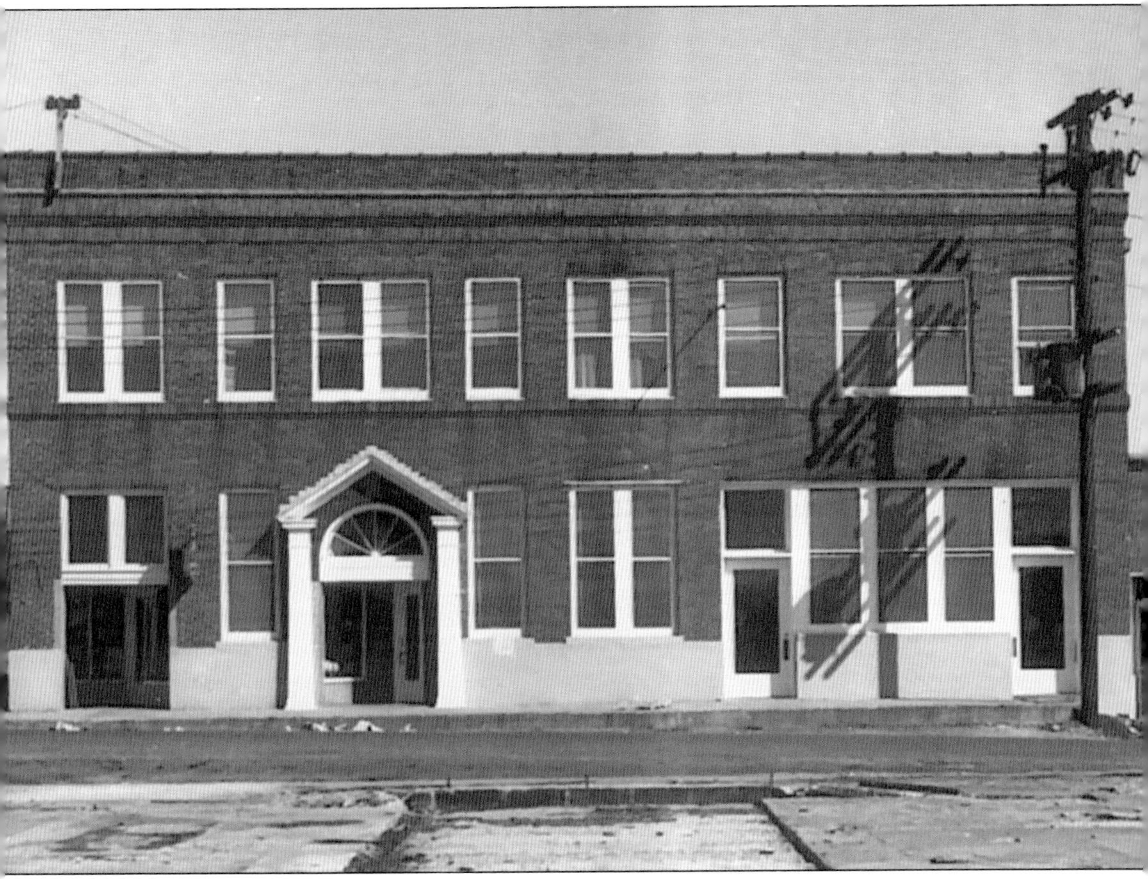

this image of the Springhill Bank was taken in 1944, during the later part of World War II. (Courtesy of Dr. A.C. Higginbotham.)

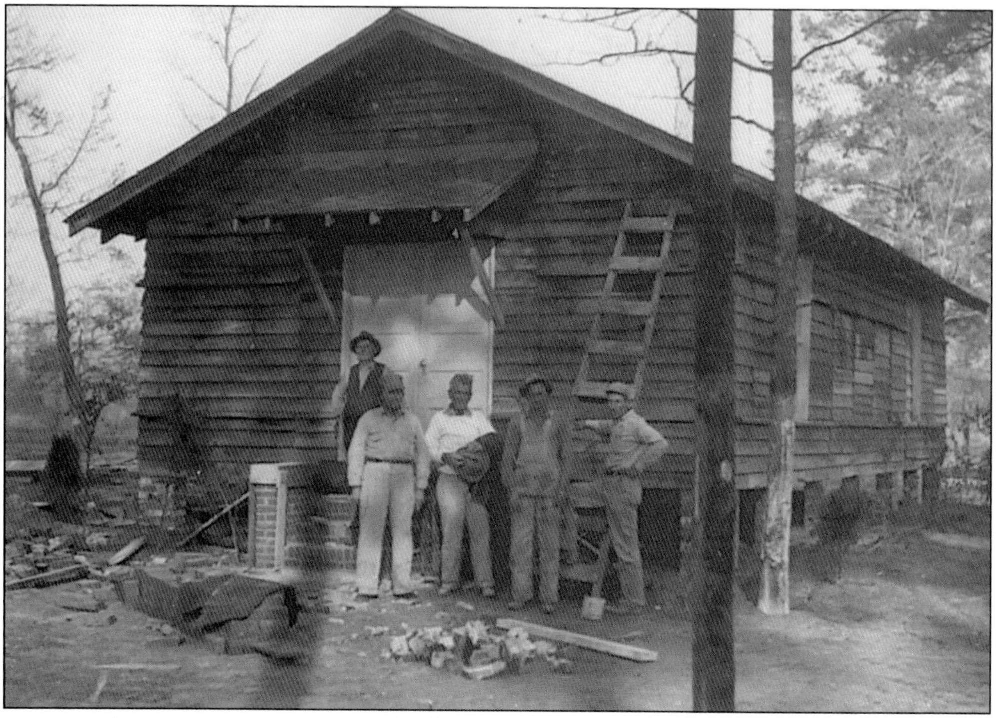

A group of men are seen working on the Springhill Boy Scout Cabin in 1945. (Courtesy of Dr. A.C. Higginbotham.)

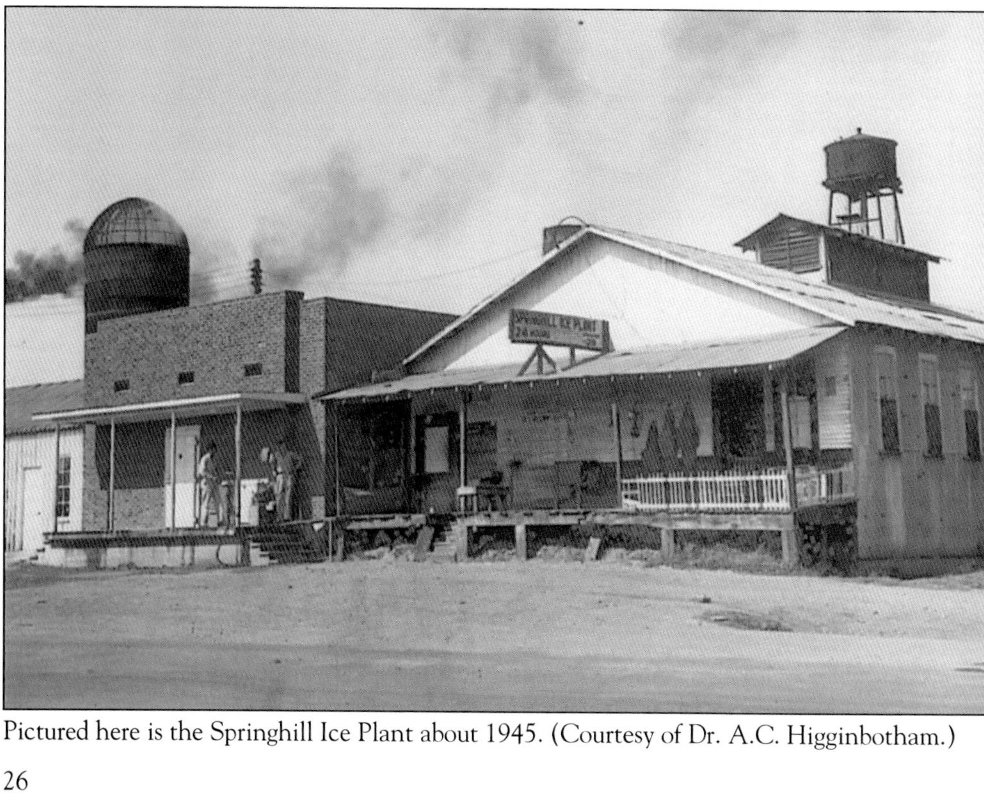

Pictured here is the Springhill Ice Plant about 1945. (Courtesy of Dr. A.C. Higginbotham.)

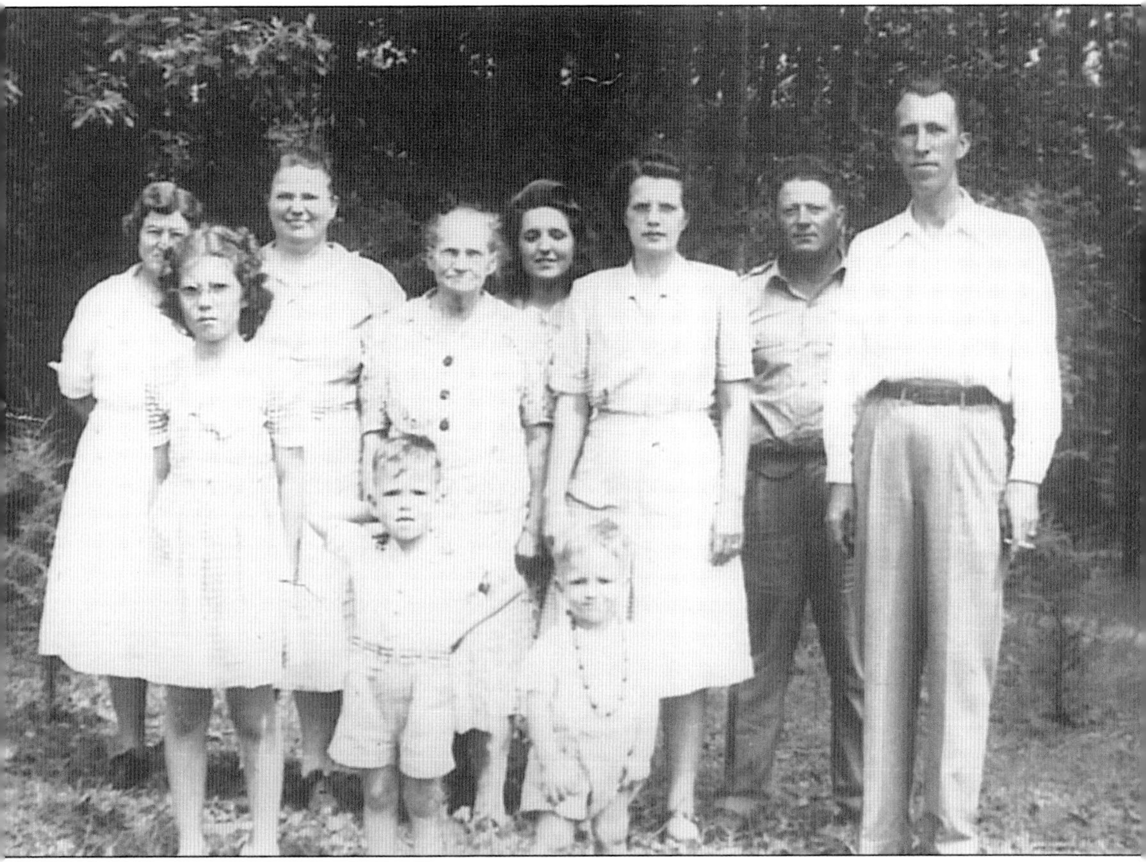

The Martin family is shown at a family gathering in 1946. Pictured from left to right are as follows: (front row) Ann Machen Harrison, R.O. Machen Jr., and Matt Martin; (back row) Winnie Martin, Emma Martin, Liz Martin, Harriet Martin, Lela Machen, Bill Martin, and R.O. Machen Sr. (Courtesy of R.O. Machen Jr.)

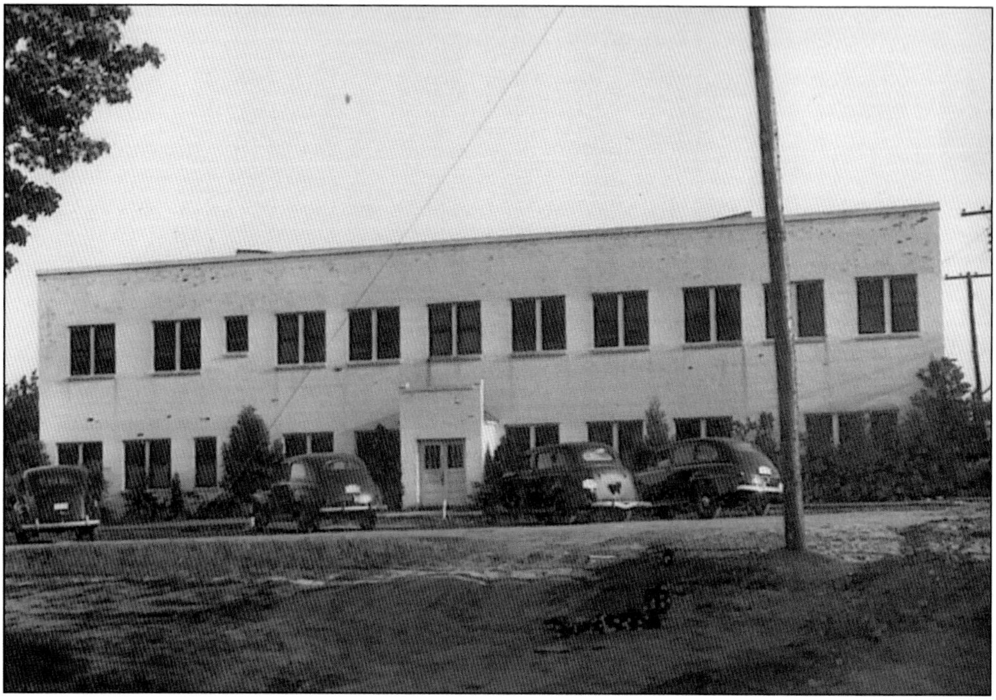

The Swann Clinic in Springhill is pictured here in April 1946. (Courtesy of Dr. A.C. Higginbotham.)

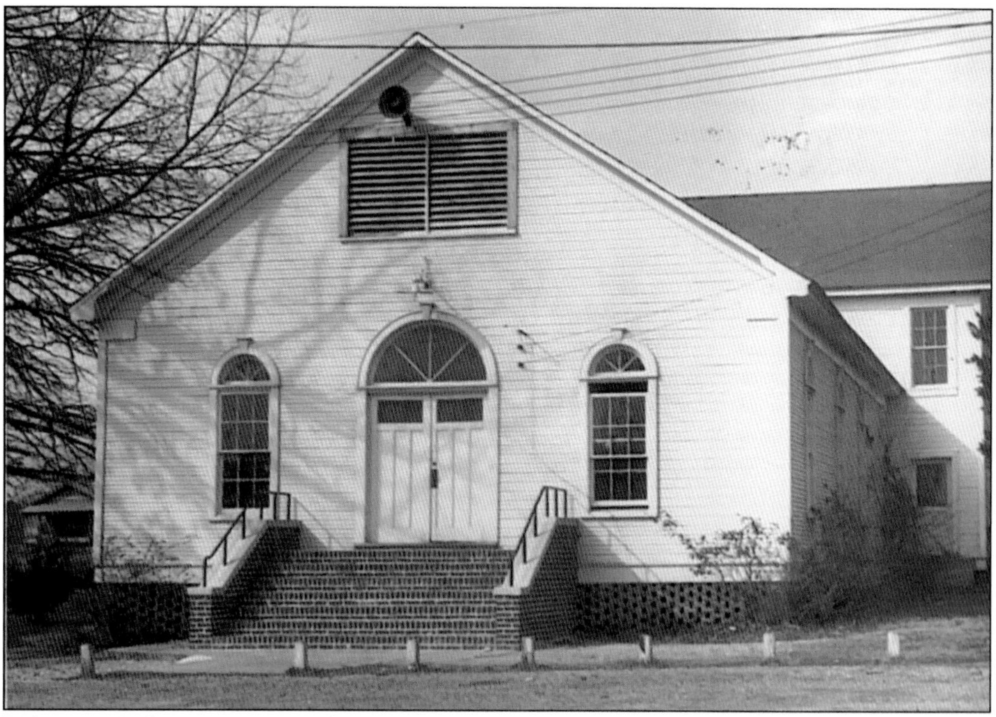

Taken on Valentine's Day, February 14, 1946, this picture shows the Springhill Methodist Church. (Courtesy of Dr. A.C. Higginbotham.)

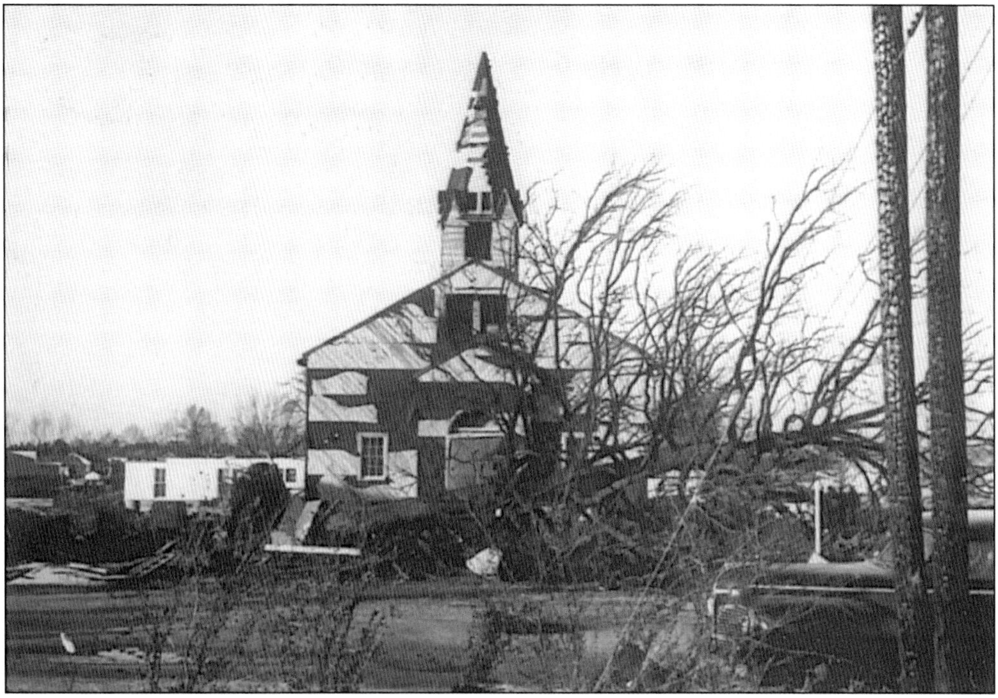

On the evening of December 31, 1947, Cotton Valley was devastated by a killer tornado that inflicted major damage on the community and claimed the lives of several local residents. Pictured above is what remained of the First Methodist Church of Cotton Valley after the storm. (Courtesy of Dr. A.C. Higginbotham.)

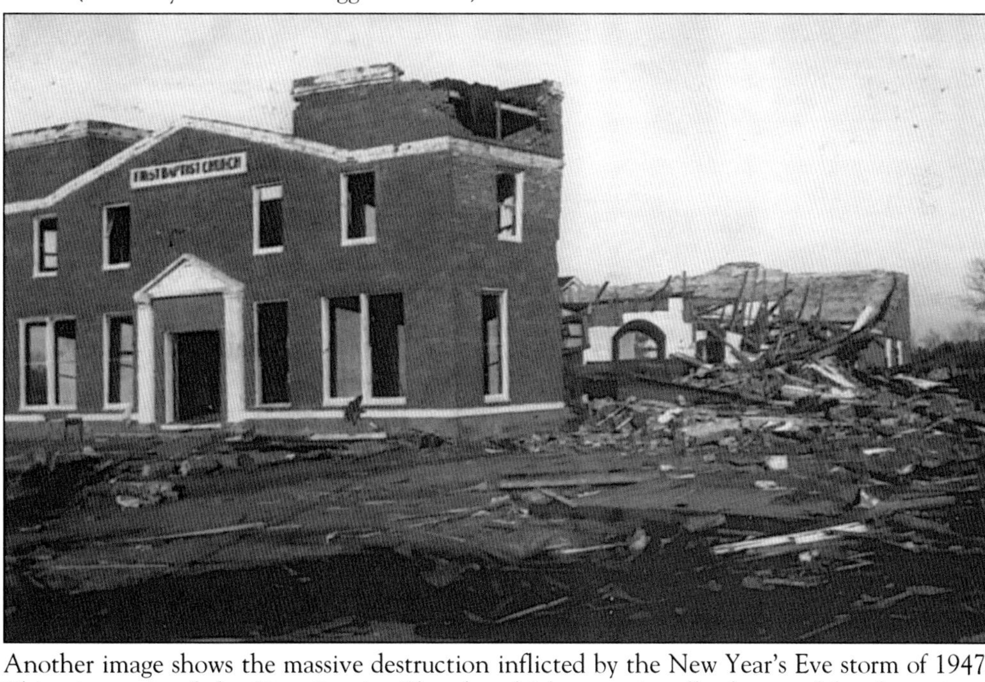

Another image shows the massive destruction inflicted by the New Year's Eve storm of 1947. This picture is of the First Baptist Church, which was virtually destroyed by the twister. (Courtesy of Dr. A.C. Higginbotham.)

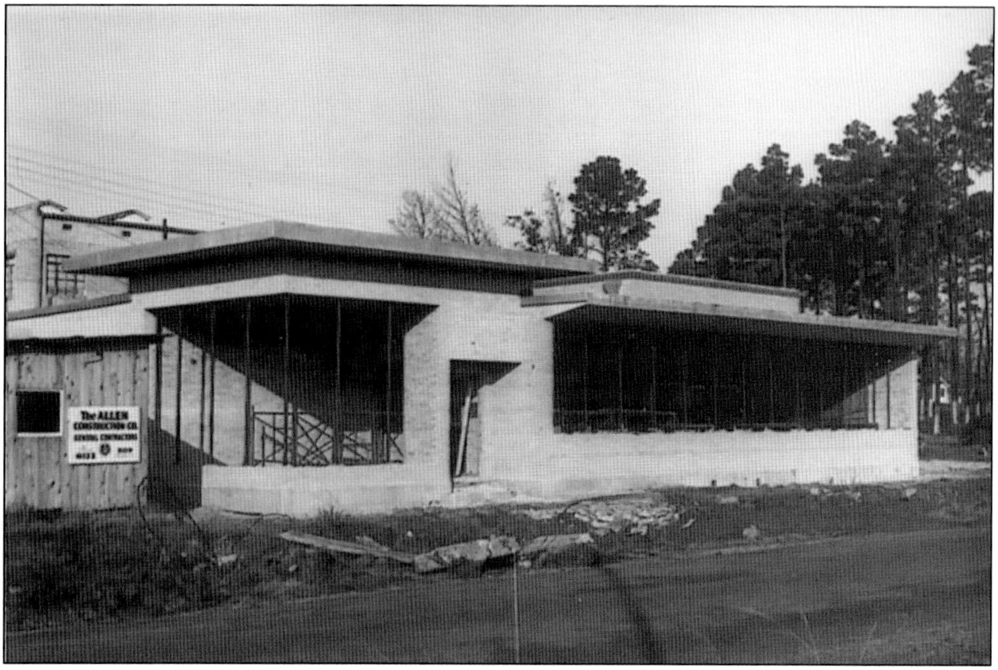

The Springhill Health Center is seen while under construction on December 7, 1949. (Courtesy of Dr. A.C. Higginbotham.)

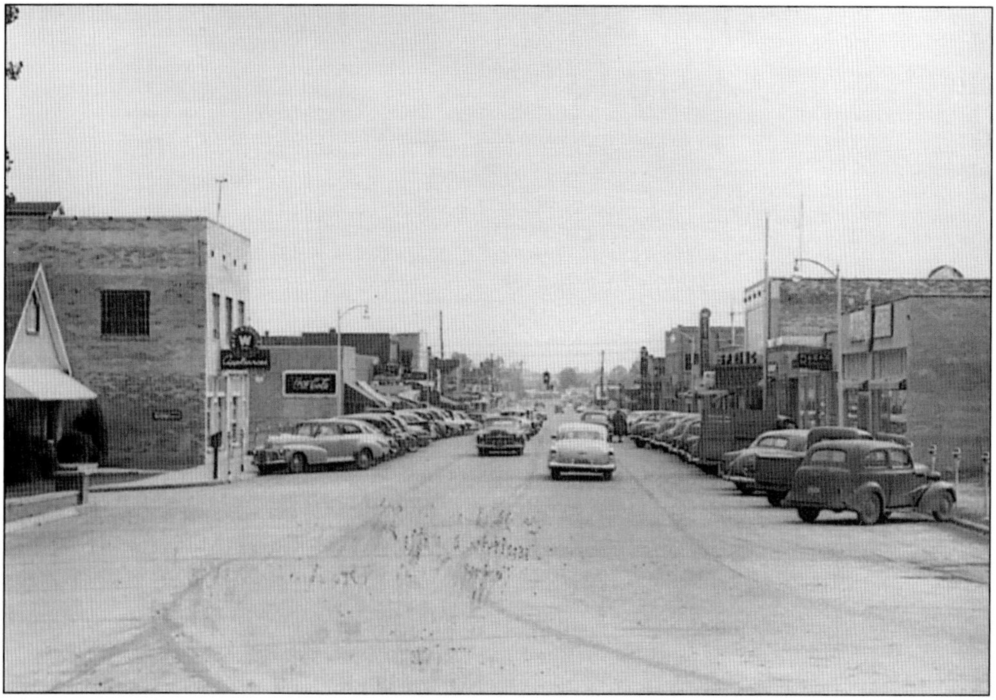

This view of downtown Springhill was taken in the 1950s. By this time not only had angle parking become the norm, but parking meters had been added to the scene. (Courtesy of Dr. A.C. Higginbotham.)

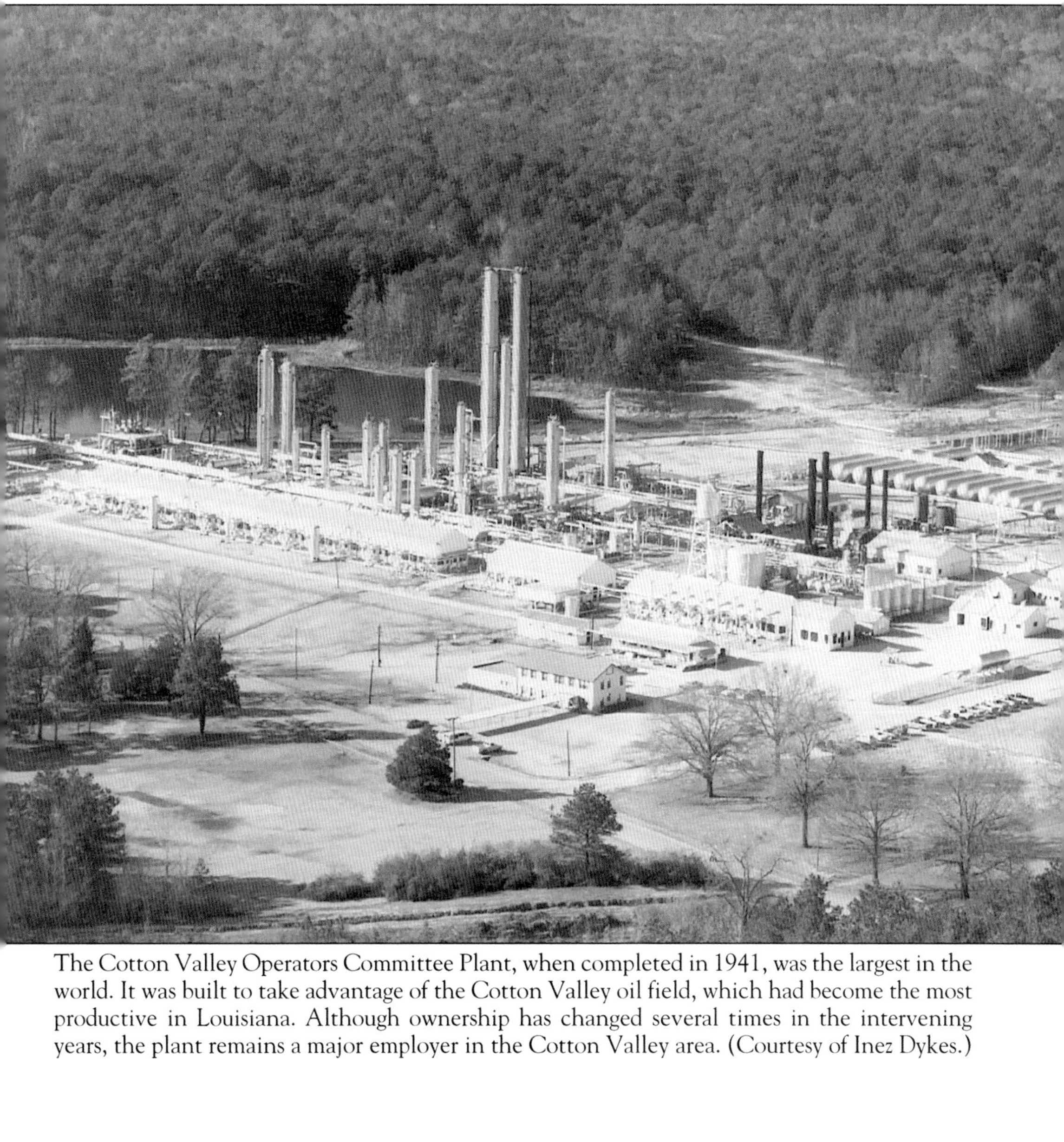

The Cotton Valley Operators Committee Plant, when completed in 1941, was the largest in the world. It was built to take advantage of the Cotton Valley oil field, which had become the most productive in Louisiana. Although ownership has changed several times in the intervening years, the plant remains a major employer in the Cotton Valley area. (Courtesy of Inez Dykes.)

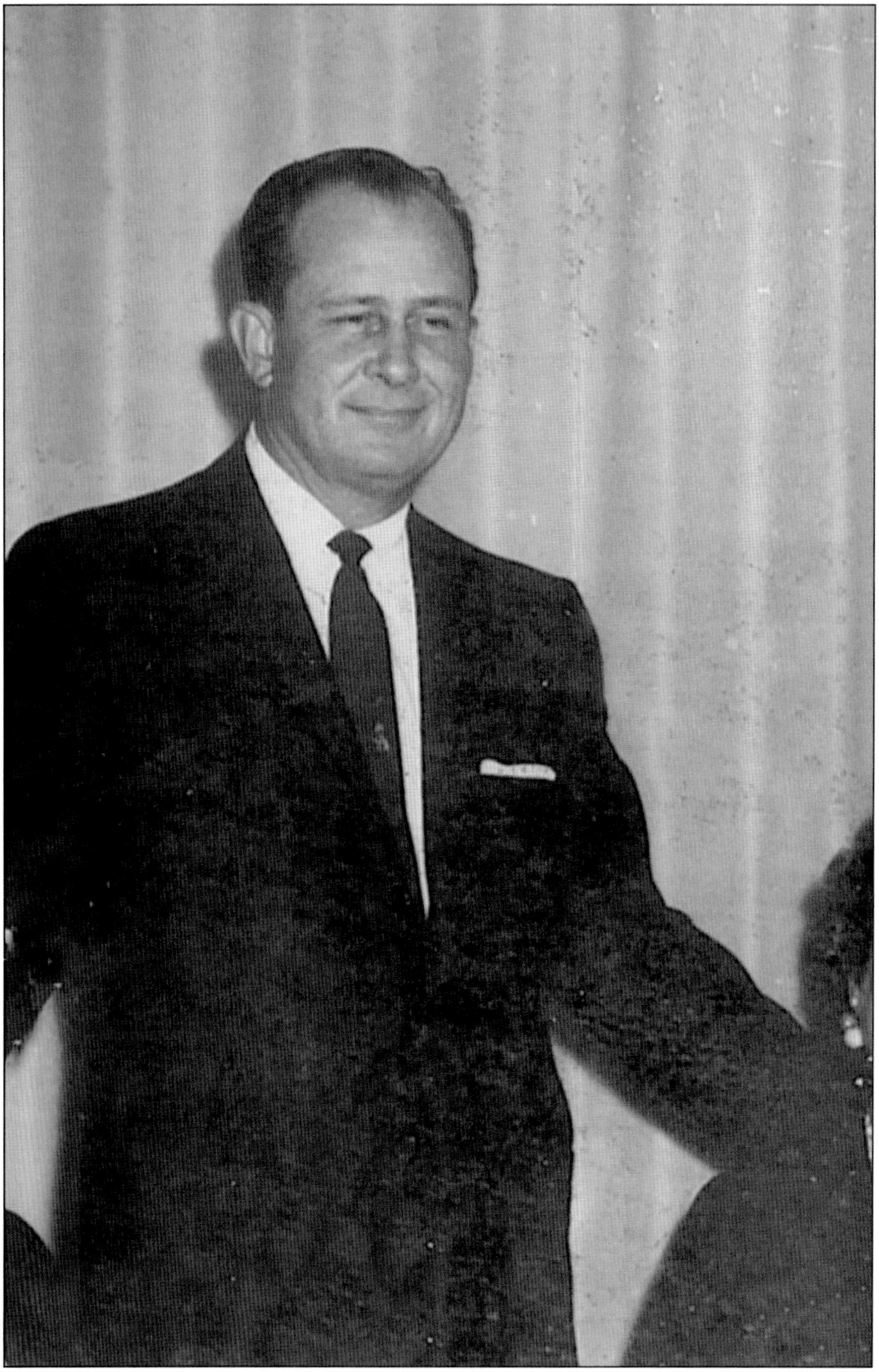

Mayor Jesse Boucher of Springhill is pictured in the early 1960s. Boucher, a star athlete at Northwestern State College of Louisiana, began his career as a Webster Parish schoolteacher. He taught at both Evergreen High School and Minden High School during the 1930s. He later formed the Boucher and Slack Insurance Agency with Wilburn Slack, and became a key business leader and extremely active in all areas of public affairs in the Springhill community. (Courtesy of Jesse Boucher.)

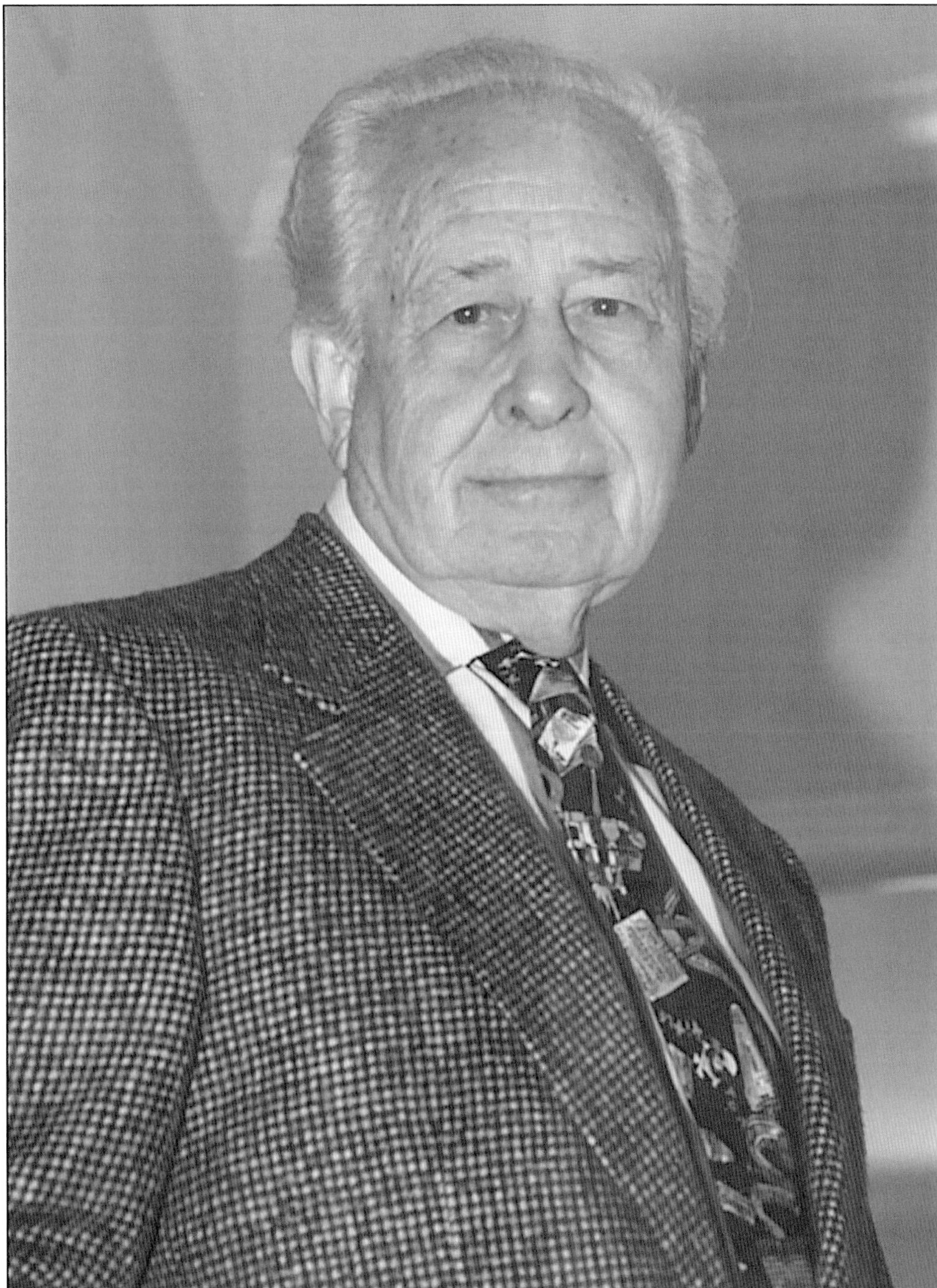

Pictured in 1994, Jesse Boucher is still actively involved in operating his business enterprises today. Boucher and Slack has branched out from the insurance business to become one of the leading residential construction firms in North Louisiana, with offices in both Springhill and Shreveport. The firm has been responsible for the construction of many of the most successful subdivisions and apartment complexes in the region, and Mr. Boucher is recognized as a leader and innovator in his field. (Courtesy of Jesse Boucher.)

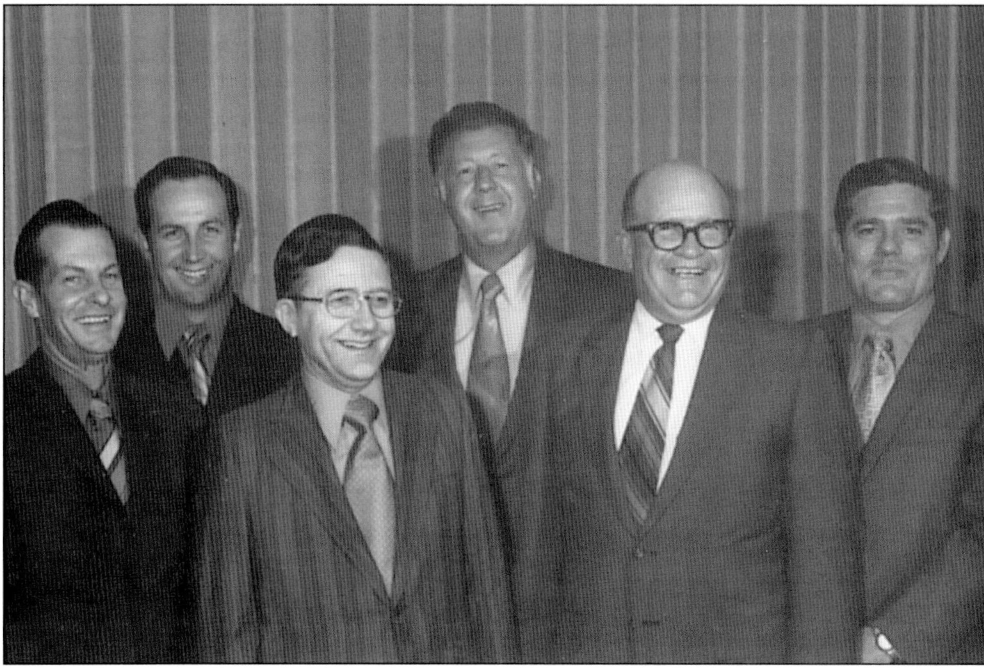

The Springhill City Council is pictured in the early 1970s. Seen from left to right are Curtis Smith, Robert Bryan, Dr. A.C. Higginbotham, H. Gray, Mayor James Allen, and James Harris. (Courtesy of Dr. A.C. Higginbotham.)

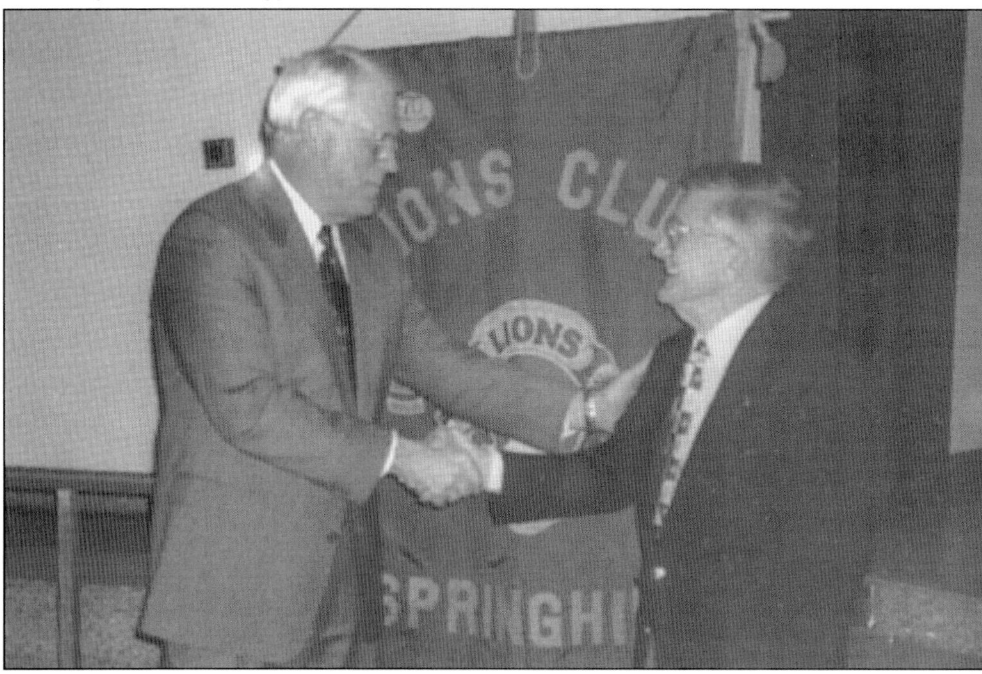

One of Springhill's famous native sons, John David Crow, is greeted by Dr. A.C. Higginbotham at a meeting of the Springhill Lions Club. Crow, who won the Heisman Trophy in 1957 while playing for Texas A&M, went on to a long and successful NFL career with the Chicago and St. Louis Cardinals, and the San Francisco 49ers. (Courtesy of Dr. A.C. Higginbotham.)

Two

GOVERNMENT

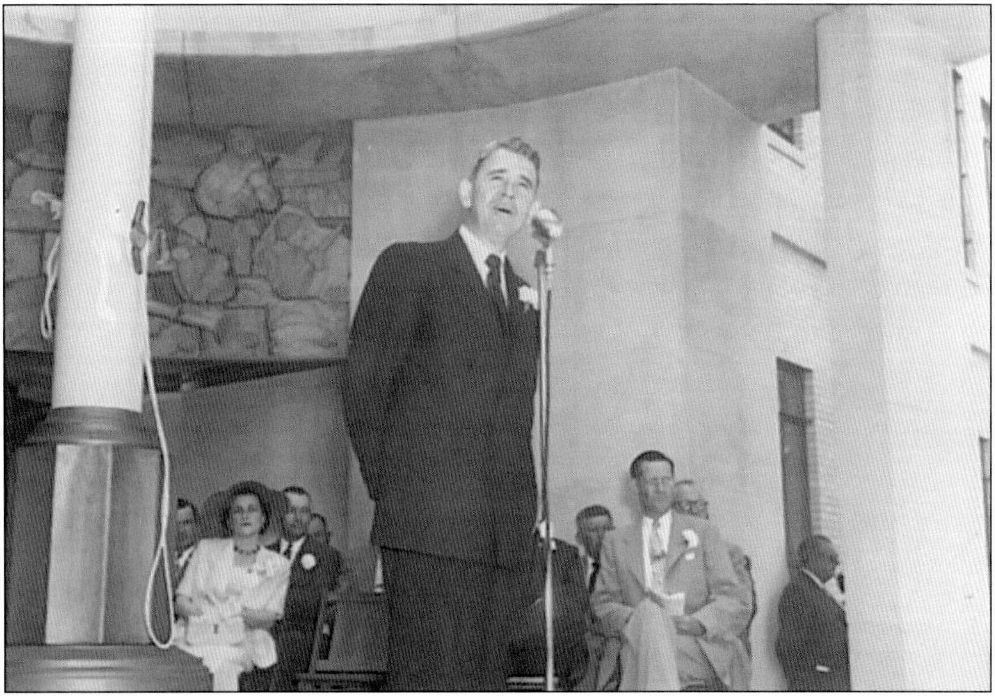

Governor Robert F. Kennon, a native of Minden, is shown dedicating the new Webster Parish Courthouse in 1953. Kennon had begun his political career at the age of 23 as mayor of Minden and later served as district attorney, district judge, and court of appeals judge before being elected governor in 1952. (Courtesy of Major DePingre.)

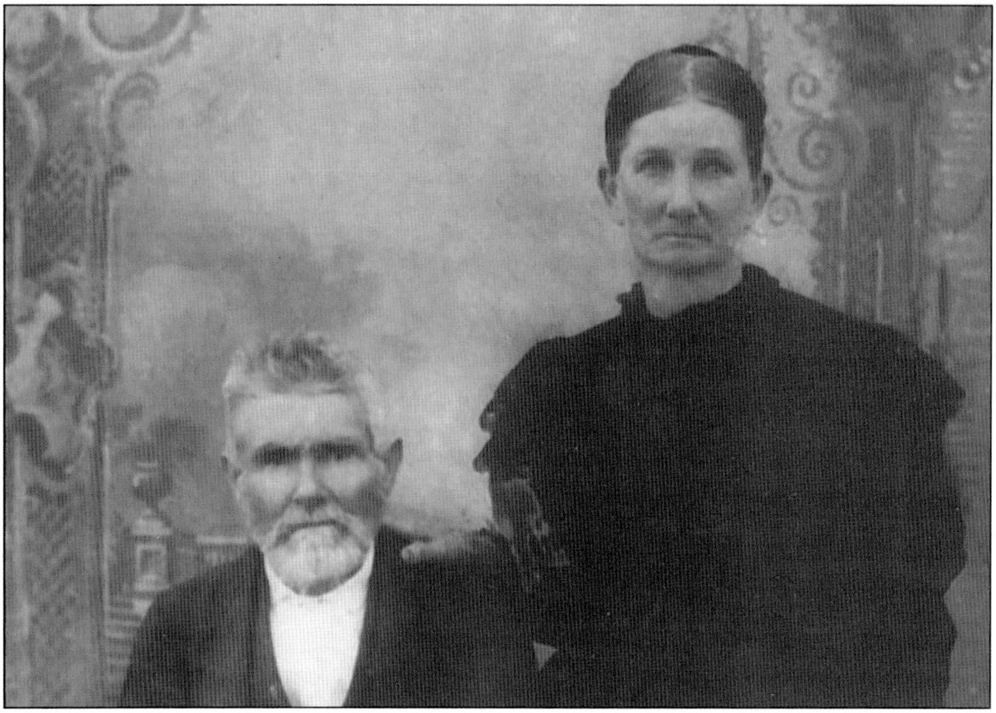

John Sidney Killen, who was the state representative from Minden when Webster Parish was created in February 1871, is pictured with his wife, Sarah Monzingo Killen, shortly before his death in 1901. (Courtesy of George Turner.)

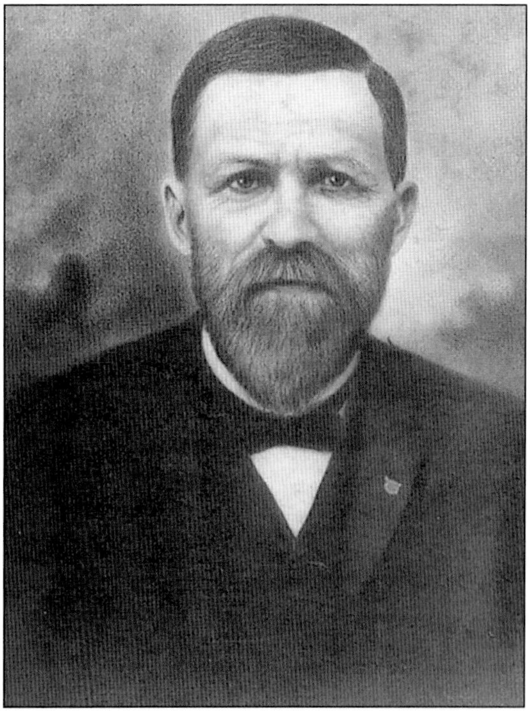

George Lovic Pierce Wren (1836–1901) was a graduate of Emory University. He represented Webster Parish in the state legislature for 12 years, serving 8 years as a state representative and 4 years as state senator. In the legislature he led the fight to abolish the Louisiana Lottery, which had come to dominate state government. (Courtesy of Marcus D. Wren Jr.)

Two future Minden mayors, Connell Fort (left) and H.H. Barnes (right), are pictured in 1895, standing in front of the first Webster Parish Courthouse. This courthouse was built in 1872 and remained in use until 1905.

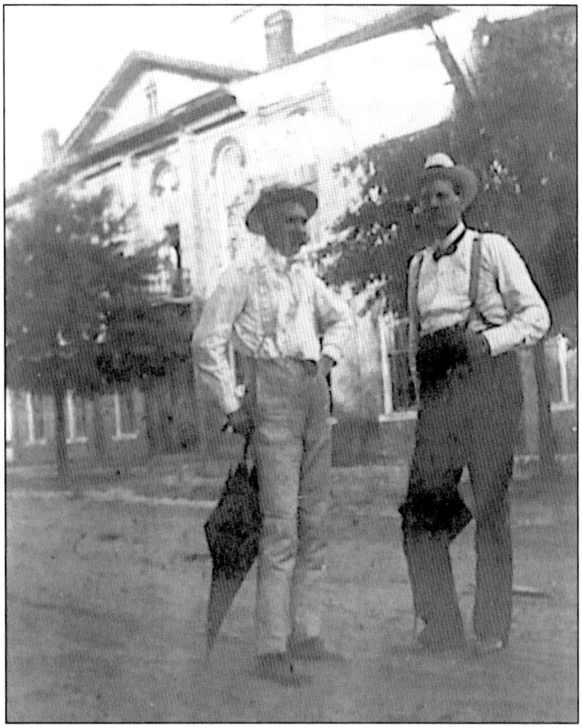

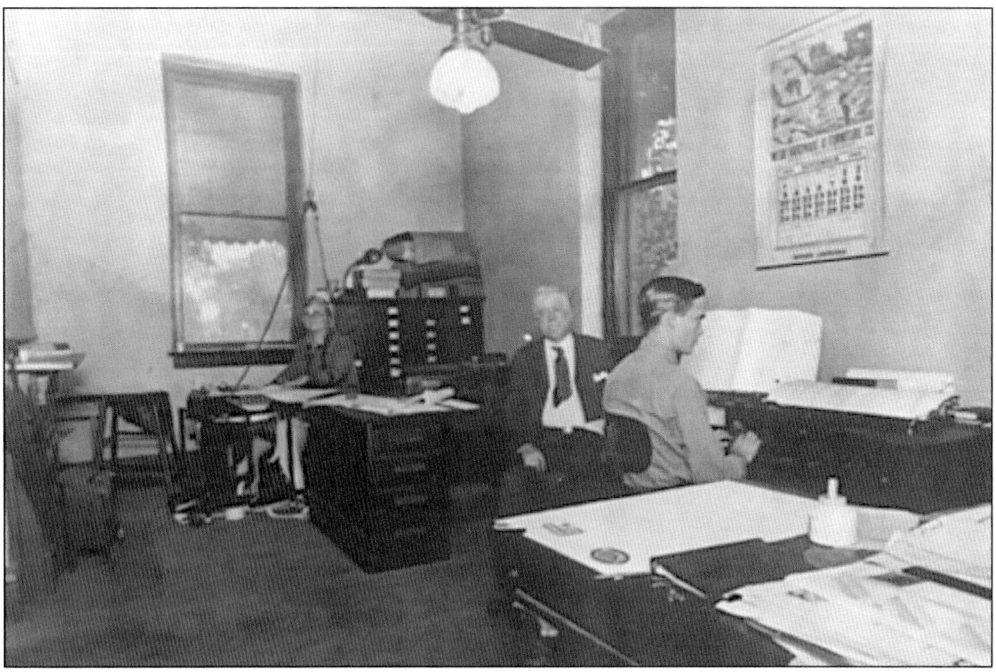

The Webster Parish Tax Assessor's Office is pictured in November 1925. Seated at the middle of the picture is McIntyre H. Sandlin, who served as assessor from 1908 through 1936. He had also served earlier as the mayor of Minden. His brother, John N. Sandlin, represented Minden and the Fourth Congressional District in Congress from 1921 to 1937. (Courtesy of Major DePingre.)

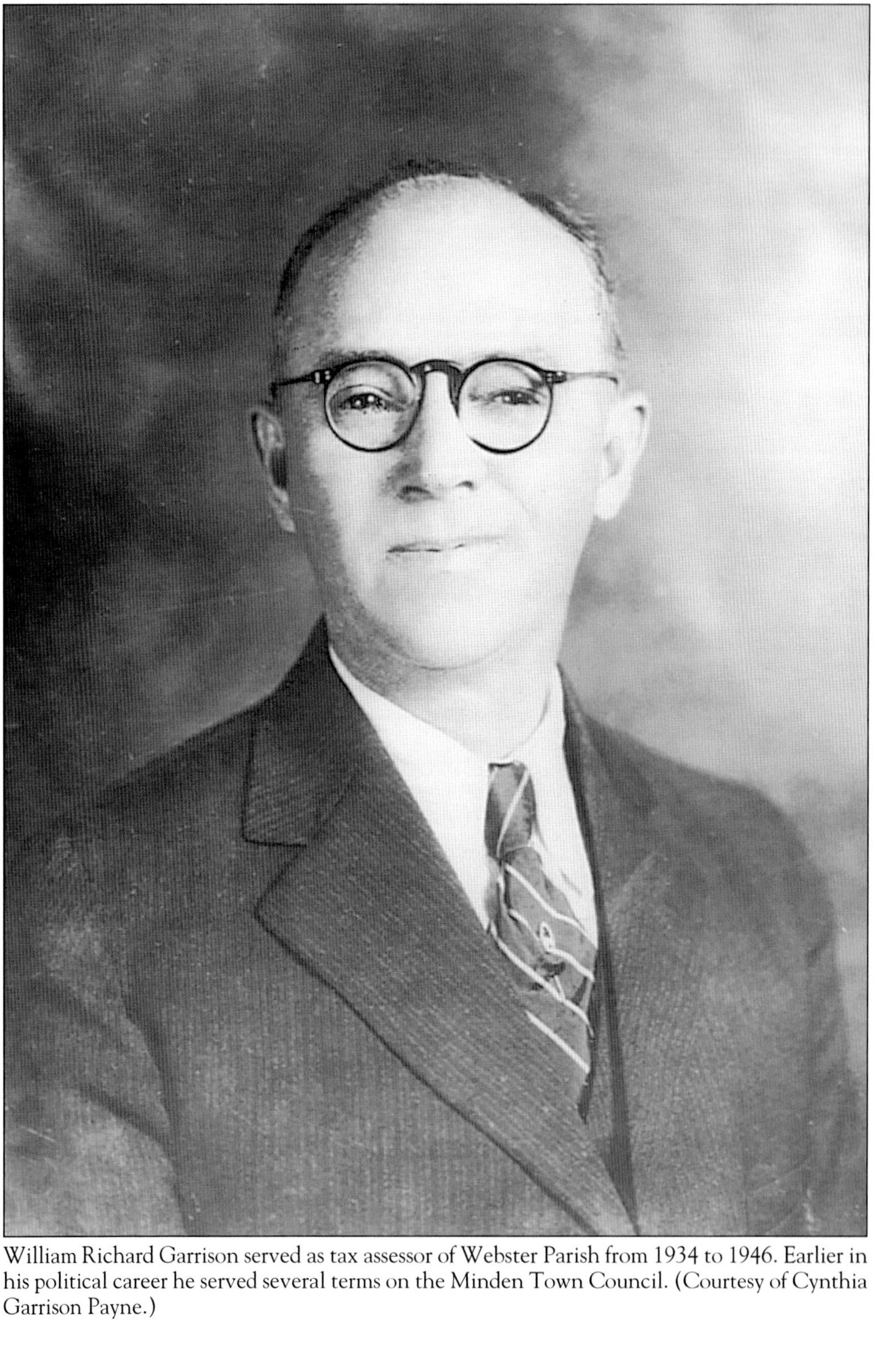

William Richard Garrison served as tax assessor of Webster Parish from 1934 to 1946. Earlier in his political career he served several terms on the Minden Town Council. (Courtesy of Cynthia Garrison Payne.)

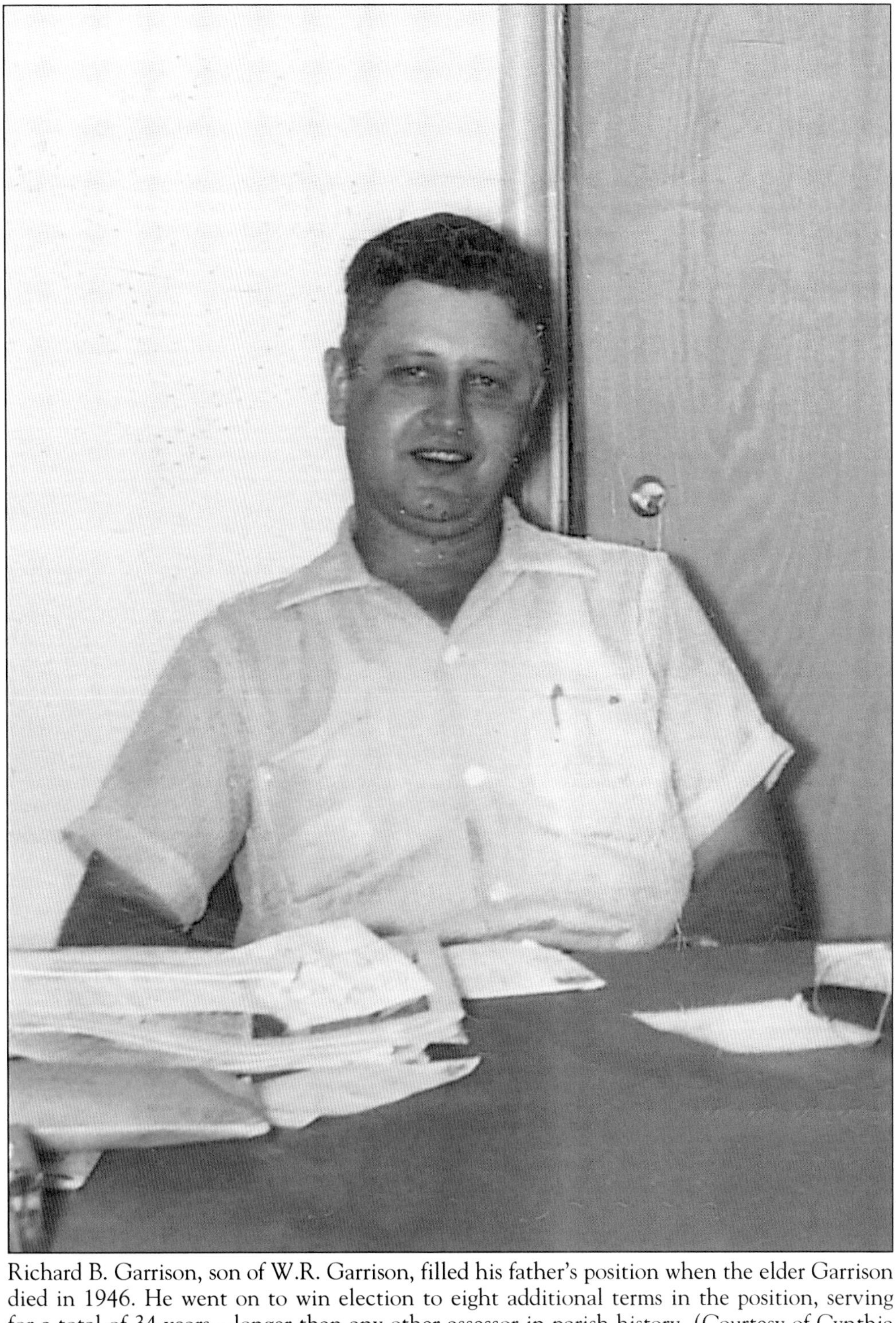

Richard B. Garrison, son of W.R. Garrison, filled his father's position when the elder Garrison died in 1946. He went on to win election to eight additional terms in the position, serving for a total of 34 years—longer than any other assessor in parish history. (Courtesy of Cynthia Garrison Payne.)

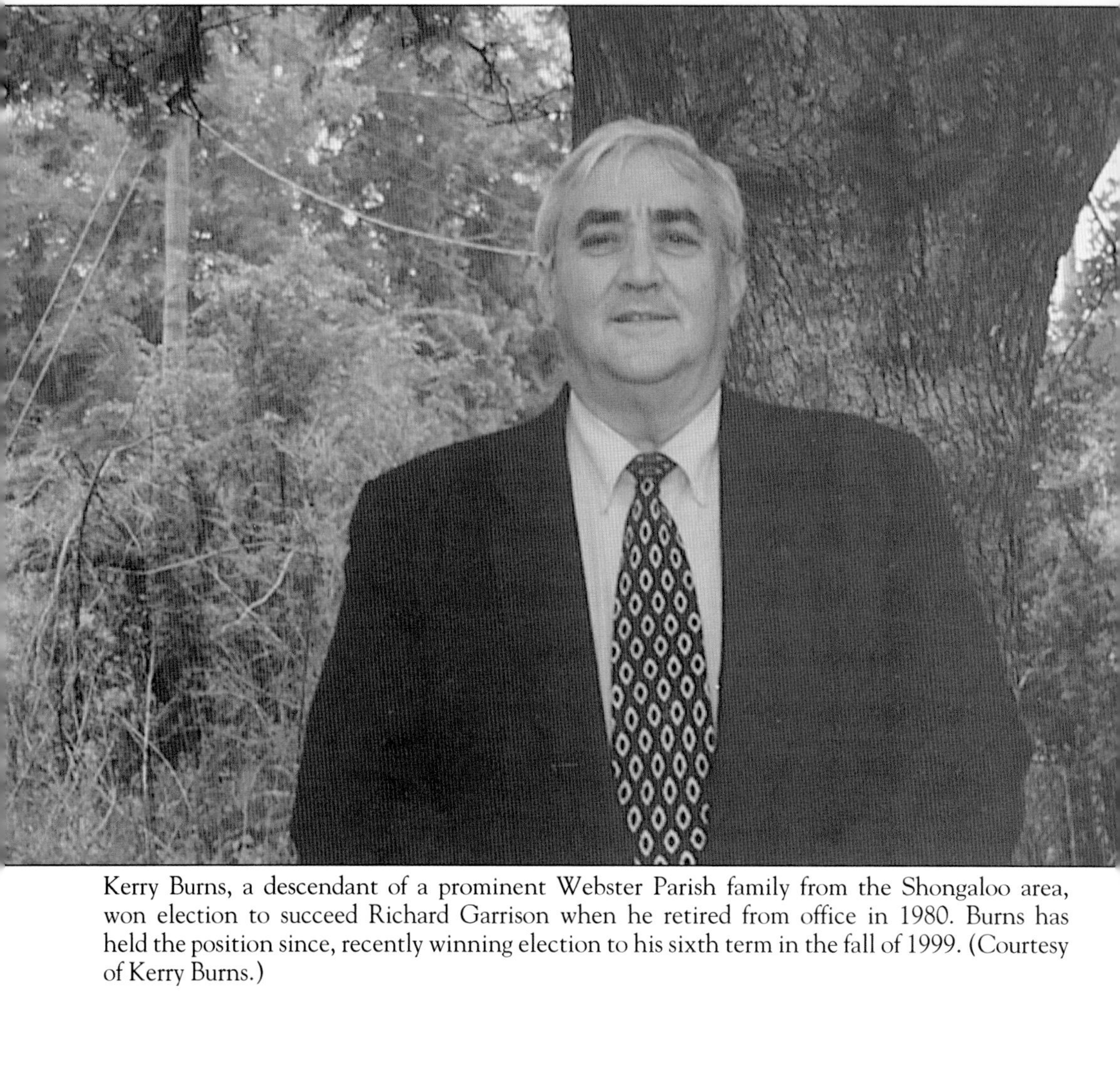

Kerry Burns, a descendant of a prominent Webster Parish family from the Shongaloo area, won election to succeed Richard Garrison when he retired from office in 1980. Burns has held the position since, recently winning election to his sixth term in the fall of 1999. (Courtesy of Kerry Burns.)

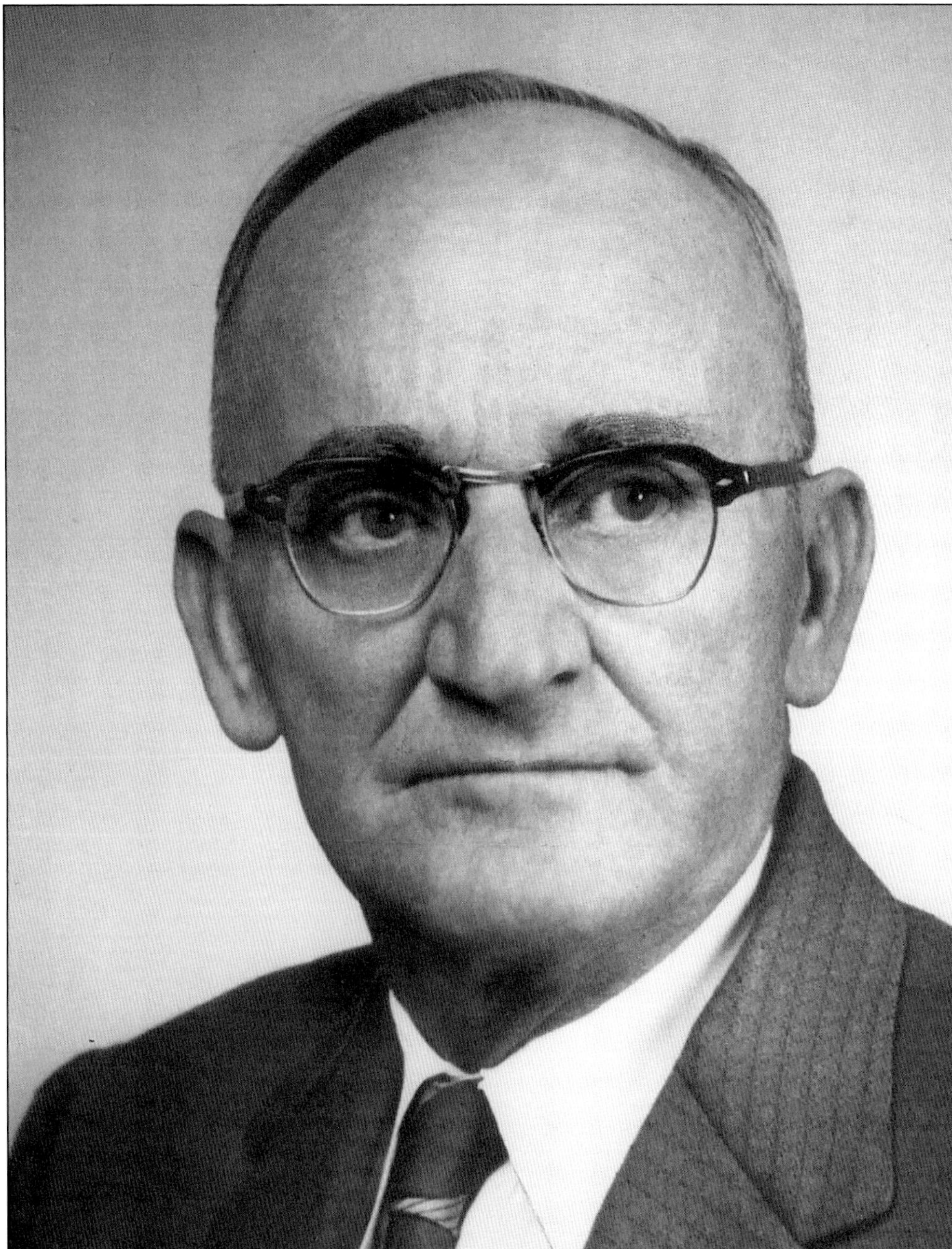

Thomas Jenkins Campbell served as the Webster Parish clerk of court from 1932 through 1956. His family has been extremely active in public affairs in Webster Parish. His two brothers, John T. and Cecil Campbell, were among the leading attorneys in Minden for over 50 years. Currently his nephew, Cecil Campbell, is a district judge, while another nephew, John C. Campbell, is Minden city judge. (Courtesy of Mary Campbell.)

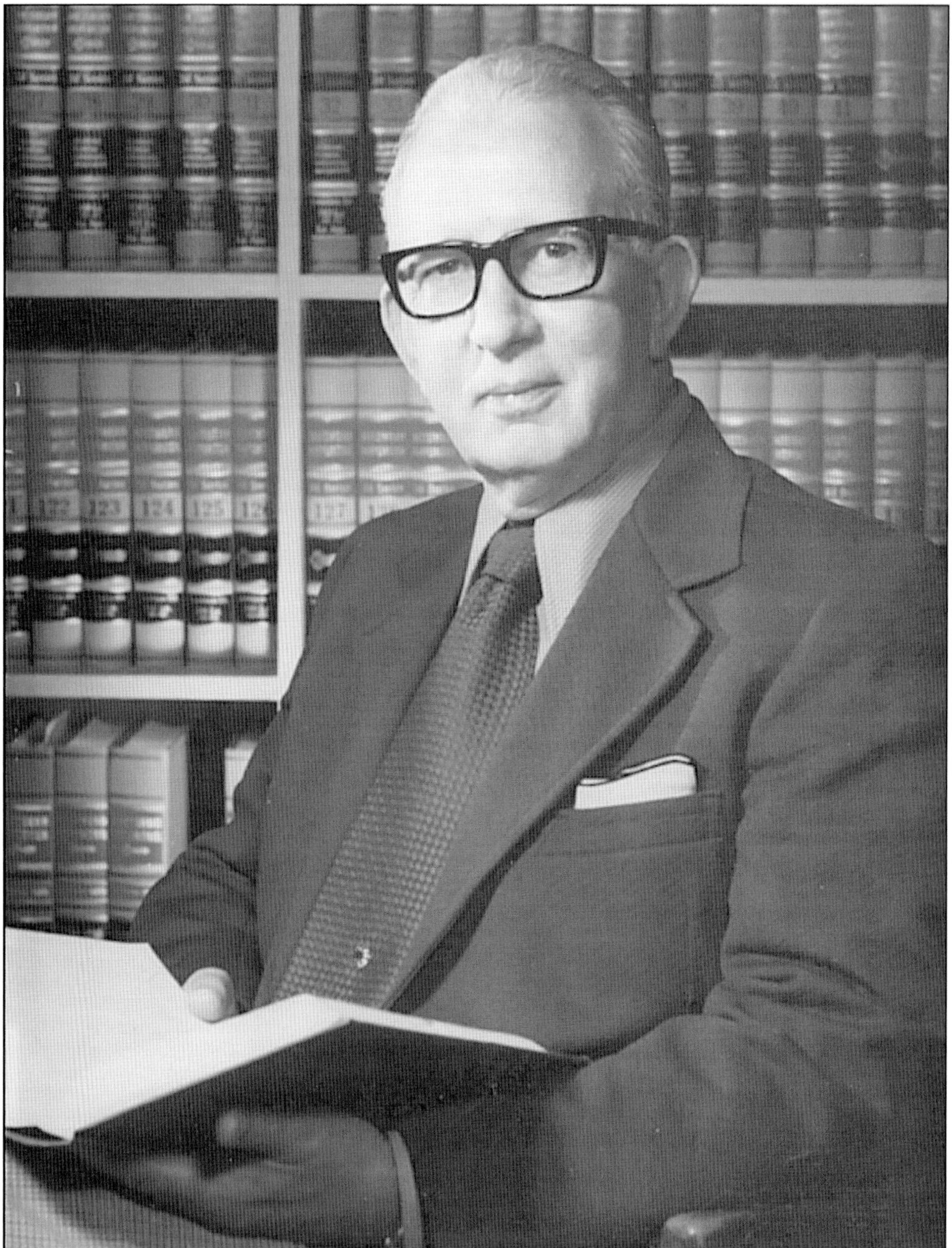

Clarence D. Wiley, after serving as deputy clerk for many years, defeated Tom Campbell for the office of clerk in 1956. He would be elected for four additional terms before retiring in 1976. He was elected to a seat on the Webster Parish Police Jury after leaving the post of clerk, but died before taking office. (Courtesy of Joan Wiley Luck.)

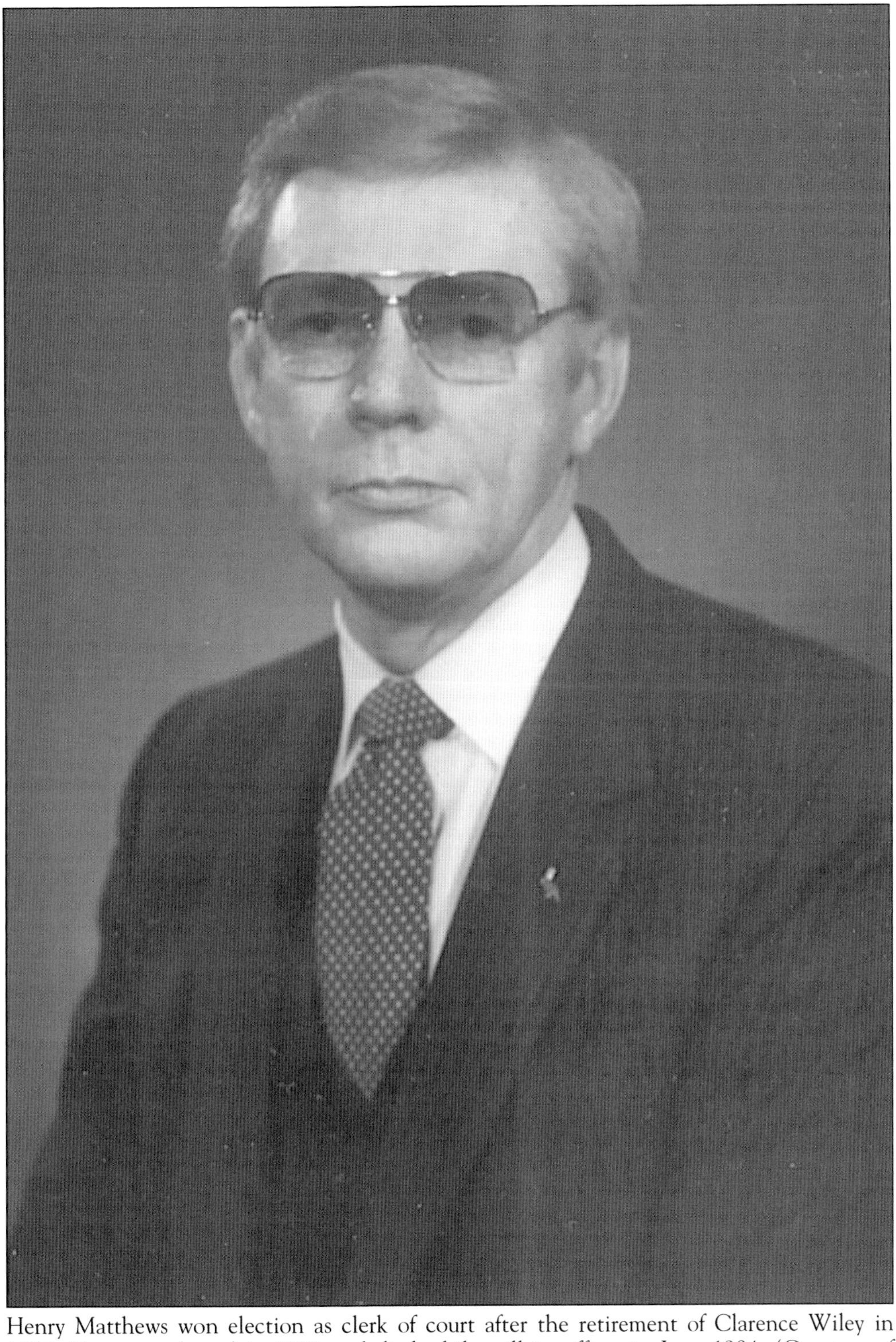

Henry Matthews won election as clerk of court after the retirement of Clarence Wiley in 1976. He was reelected in 1980 and died while still in office, in June 1984. (Courtesy of Doris Matthews.)

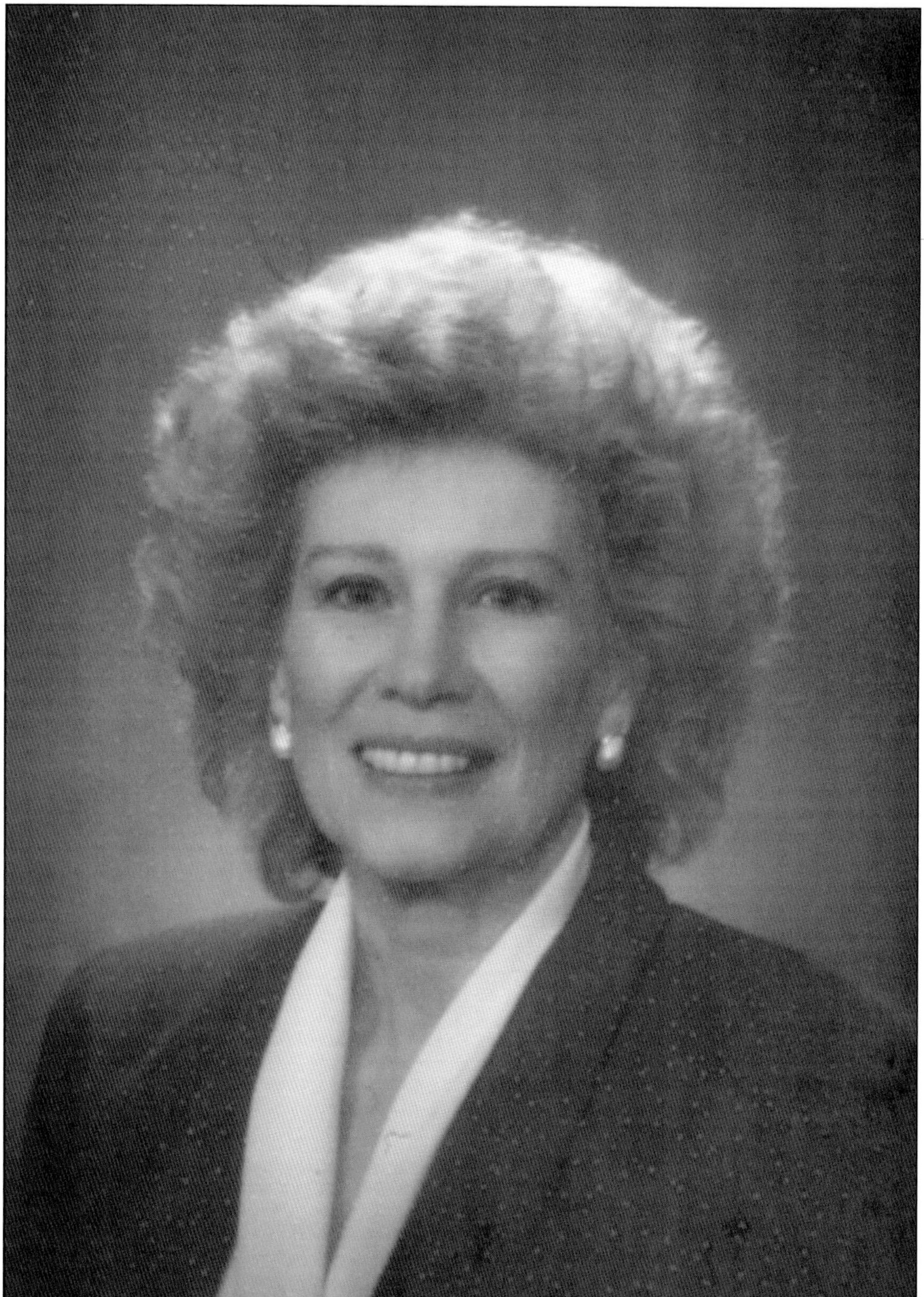

Winnie Brinkley, a native of Cotton Valley, was serving as deputy clerk when Henry Matthews died and assumed the office of clerk. In September 1984, she won election on her own right, becoming the first woman to be elected to a parish-wide office in history. She served four terms before retiring in 2000. (Courtesy of Winnie Brinkley.)

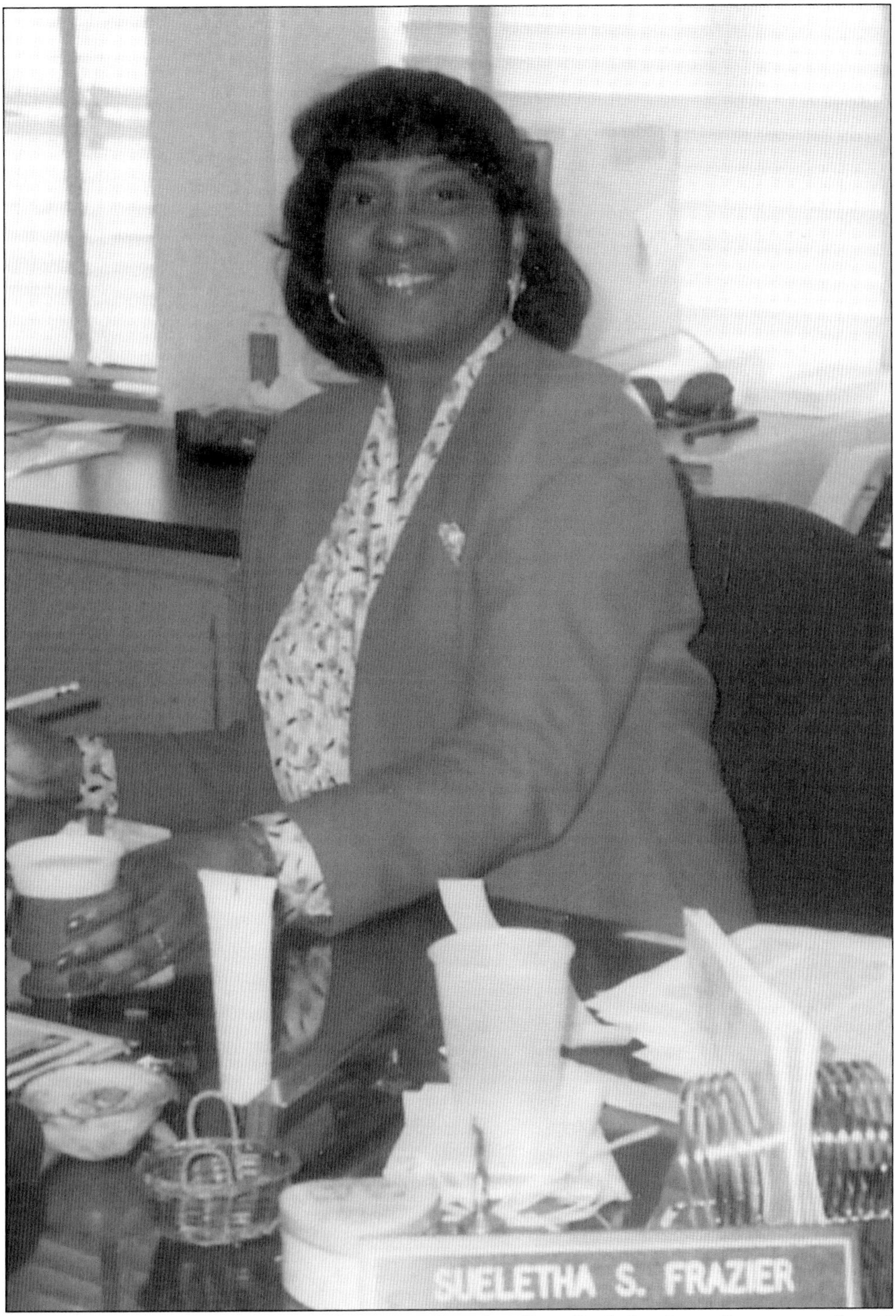

The first African American elected to a parish-wide office, Sueletha Scott Frazier was elected clerk of court in the fall of 1999. She had served for many years as deputy clerk to Winnie Brinkley and succeeded her in 2000. (Courtesy of Sueletha Scott Frazier.)

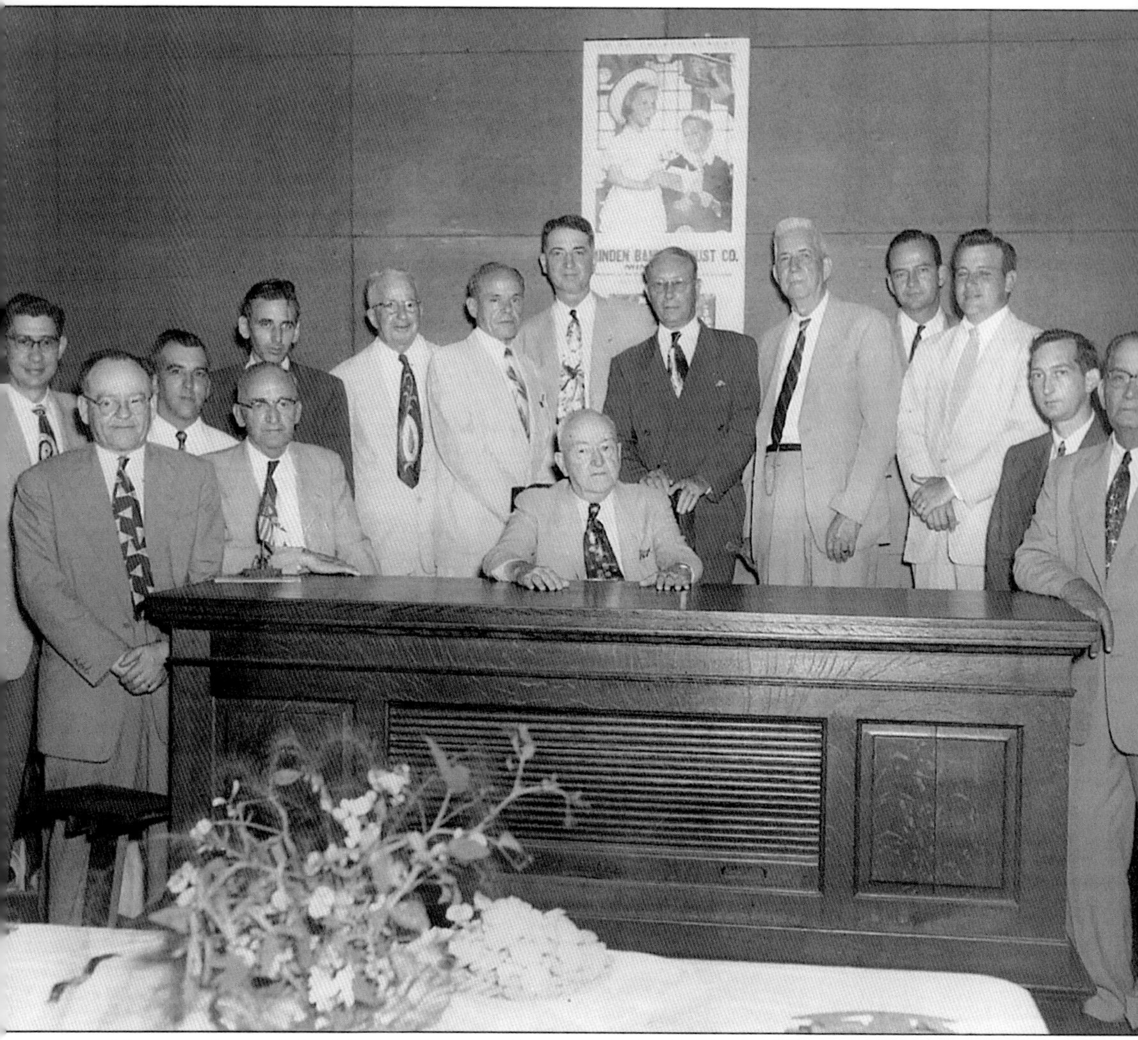

The members of the Minden bar are shown in May 1952 as Judge J. Frank McInnis (seated) left his position as district judge to become a judge on the state court of appeals in Shreveport. McInnis had also served as Webster Parish clerk of court from 1919 to 1924, before being admitted to the bar. Pictured from left to right are George W. Fort; Cecil P. Campbell; Enos C. McClendon Jr., later to serve as a 26th judicial district judge; Clerk of Court Tom J. Campbell; Cecil C. Lowe, later Minden city judge and 26th judicial district judge; David W. Thomas, mayor of Minden from 1936 to 1940; John T. Campbell; Graydon K. Kitchens, district attorney from 1941 to 1942; Dan W. Stewart Jr.; Will C. McKinney, longtime chief deputy clerk of court; R. Harmon Drew, later Minden city judge and state representative; John B. Benton Jr., later to serve as district attorney; Henry G. Hobbs; and Sheriff O.H. Haynes Sr. (Courtesy of Henry Hobbs.)

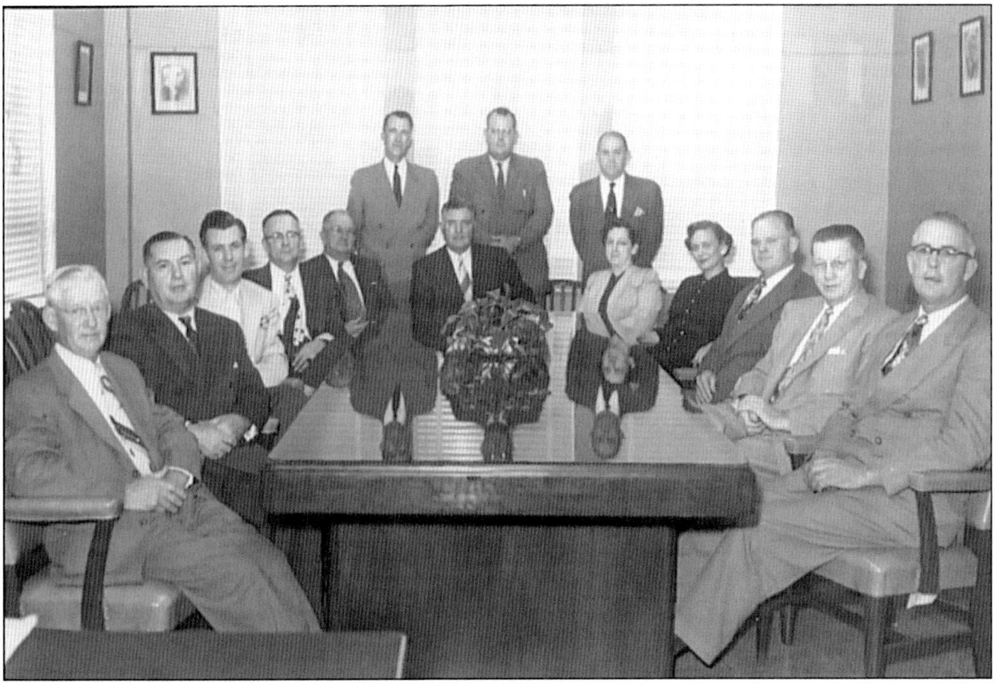

Members and administrators of the Webster Parish School Board are shown in this picture from the late 1950s. Seated at the head of the table is president J.E. Harper. Standing in the rear, from left to right, are assistant superintendent R.O. Machen Sr.; assistant superintendent R.H. Manning; and superintendent J.E. Pitcher. (Courtesy of R.O. Machen Jr.)

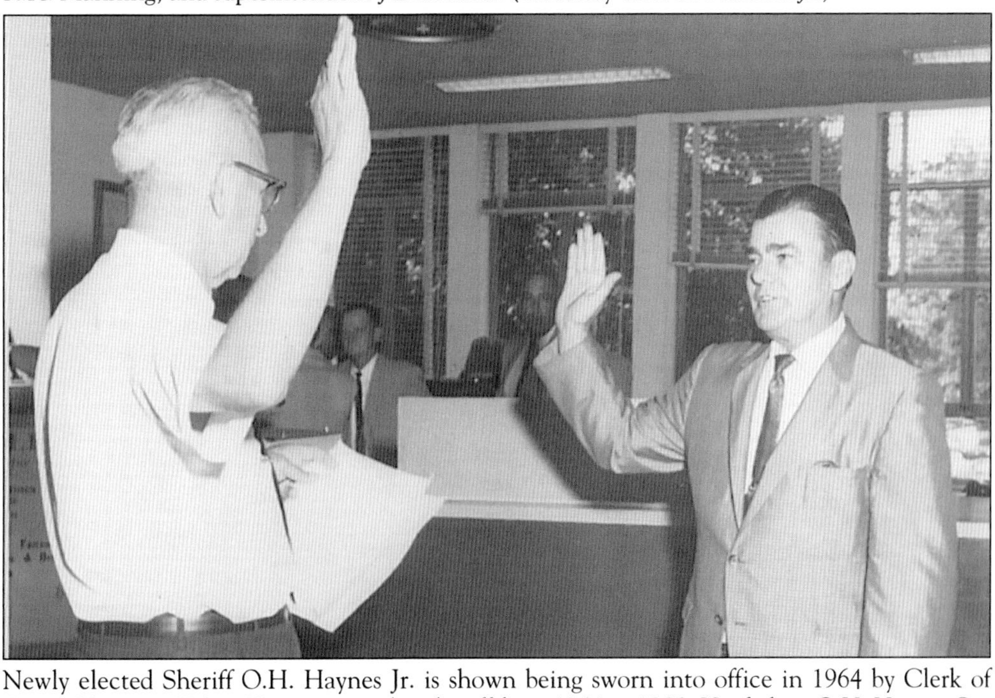

Newly elected Sheriff O.H. Haynes Jr. is shown being sworn into office in 1964 by Clerk of Court Clarence Wiley. Haynes served as sheriff from 1964 to 1980. His father, O.H. Haynes Sr., had been sheriff from 1933 to 1952. (Courtesy of Freddie Louise Haynes.)

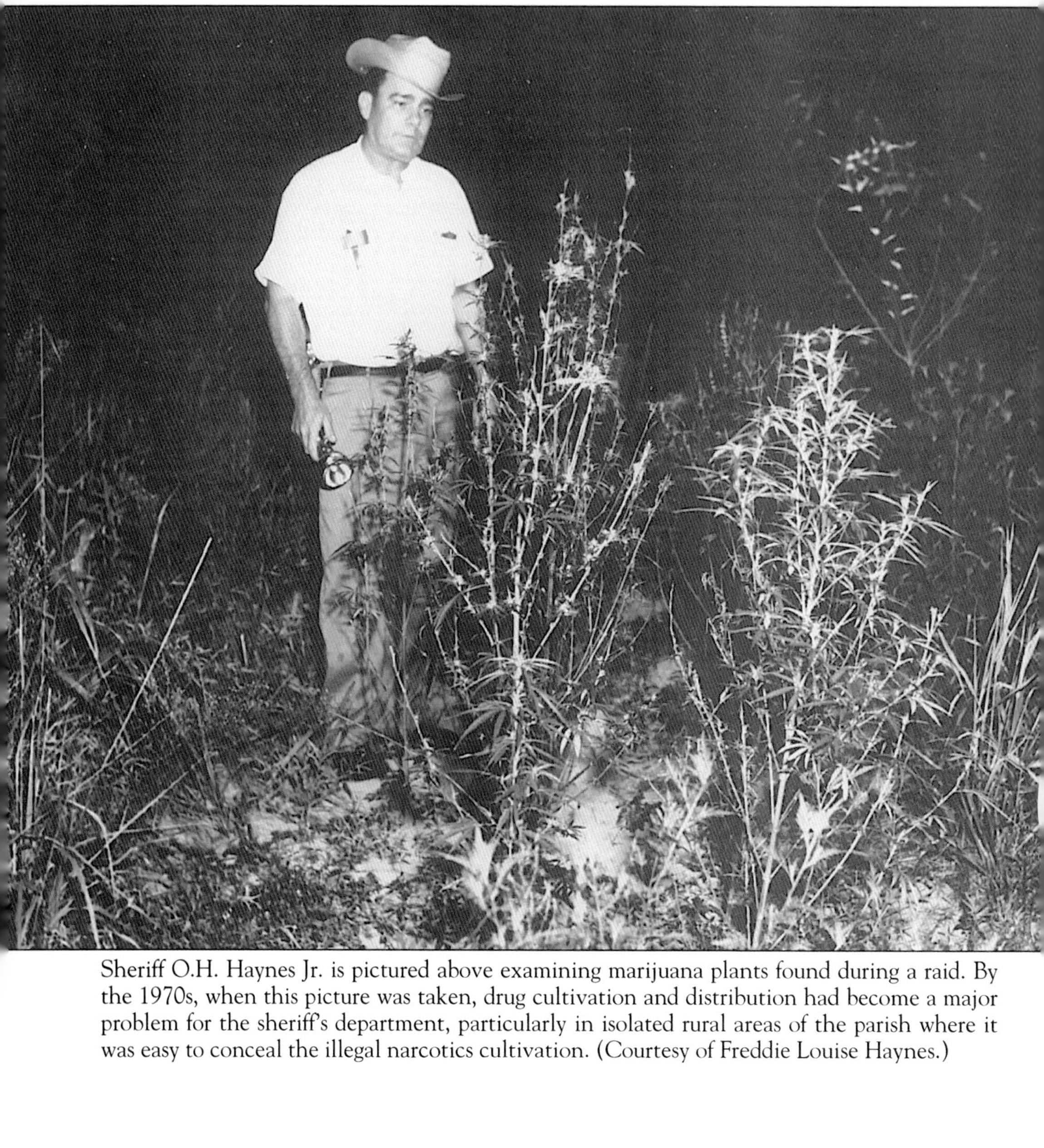

Sheriff O.H. Haynes Jr. is pictured above examining marijuana plants found during a raid. By the 1970s, when this picture was taken, drug cultivation and distribution had become a major problem for the sheriff's department, particularly in isolated rural areas of the parish where it was easy to conceal the illegal narcotics cultivation. (Courtesy of Freddie Louise Haynes.)

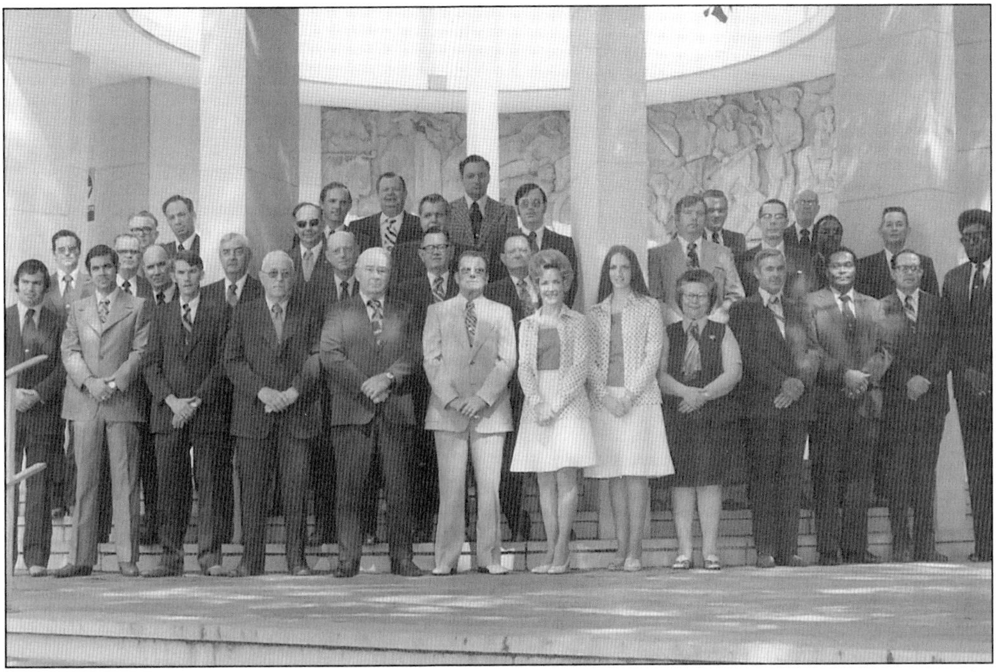

The Webster Parish sheriff's deputies and Sheriff O.H. Haynes Jr. are pictured above in the mid-1970s. Sheriff Haynes is standing at the center of the front row, and to his right is Deputy Royce McMahen, who would succeed Haynes as sheriff. In the center of the back row is Deputy Sheriff T.C. Bloxom, who would go on to become police chief of Minden. (Courtesy of Freddie Louise Haynes.)

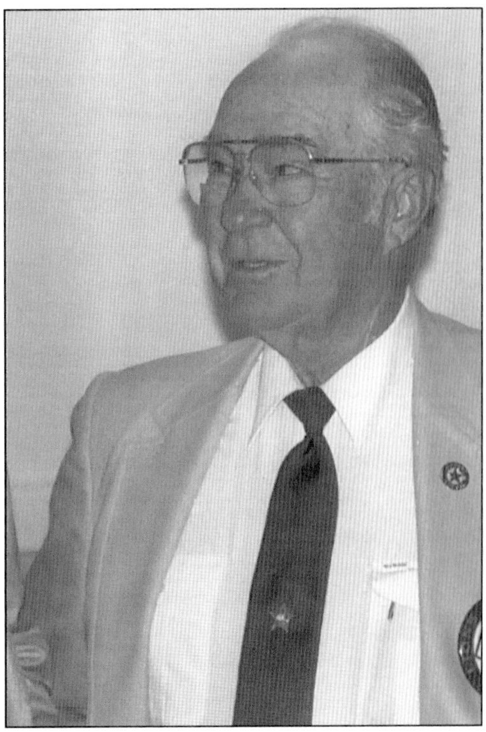

Sheriff Royce "Doc" McMahen of Springhill served from 1980 to 1996. A veterinarian by profession, McMahen joined the sheriff's office as the chief deputy in North Webster Parish under Sheriff O.H. Haynes Jr. (Courtesy of Minden *Press-Herald*.)

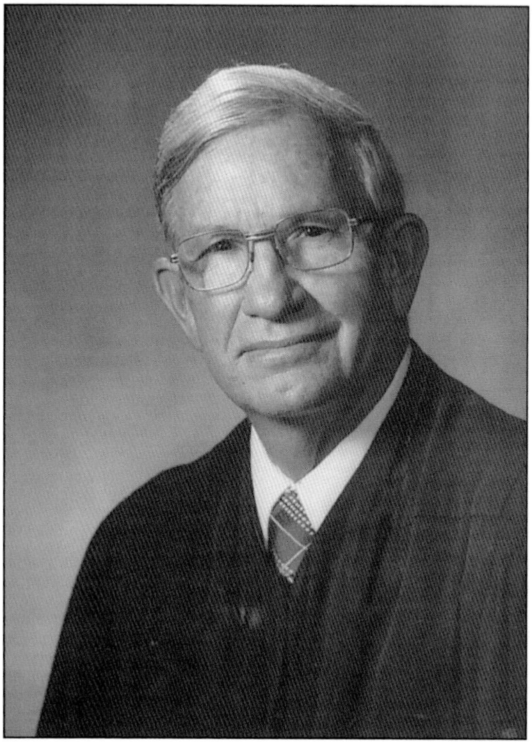

James E. Bolin was judge of the second circuit court of appeals. A native of Doyline, Bolin had earlier served as state representative for Webster Parish while a resident of Springhill. After moving to Minden he served as district attorney, district judge, and eventually judge of the court of appeals. (Courtesy of Minden *Press-Herald*.)

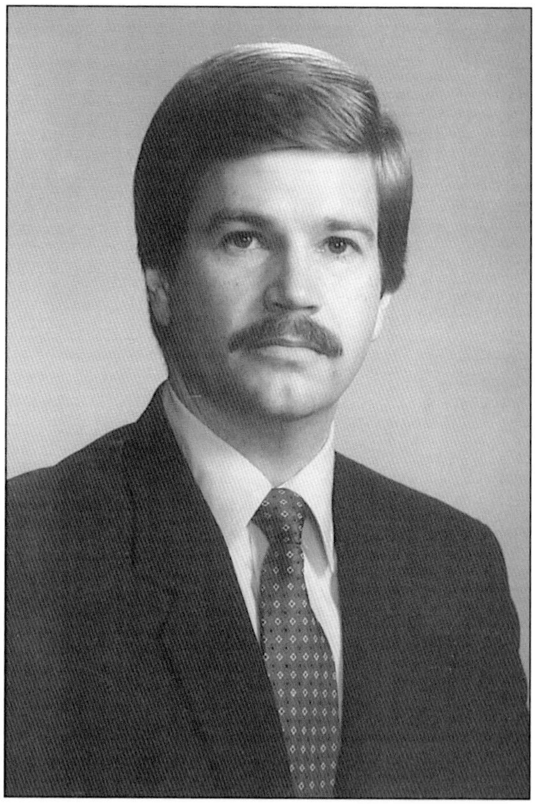

Judge Bruce Bolin, son of James E. Bolin, followed in his father's footsteps by first serving as Webster Parish representative in the Louisiana Legislature before being elected as a judge of the 26th judicial district. (Courtesy of Minden *Press-Herald*.)

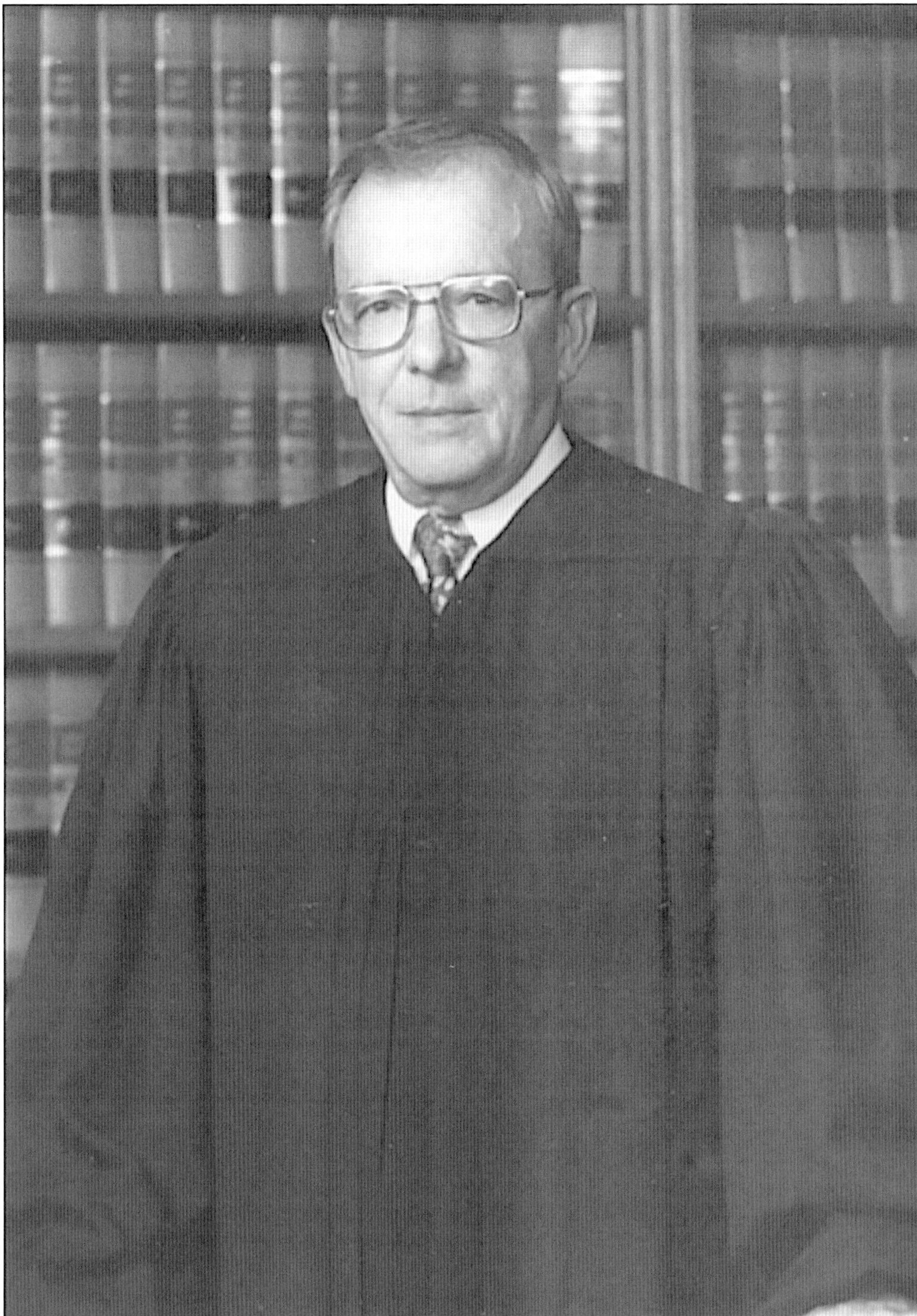

Charles A. "Corky" Marvin is shown while serving as judge of the Louisiana second circuit court of appeals. Marvin, son-in-law of long-time Minden attorney John T. Campbell, had earlier served as district attorney and district judge of the 26th judicial district. (Courtesy of C.A. Marvin.)

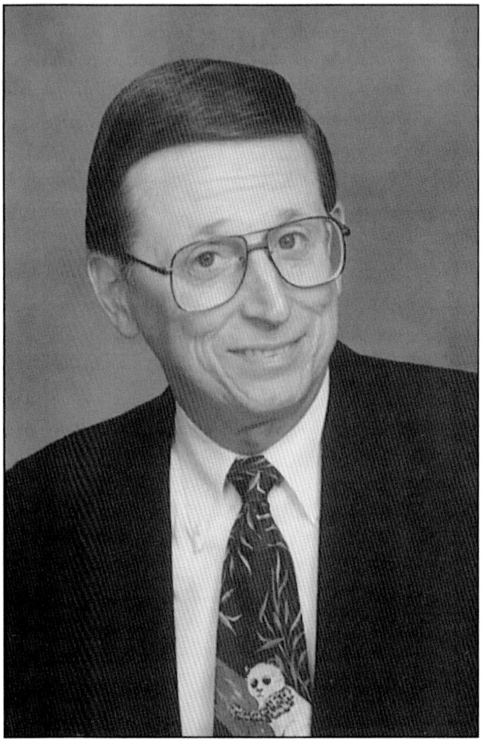

Judge Graydon K. Kitchens Jr. served as both Minden city judge and judge of the 26th judicial district. He is also a member of a family law firm that included at various times his father, Graydon K. Kitchens Sr., who served as district attorney; his first cousin, John B. Benton, who also served as district attorney; his brother, Paul; and his son, Graydon K. Kitchens III. (Courtesy of G.K. Kitchens Jr.)

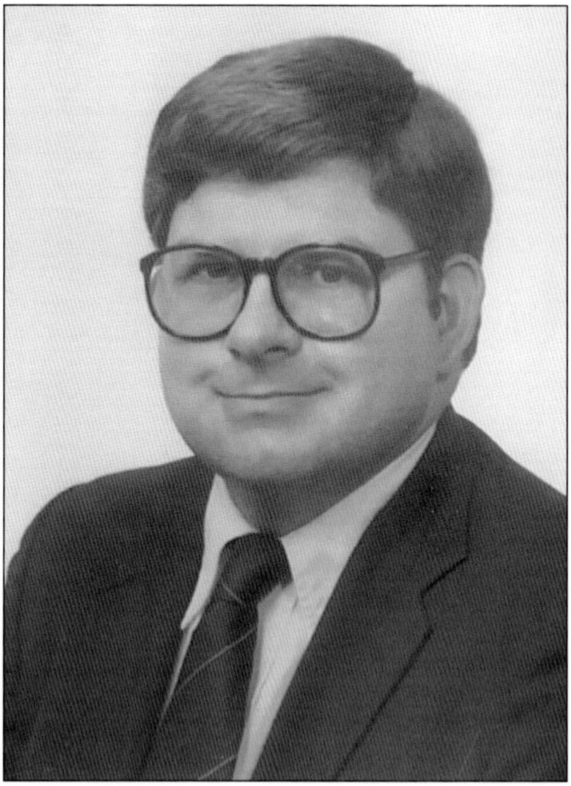

Judge R. Harmon Drew Jr. is the latest in a line of Drews to serve as judges in the Minden area, beginning in the 1850s. He served as a judge of the 26th judicial district and then was elected to the second circuit court of appeals. In addition, Judge Drew has a regional reputation as a musician and entertainer as the leader of the Harmon Drew Group. (Courtesy of R. Harmon Drew Jr.)

Harold Newsom, a retired teacher, served as president of the Webster Parish School Board during the 1980s and 1990s. (Courtesy of Minden *Press-Herald.*)

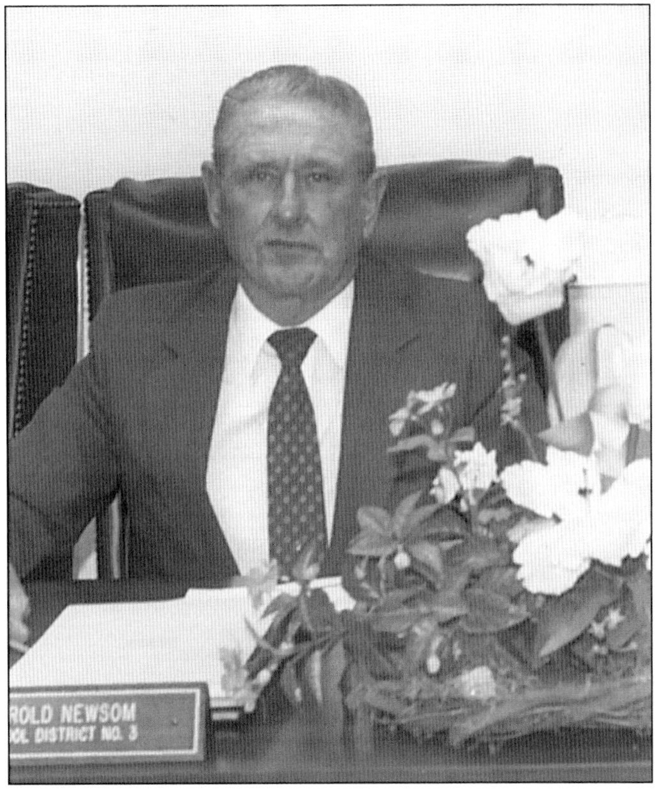

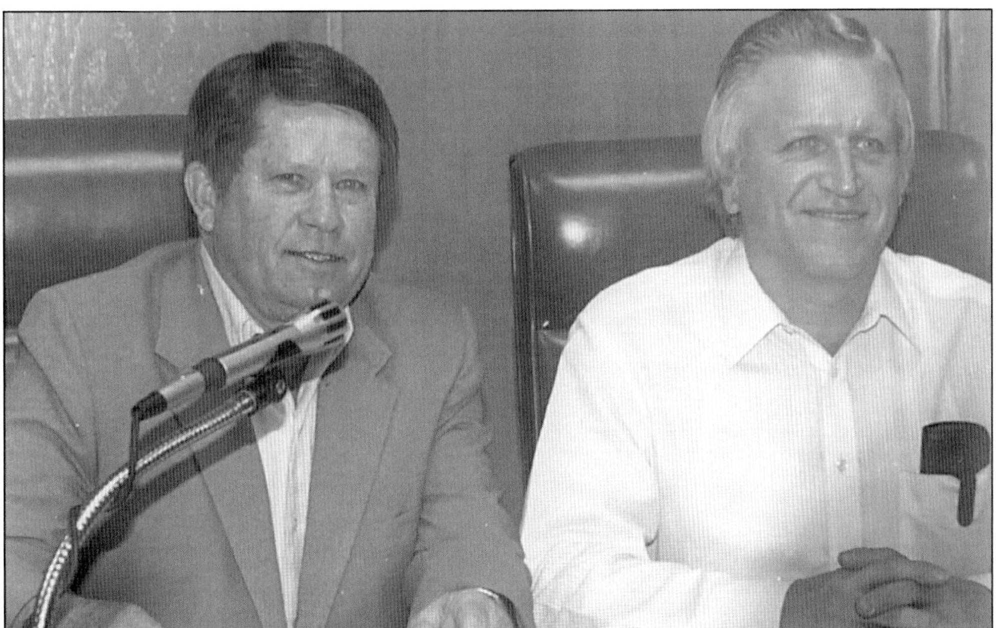

Police Jurors M.S. "Digger" O'Dell of Minden and John Blake of Springhill are pictured during a jury meeting in the 1970s. (Courtesy of Minden *Press-Herald.*)

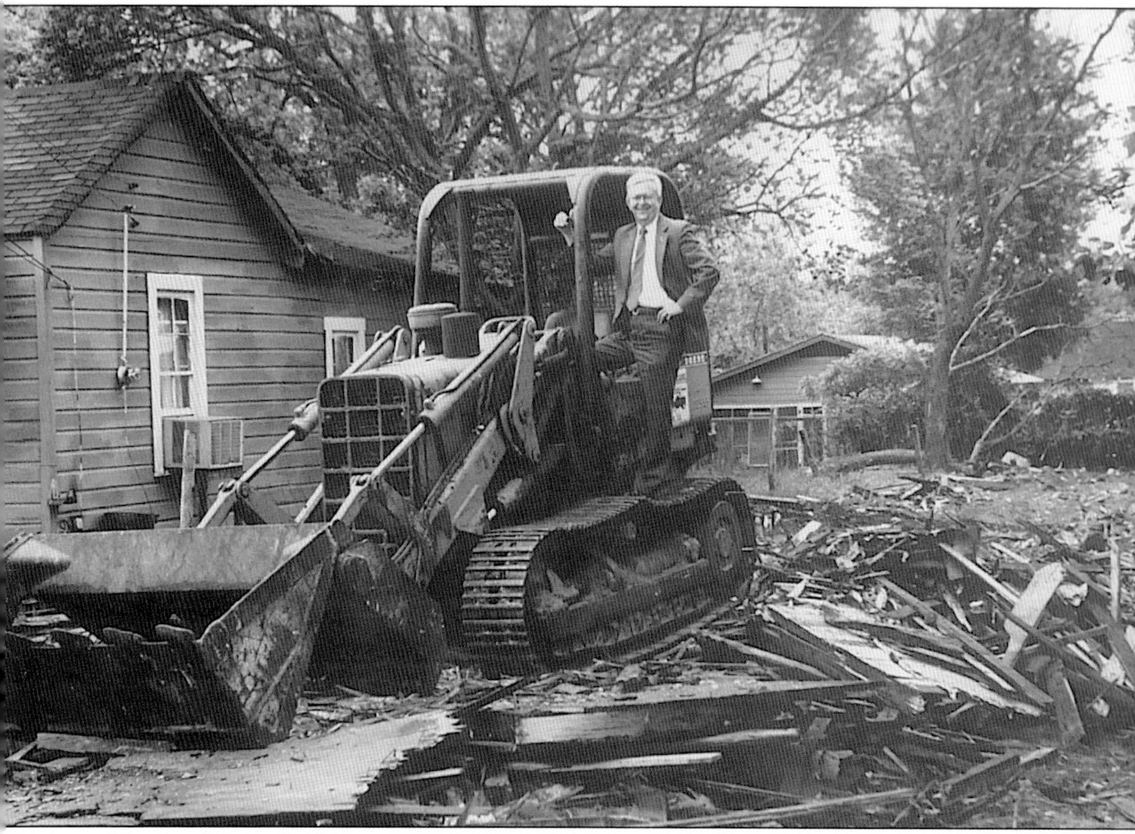

Minden Mayor Paul Brown is shown standing on a bulldozer that has just demolished an abandoned house. Brown won election as mayor following a trouble-filled period that had seen the previous mayor recalled by the voters. Brown promised to clean up the city both figuratively and literally. This picture was taken as his administration was calling for the removal of abandoned and decaying property from Minden. (Courtesy of Minden *Press-Herald*.)

Charles Minnifield became the first African American to serve as Minden city attorney during the late 1980s. (Courtesy of Minden *Press-Herald*.)

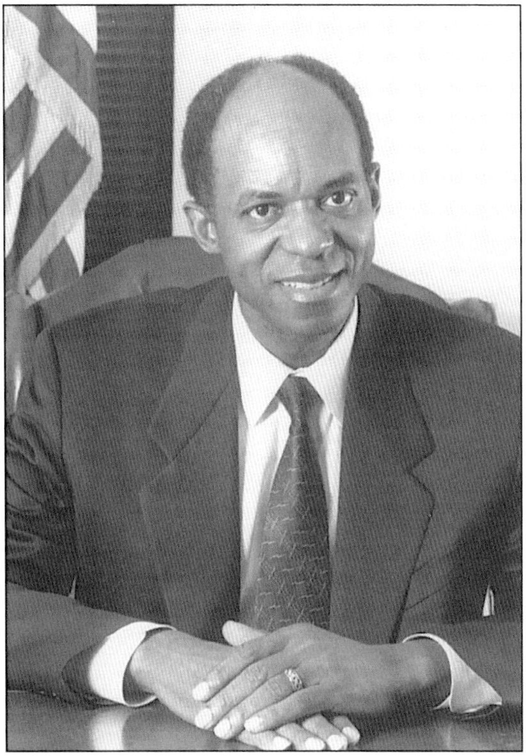

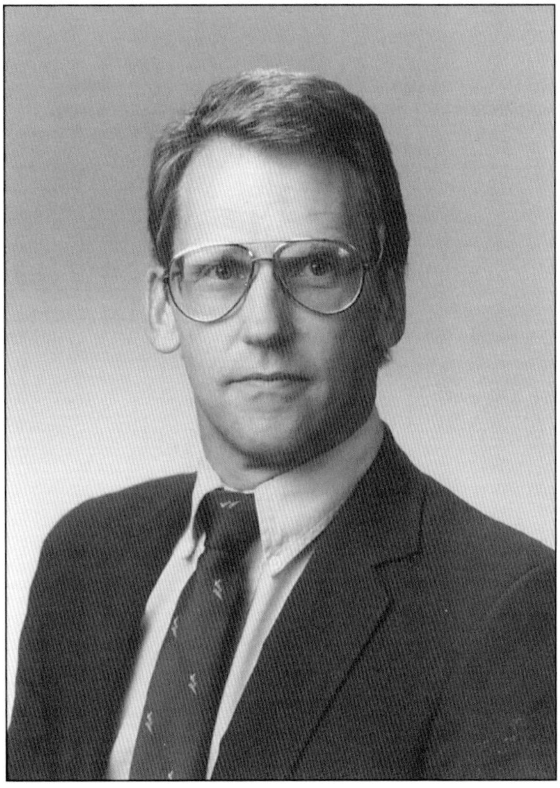

Jim Bullers of Bossier City is the current district attorney of the 26th judicial district. (Courtesy of Minden *Press-Herald*.)

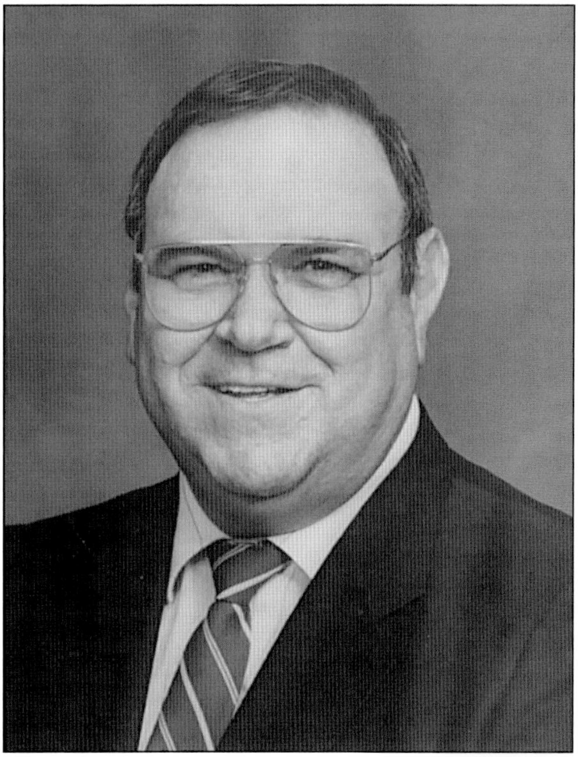

Dr. Everett G. Doerge, a retired teacher, coach, principal, and administrator in the Webster Parish School system, gained election as state representative for Webster Parish. He fought particularly hard for education issues in the legislature before suffering a fatal heart attack. (Courtesy of Minden *Press-Herald.*)

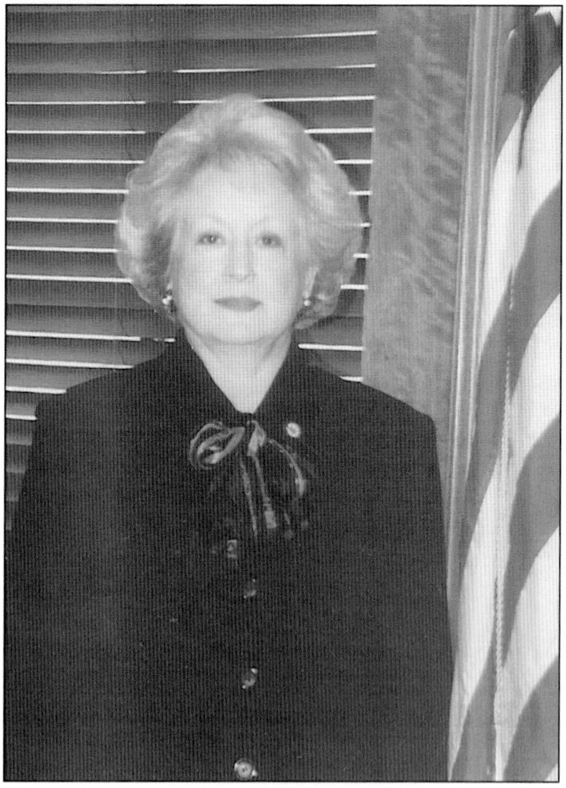

Dr. Doerge's term was filled by his widow, Jean Doerge, also a retired educator. She finished his term with distinction and then won election in her own right in the fall of 1999. (Courtesy of Minden *Press-Herald.*)

Three

EDUCATION

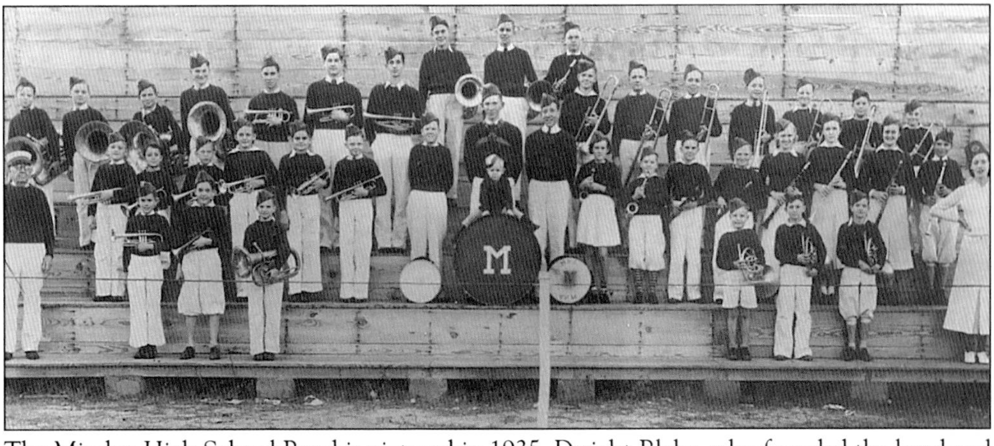

The Minden High School Band is pictured in 1935. Dwight Blake, who founded the band and led it for 20 years, is seen at the front left. The band mascot, seated on top of the bass drum, is 5-year-old Alan Bean, who later become the fourth man to walk on the moon as an astronaut on Apollo 12. (Courtesy of Major DePingre.)

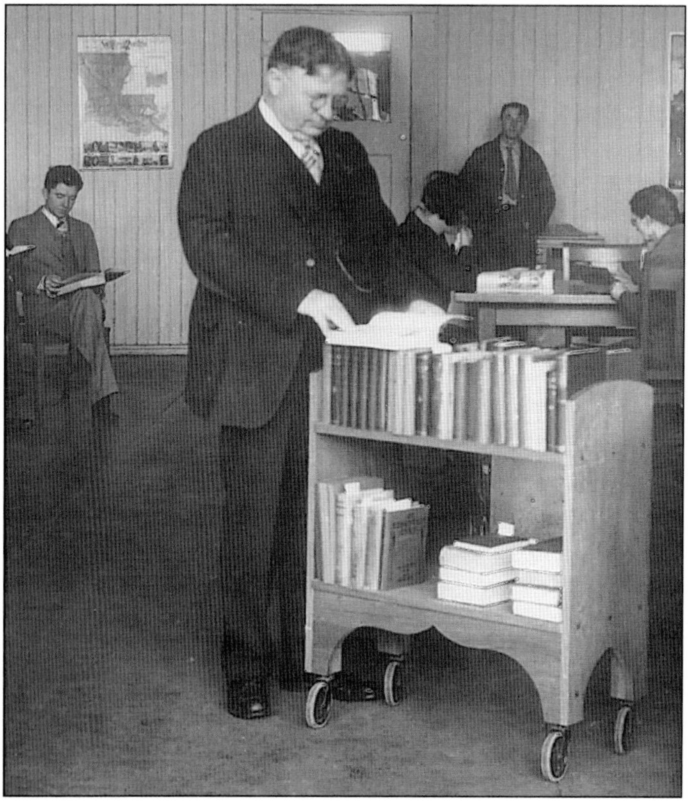

Superintendent E.S. Richardson, with the cooperation of the Webster Parish School Board, transformed a system that included 39 decaying frame schools, as seen on later pages, into a system with 11 modern brick buildings between 1919 and 1927. He also pioneered the use of school buses to make his consolidation program possible.

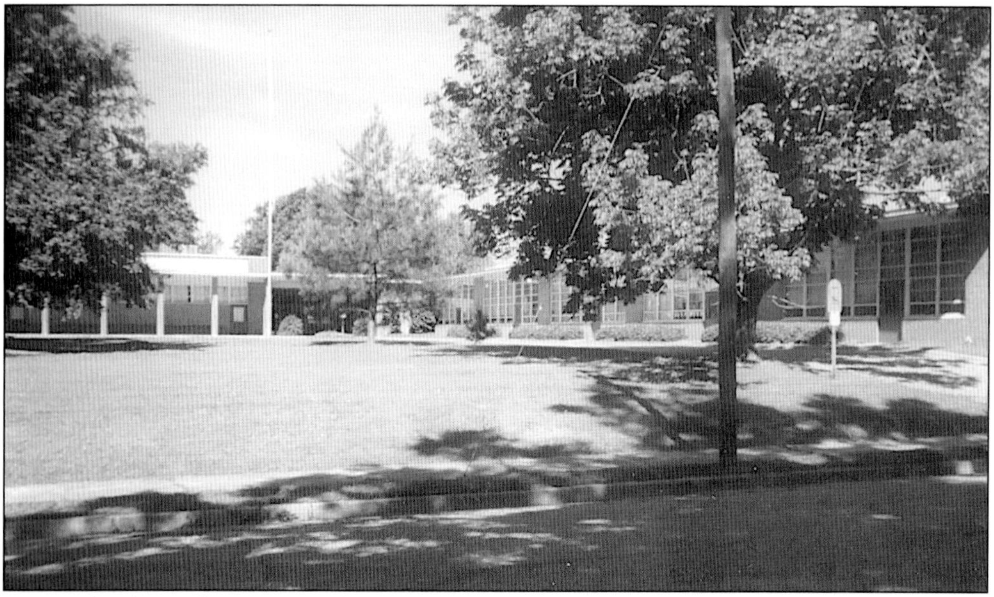

E.S. Richardson Elementary School was erected in Minden in 1948 and named after the superintendent responsible for reforming and modernizing the Webster Parish Schools.

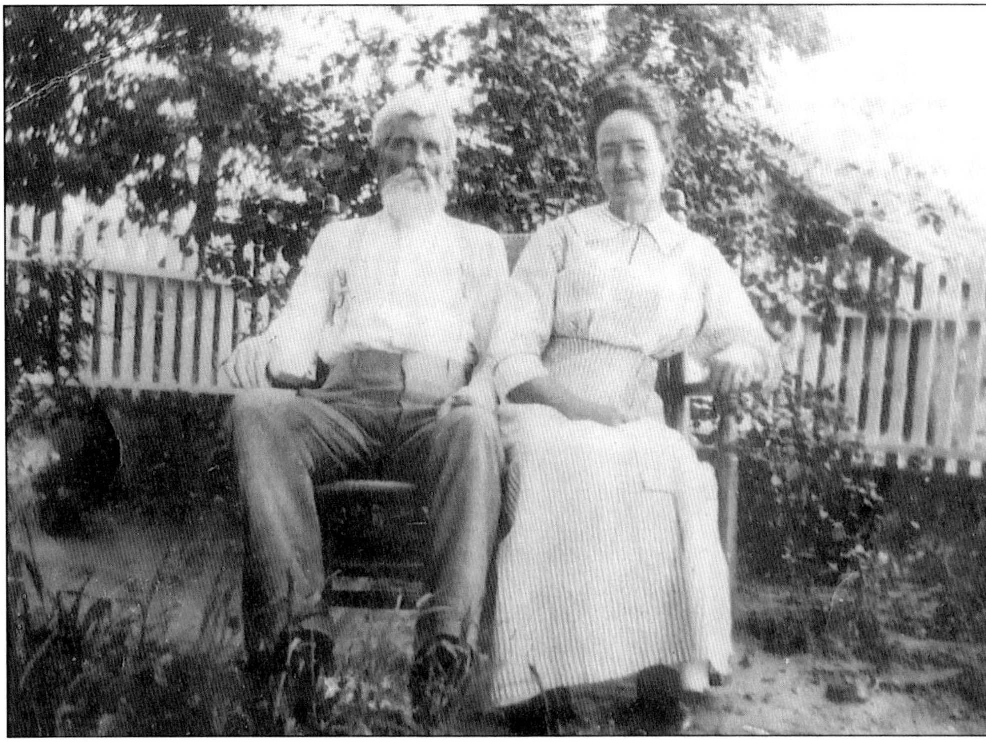

William G. Stewart and his wife, Nora Killen Stewart, are pictured at home around 1920. Mr. Stewart was president of the Webster Parish School Board when E.S. Richardson was hired in 1919, and worked with Richardson to make the modernization of Webster Parish Schools a success. (Courtesy of Virginia Fox.)

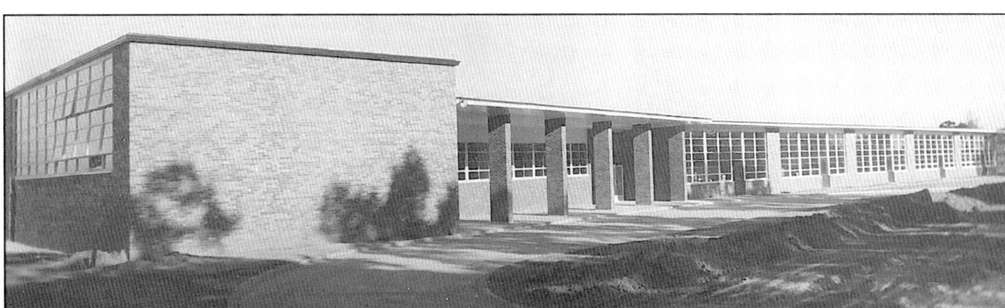

W.G. Stewart Elementary School was built on the west side of Minden in 1948, and named in honor of the school board president who worked so closely with E.S. Richardson to bring about progress in the parish schools. (Courtesy of W.W. Williams Sr.)

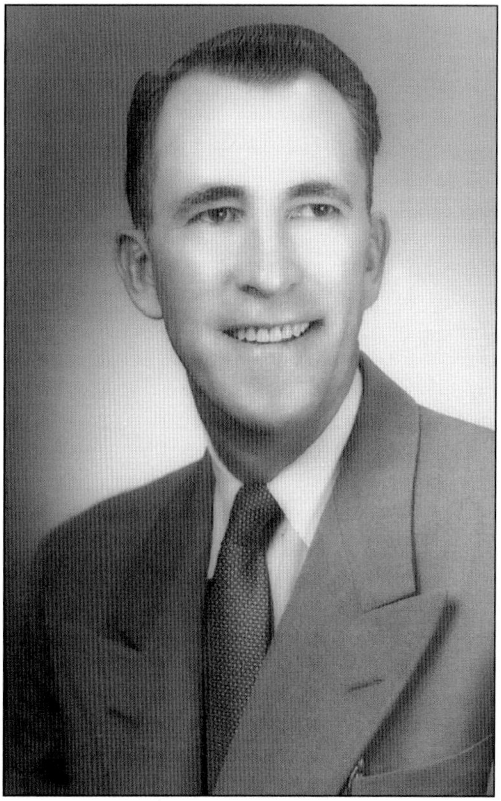

R.O. Machen Sr. served for many years as a teacher, coach, and principal in the Webster Parish School System. He then became an assistant superintendent under superintendent J.E. Pitcher, before becoming superintendent of Webster Parish Schools in the early 1960s. (Courtesy of R.O. Machen Jr.)

This frame school at Springhill was in use in the early years of the 20th century, before consolidation and modernization. (Courtesy of Webster Parish School Board.)

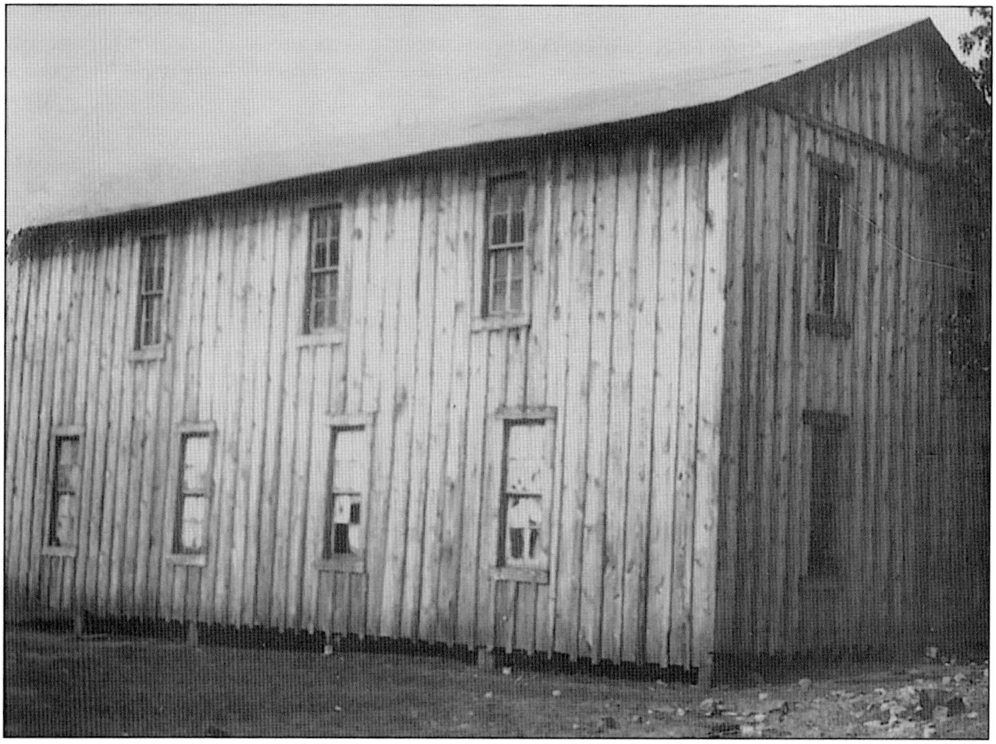

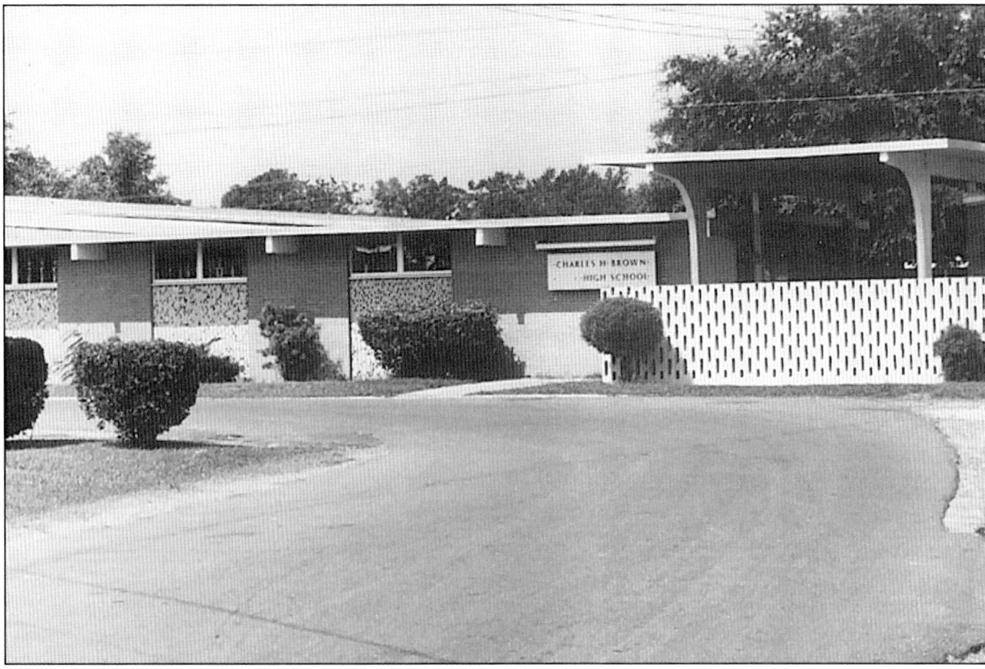

Charles Brown High School in Springhill served as the African-American high school for Springhill before school desegregation. It was later converted to a junior high school. (Courtesy of W.W. Williams Sr.)

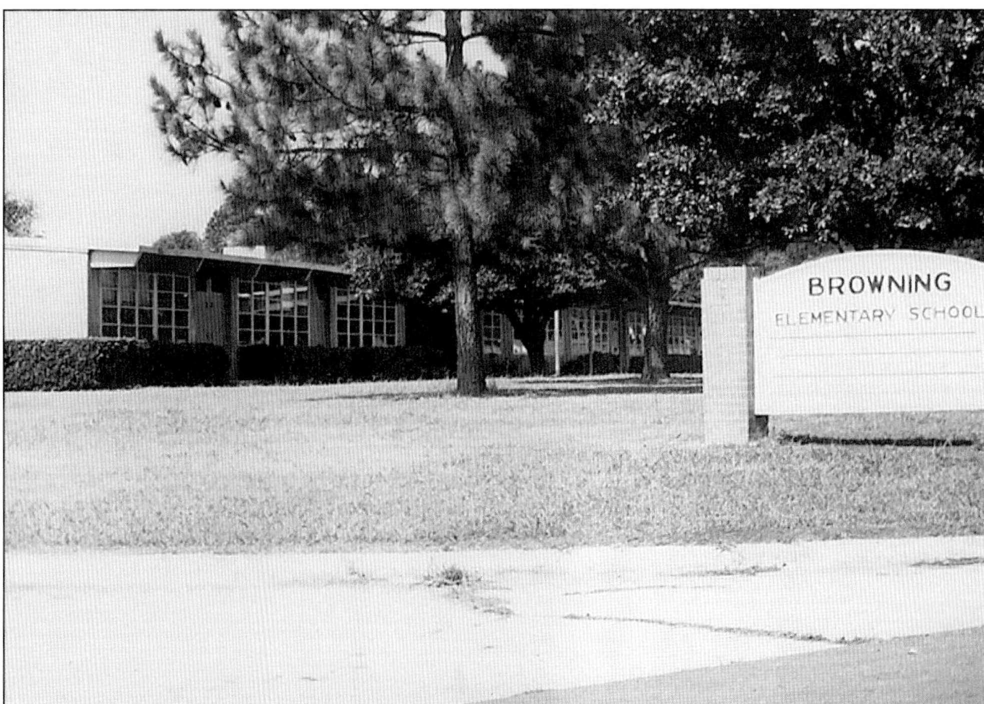

Browning Elementary School in Springhill was named for a longtime educational leader in the Springhill area. (Courtesy of W.W. Williams Sr.)

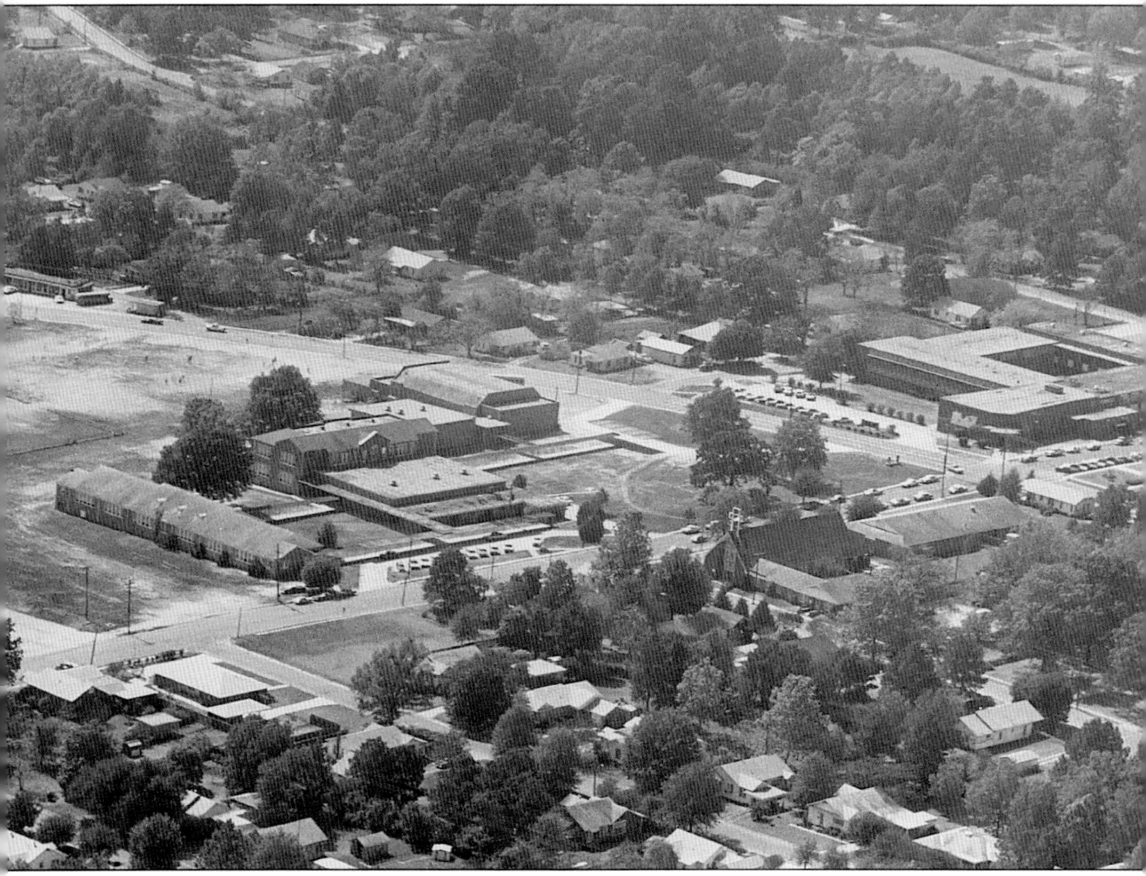

An aerial view of the current Springhill High School and Springhill Junior High School campuses was taken in October 1975. The high school is seen to the far right of the picture, with the junior high school across the street in the left side of the image. (Courtesy of W.W. Williams Sr.)

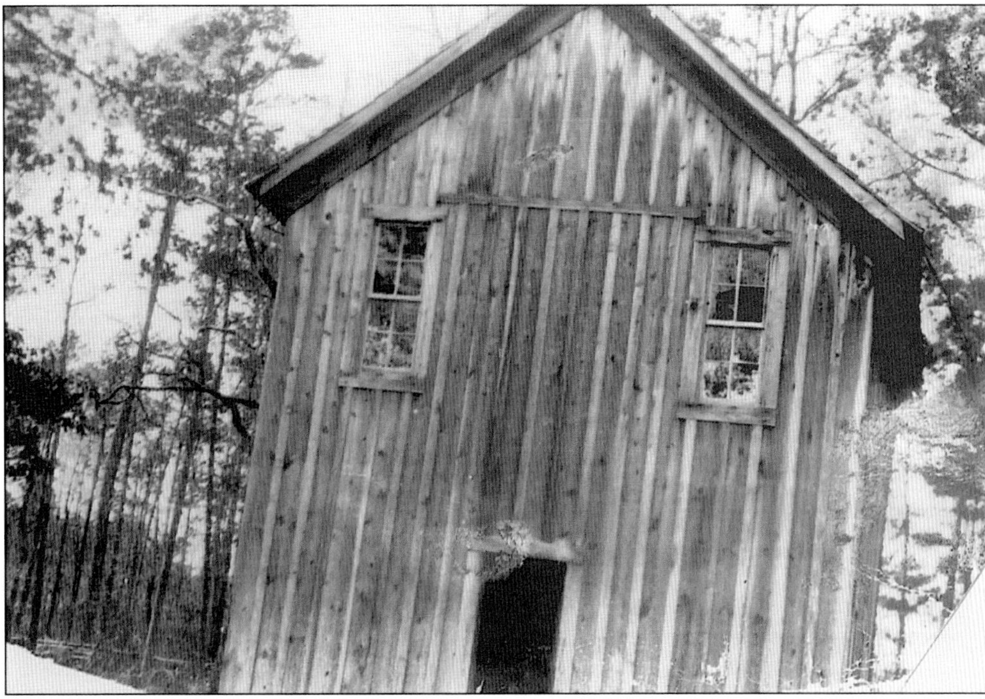

The Thomasville School in the Sarepta area is pictured during the early 1900s. (Courtesy of Webster Parish School Board.)

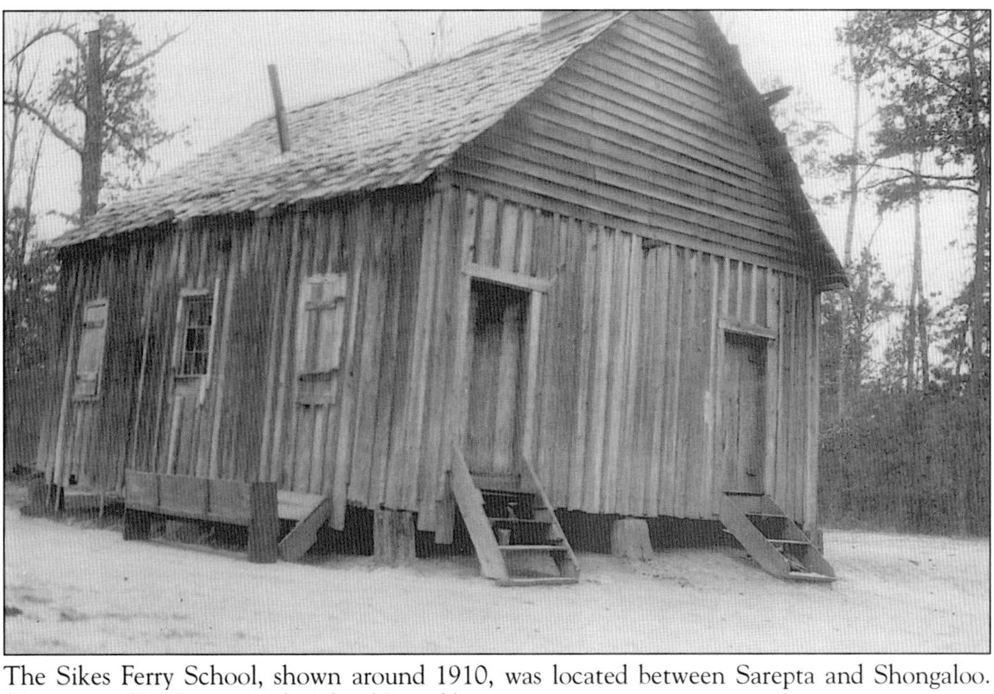

The Sikes Ferry School, shown around 1910, was located between Sarepta and Shongaloo. (Courtesy of Webster Parish School Board.)

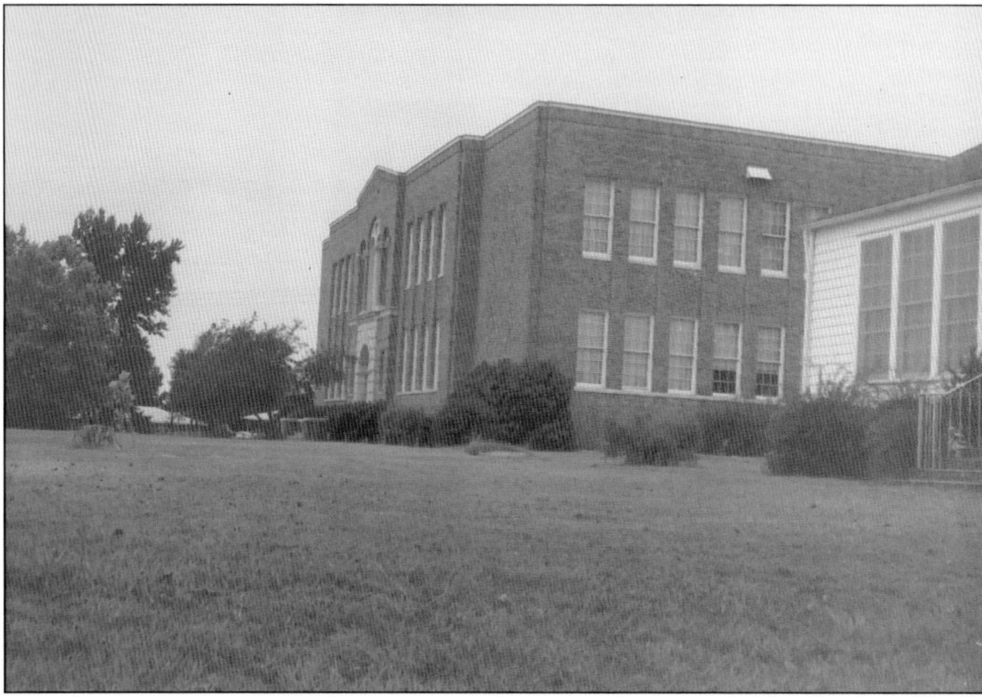

Sarepta High School was constructed in the mid-1920s, during the tenure of E.S. Richardson. Shown during the 1950s, the building is still in use today. (Courtesy of W.W. Williams Sr.)

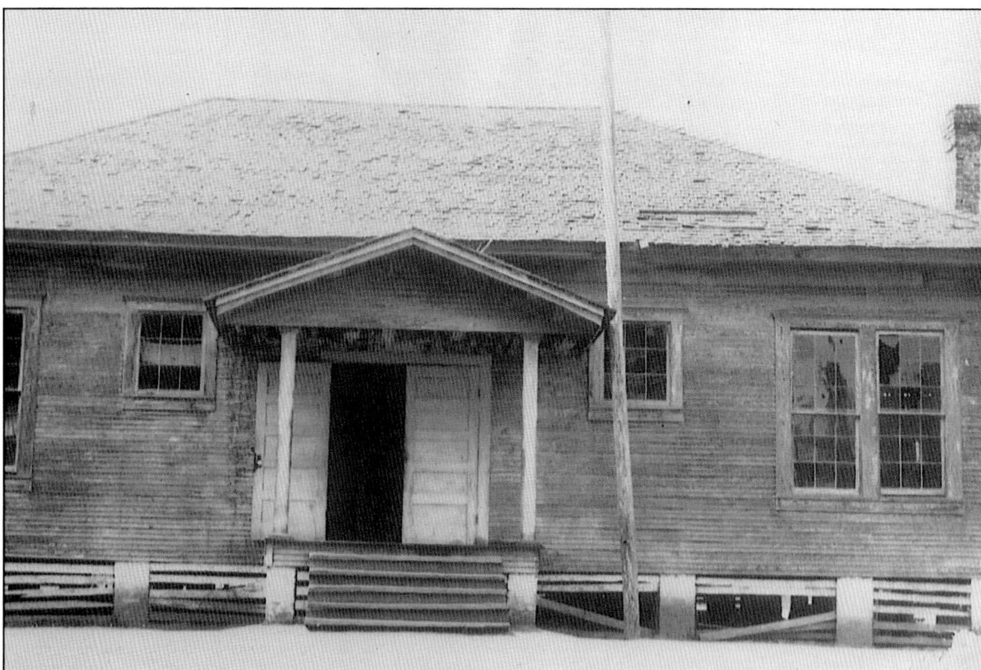

In a picture taken shortly after it was abandoned is the Cotton Valley School, which was replaced in the consolidation and construction program of the 1920s. (Courtesy of Webster Parish School Board.)

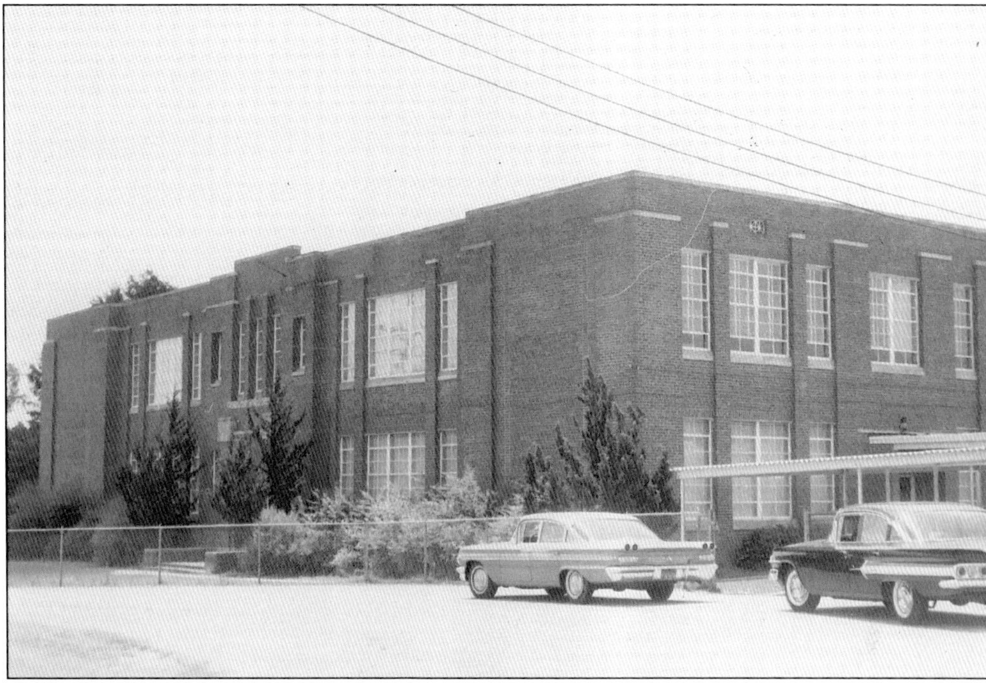

The new Cotton Valley school built by the Richardson administration of the school board is pictured in the 1950s. This building has been replaced by a newer school complex. (Courtesy of W.W. Williams.)

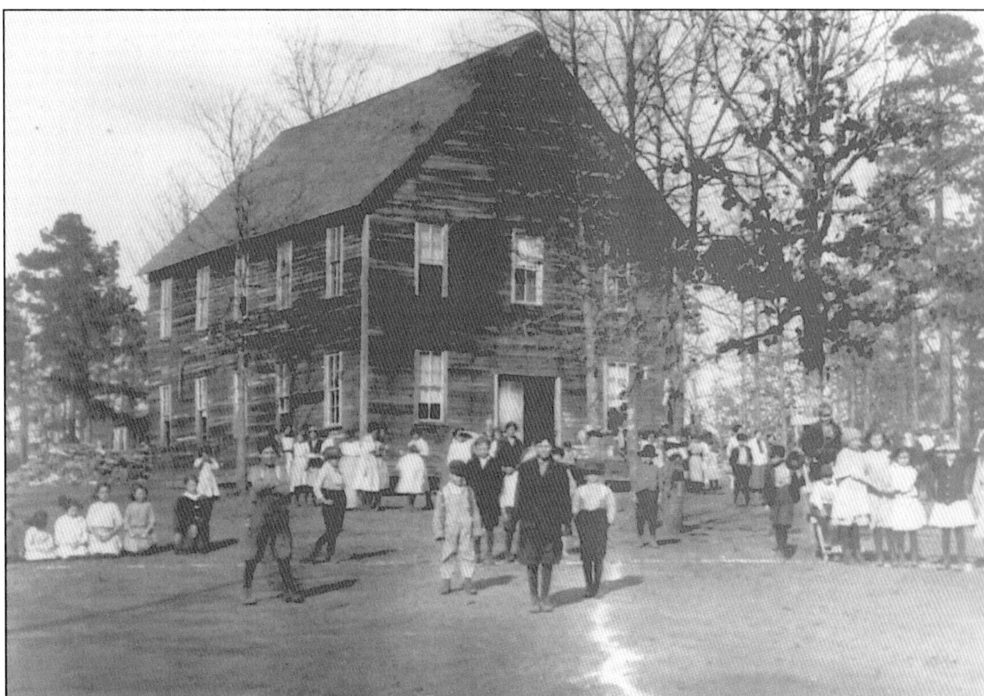

Children are seen at recess in this picture of the Shongaloo School, taken *c.* 1895. (Courtesy of Webster Parish School Board.)

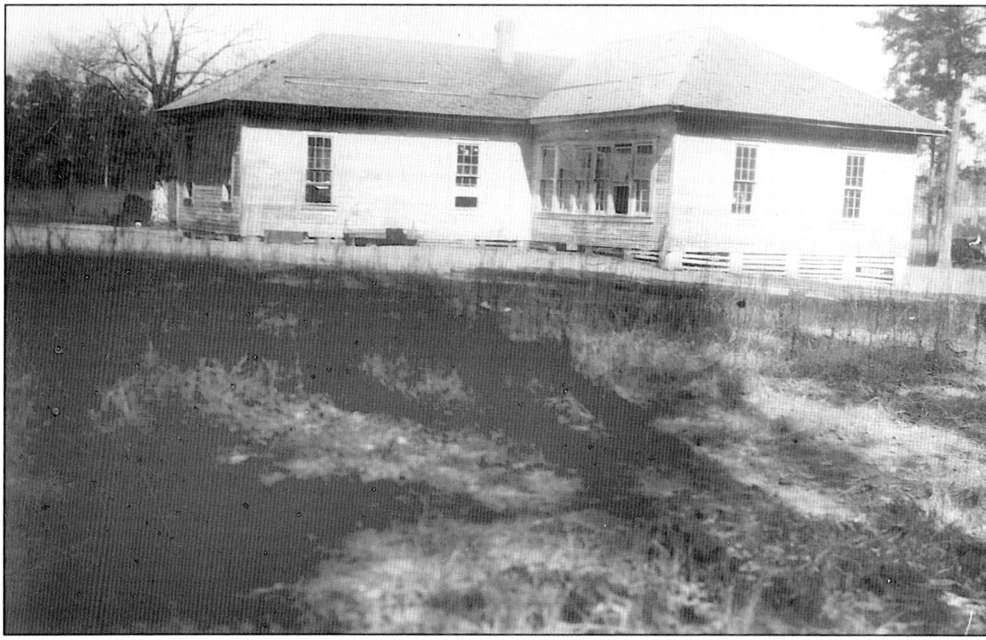

Shown after it had been abandoned is the Thomas and Rhone School, near Shongaloo in Northern Webster Parish. (Courtesy of W.W. Williams.)

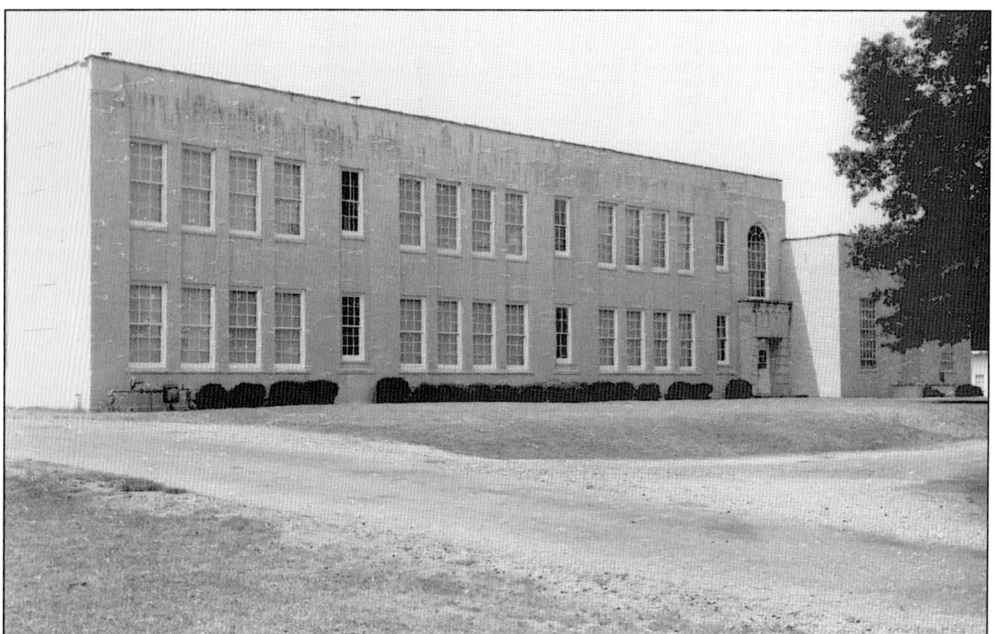

The Shongaloo School was built under the administration of E.S. Richardson in the 1920s. The building remained in use until the 1990s. (Courtesy of W.W. Williams Sr.)

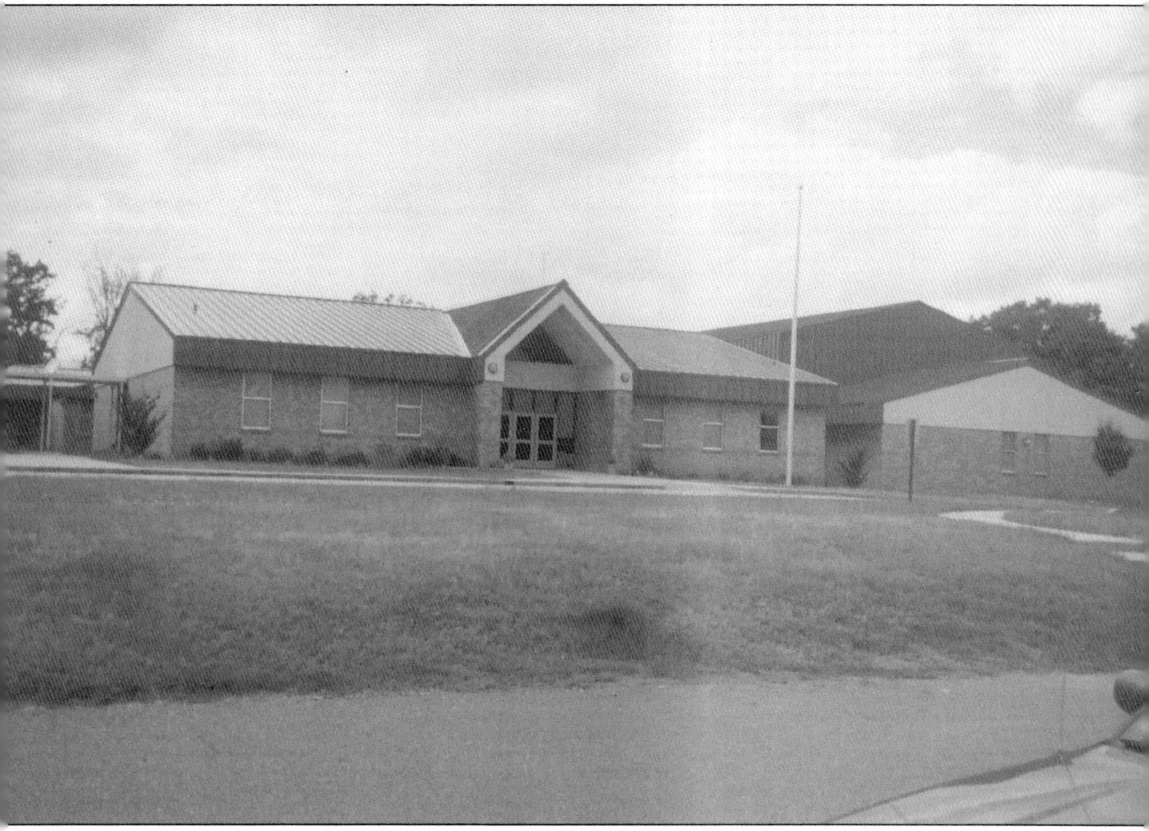

The new Shongaloo School, funded by a bond issue passed in the 1990s, replaced the old building, which dated from the 1920s.

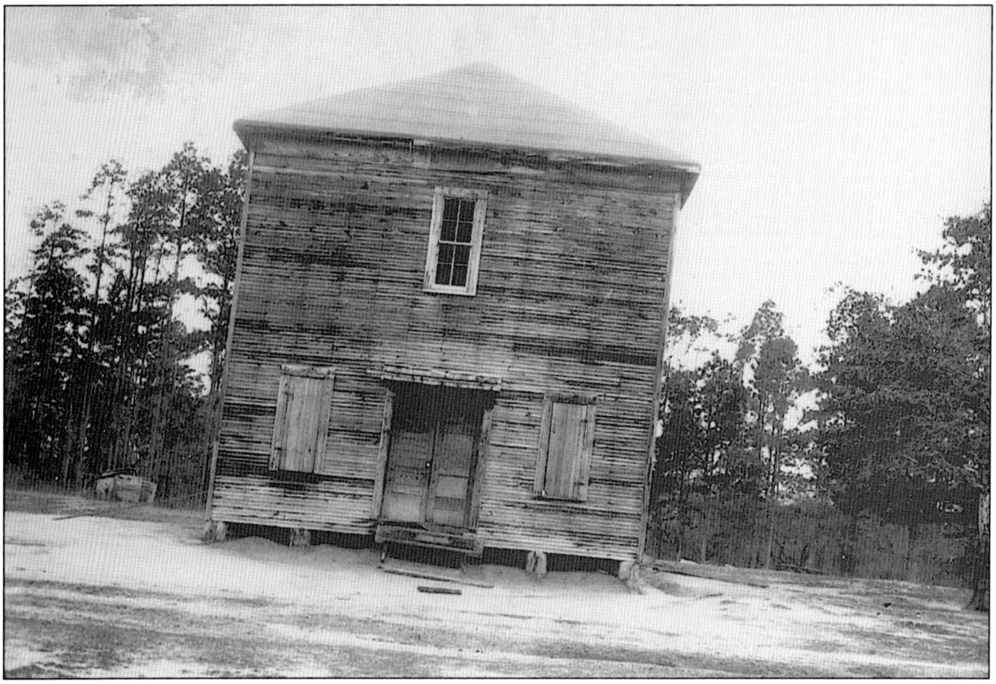

Another of the old inadequate frame schools was the New Hortman School, located at Couchwood between Minden and Cotton Valley. (Courtesy of Webster Parish School Board.)

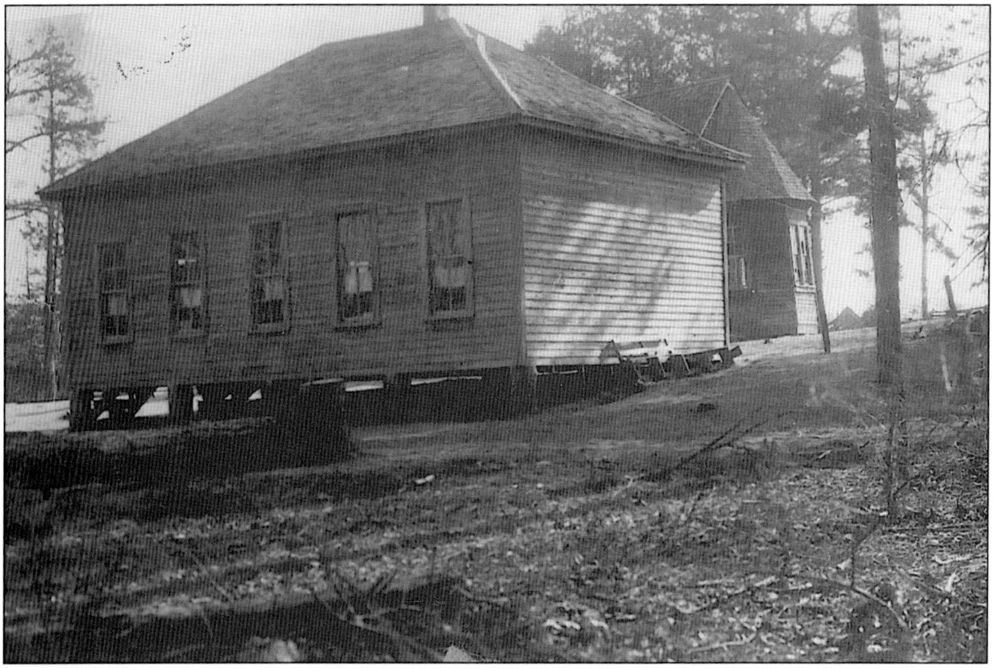

The Growing Valley School, located at Hortman, also between Minden and Cotton Valley, is pictured in the early years of the 20th century. (Courtesy of Webster Parish School Board.)

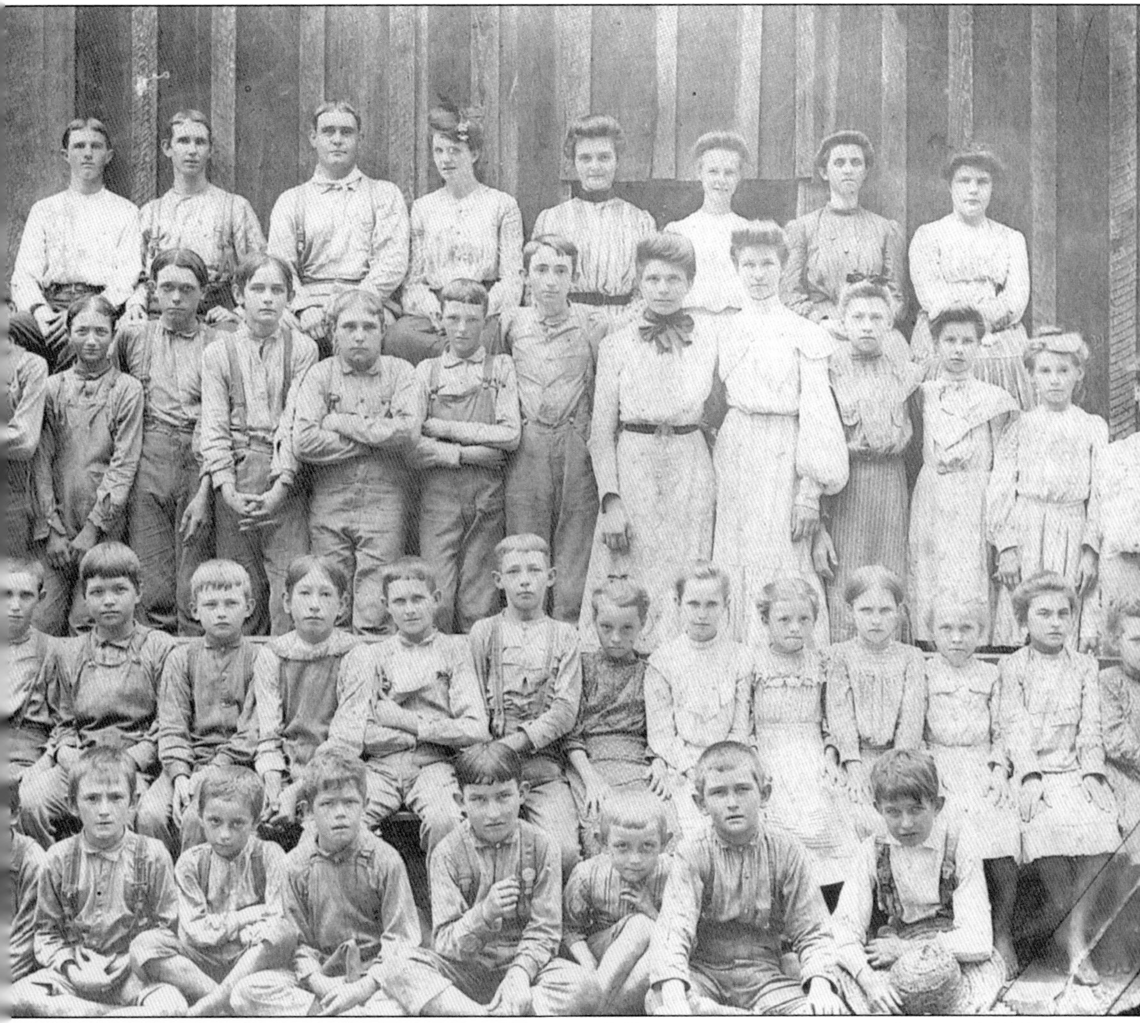

Students of the Rocky Ridge School in the area of Germantown are pictured around 1900. Seen here from left to right are as follows: (first row) Allen Gamble, Luther Botzong, Ike Chanler, Wess Gamble, Lonnie Gruner, John Lanier Miller, Alvin D. Miller, and Howard Davenport; (second row) Ralph Gamble, unidentified, Ernest Cook, Ruben A. Gruner, Johnny Gamble, Emile Krouse, Eunice Krouse, Sally Gamble, Annie Chanler, Mary Lou Gamble, Ida Belle Cook, Irma Cook, and Iona Rosura Krouse; (third row) unidentified, unidentified, Floyd Gamble, Will T. Miller, James Botzong, Arthur Krouse, Robert Botzong, Florence Gamble, Alice Carter, Exa Cole, Minnie Carter, Sophia Gruner, and Cleo Gail; (fourth row) Ernest Carter, Arthur Gamble, John Botzong, Eva Gamble, Jodie Miller, Edna Davenport, Addie Miller, and Kate Botzong.

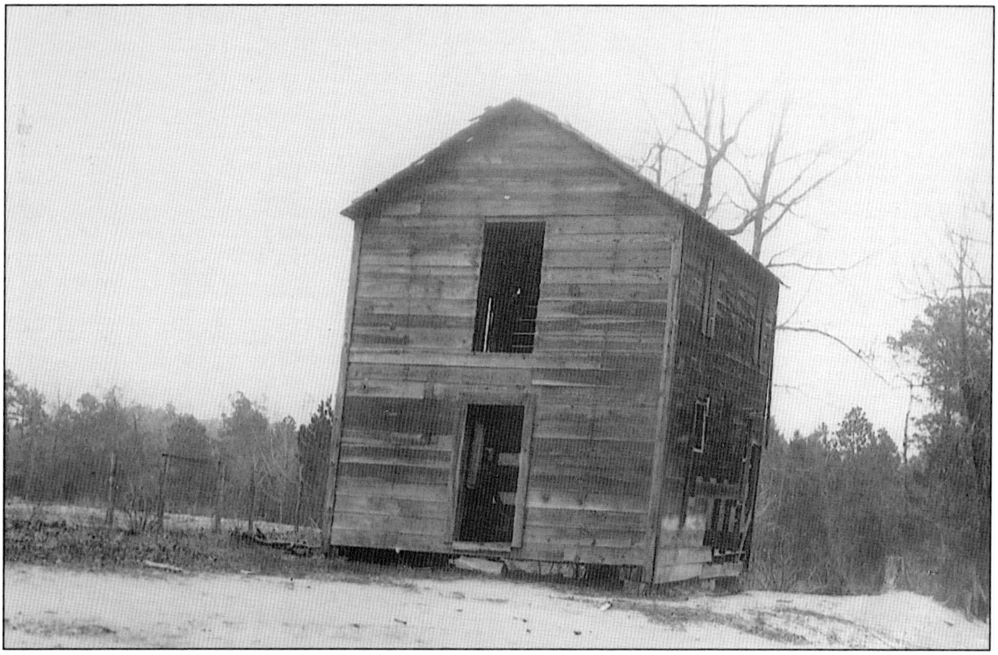

The Long Springs and Martin School for African Americans was located north of Minden. (Courtesy of Webster Parish School Board.)

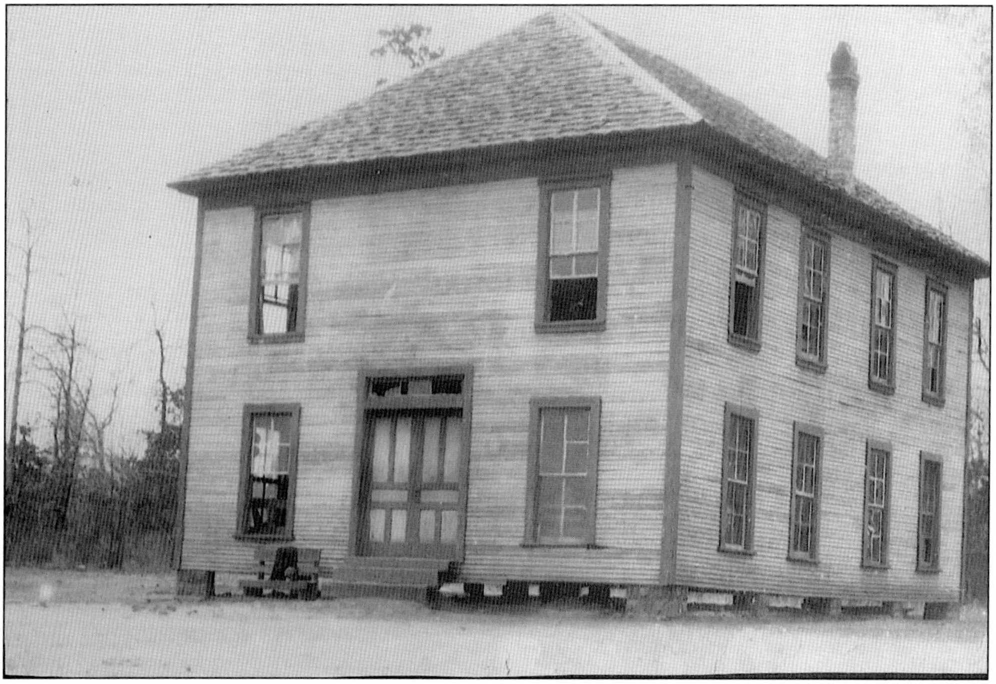

Another African-American School, the Blue Run School, was located further north than the Long Springs School, also north of Minden. (Courtesy of Webster Parish School Board.)

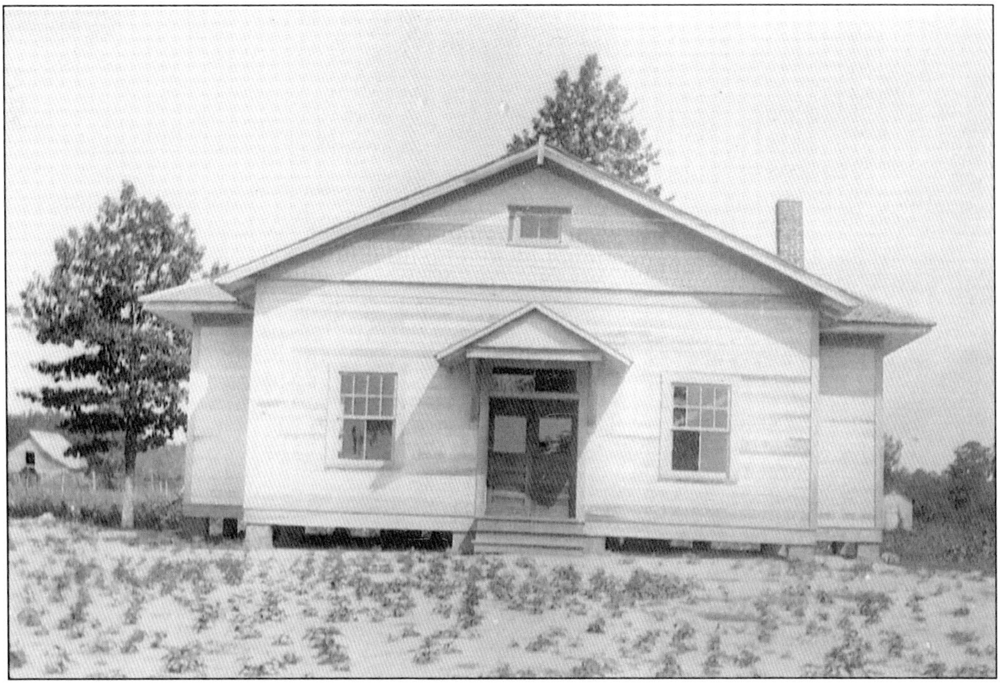

The Union Grove School is shown during the early 1900s. (Courtesy of Webster Parish School Board.)

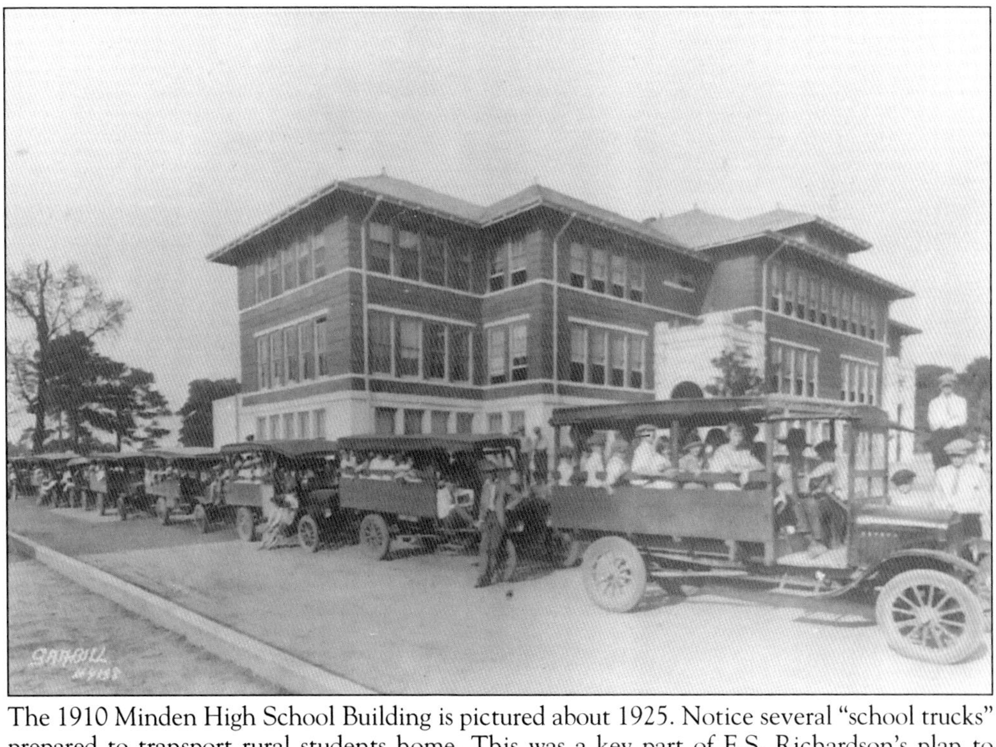

The 1910 Minden High School Building is pictured about 1925. Notice several "school trucks" prepared to transport rural students home. This was a key part of E.S. Richardson's plan to consolidate the rural schools into larger, better-equipped schools in the towns.

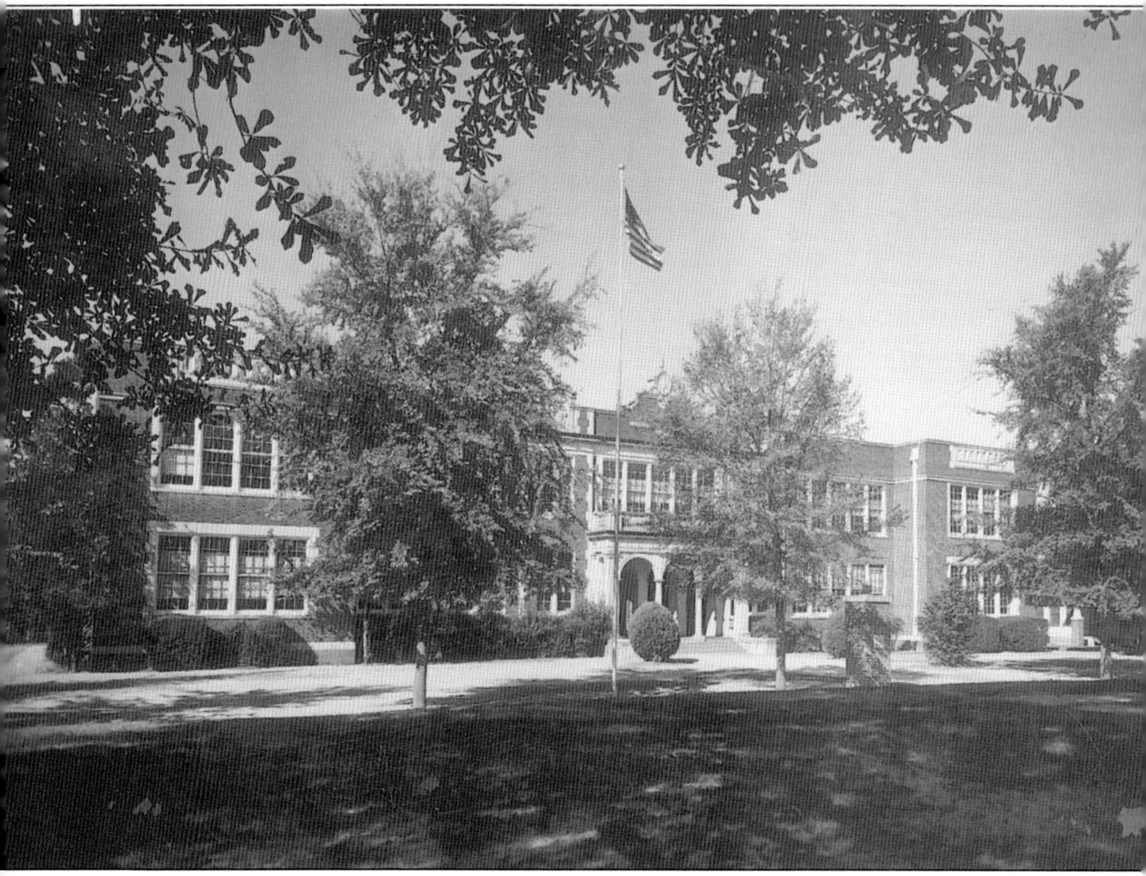

The Minden High School building was erected by E.S. Richardson in 1924. This building served as Minden High School from 1924 to 1953. It then served for several years as Minden Junior High before becoming an annex to the high school 1960. It was partially renovated in 1973, and is still in use today as a classroom building at Minden High School. (Courtesy of W.W. Williams Sr.)

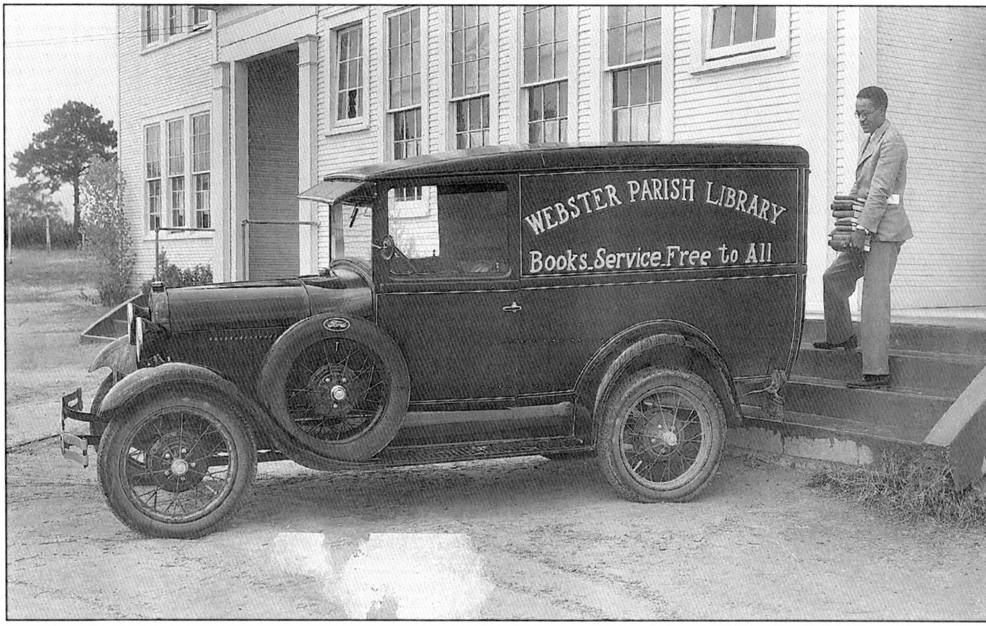

One part of Richardson's program was to place branches of the Webster Parish Library, established in 1929, in the schools. Here, a delivery vehicle from the library is seen picking up books from the library branch located in the Webster Training School in Minden, the forerunner of Webster High School. (Courtesy of Webster Parish School Board.)

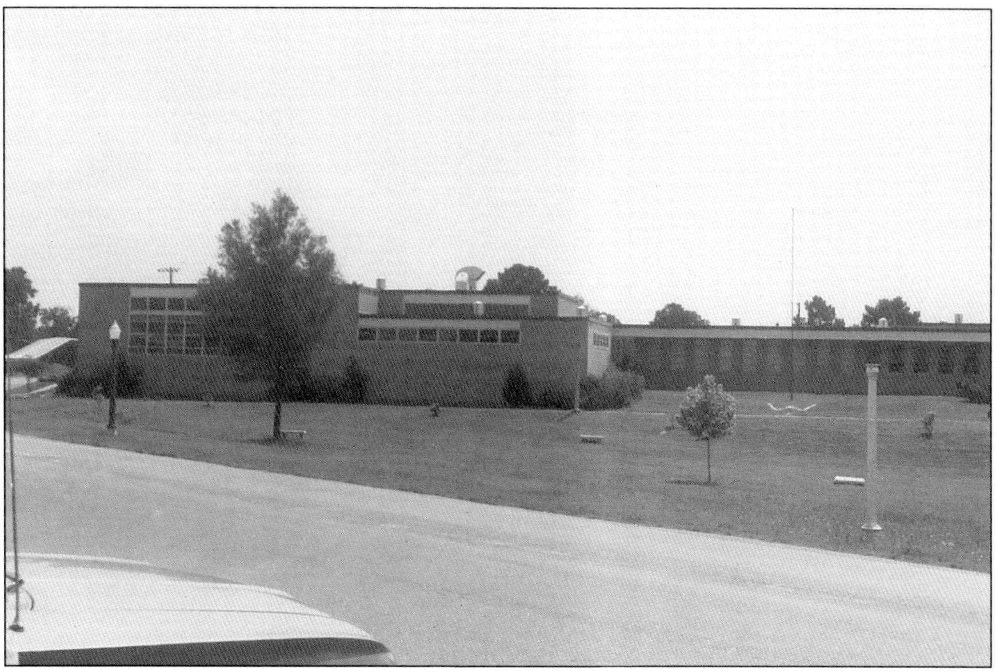

The new Webster High School was constructed for African-American high school students in Minden in 1953. When Webster Parish Schools were desegregated in 1974, this building became Webster Junior High School and remains in use today. (Courtesy of W.W. Williams Sr.)

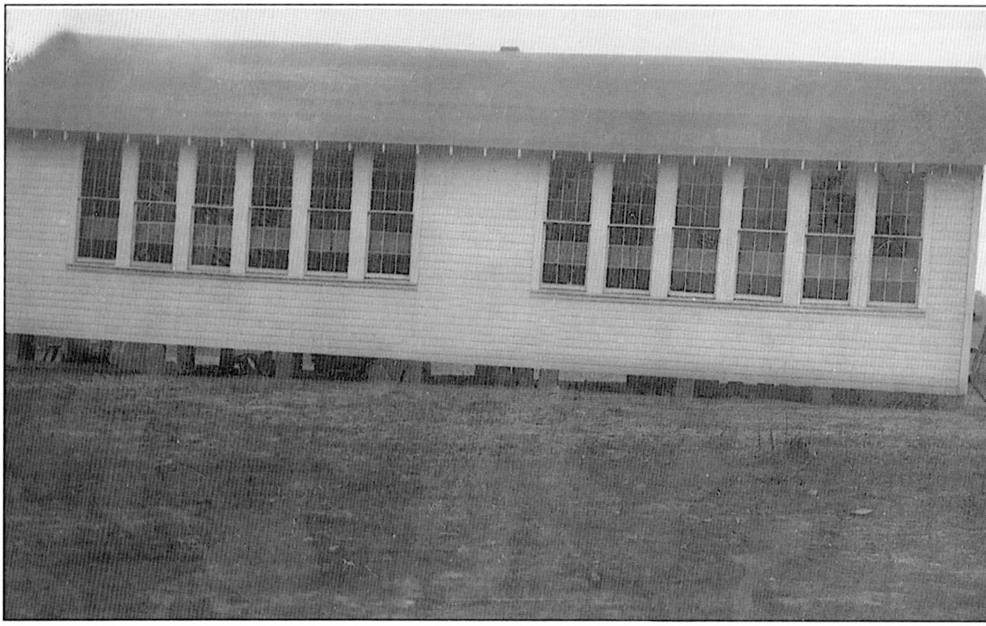

The New Hope School near Minden is shown during the early 1900s. (Courtesy of Webster Parish School Board.)

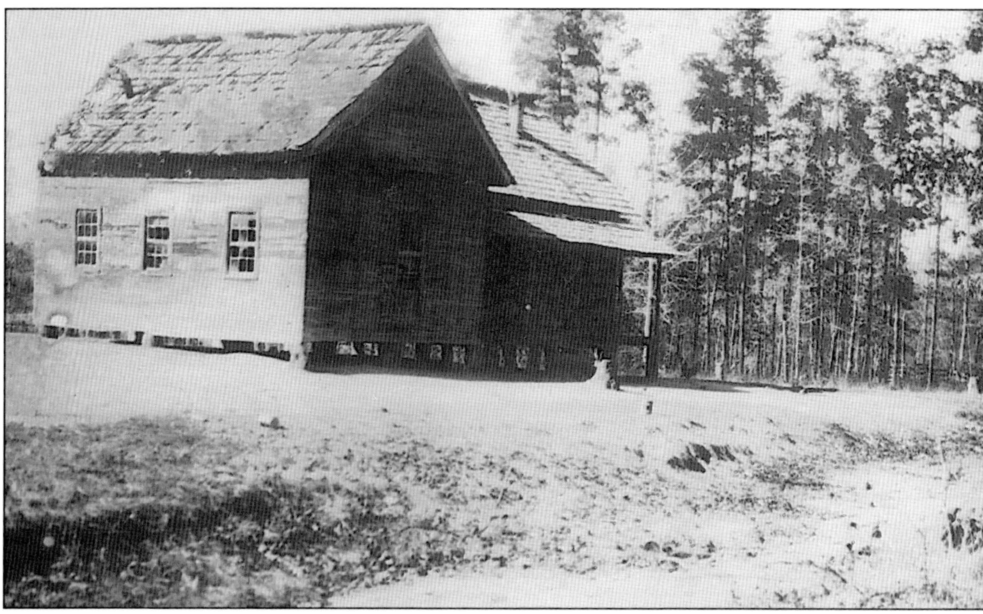

The Mt. Pero School for African Americans was located between Dubberly and Sibley in the early years of the 20th century. This school was located near the Mt. Pero Church, as most of the African-American schools of that era looked to the churches for additional support. (Courtesy of Webster Parish School Board.)

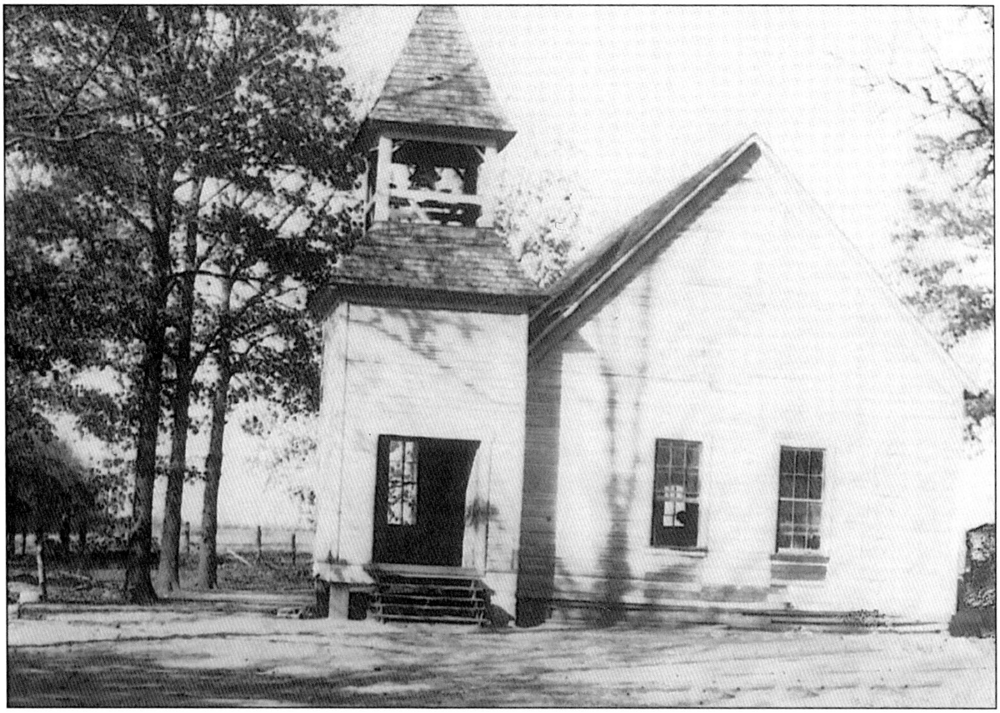

Another example of the tie between African-American schools and churches is seen in the Birt School near Sibley, located in this church building. (Courtesy of Webster Parish School Board.)

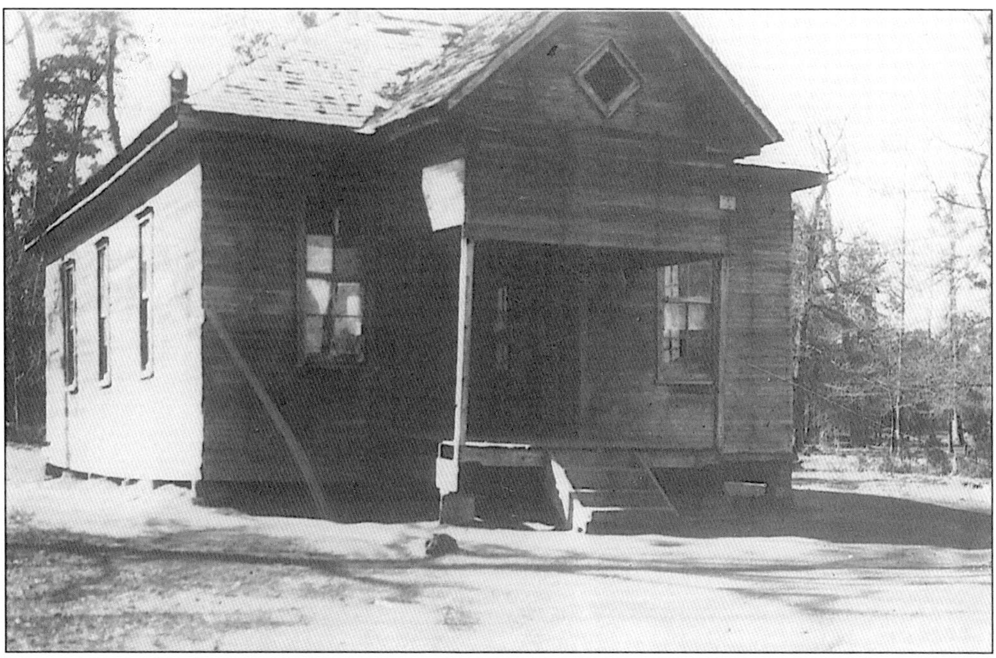

The Sibley School is shown after it was abandoned in the early 1920s and replaced by a new brick structure. (Courtesy of Webster Parish Schools.)

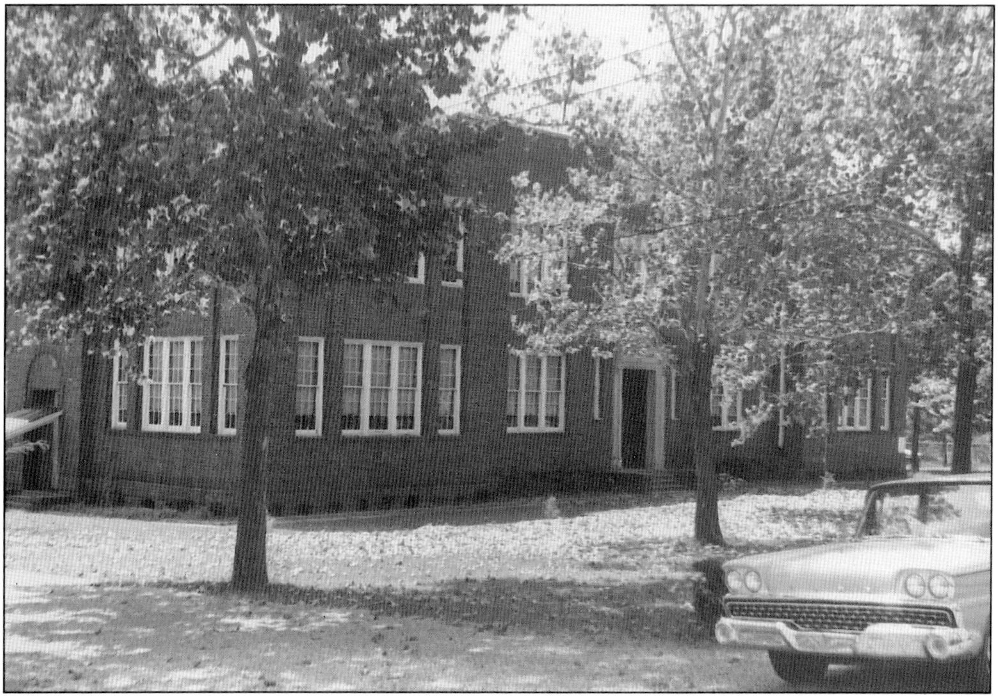

The second brick school was erected at Sibley by the Richardson administration after the first school opened in the fall of 1924 and burned in December of that year. The building, shown here in the 1950s, was built from the insurance proceeds received in compensation for the loss of the first brick building. (Courtesy of W.W. Williams Sr.)

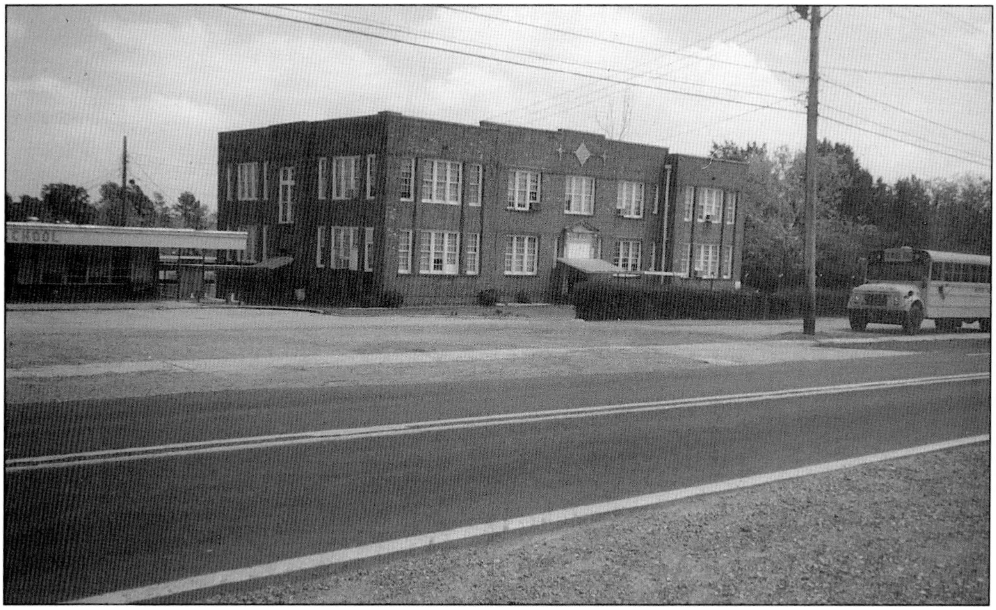

The old building at Sibley High School is shown during its last year of use, the 1999–2000 school year. From 1974 through 2000, Sibley housed the high school students from the old Central, Heflin, and Dubberly High Schools. Beginning in the fall of 2000, these students will attend the new Lakeside High School, constructed south of Sibley.

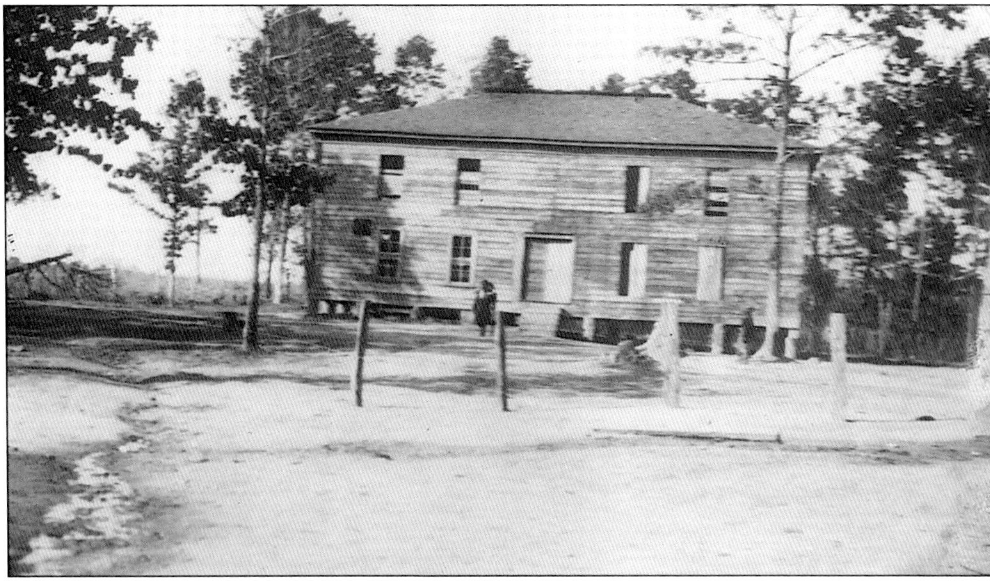

The Jenkins School for African-American students in the Doyline area is shown around 1910. (Courtesy of Webster Parish School Board.)

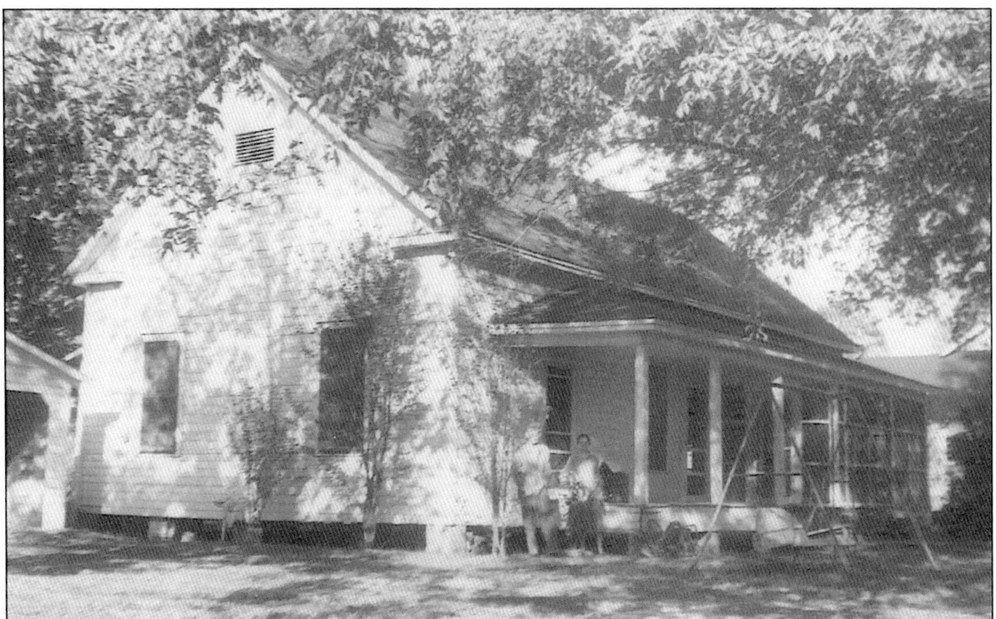

The first Doyline School was later converted into the home of J.A. Cawthon. Mr. Cawthon's daughter still lives in the home today. (Courtesy of Lee C. McIntyre.)

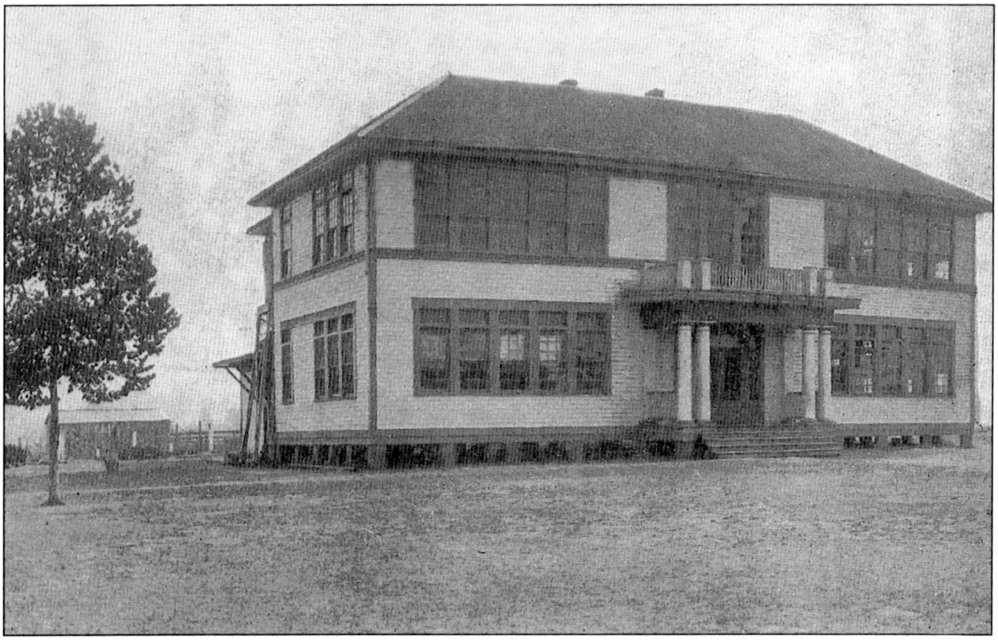

The second Doyline School is shown about 1920. It was used until replaced by the brick building constructed in Richardson's building program in about 1927. (Courtesy of Lee C. McIntyre.)

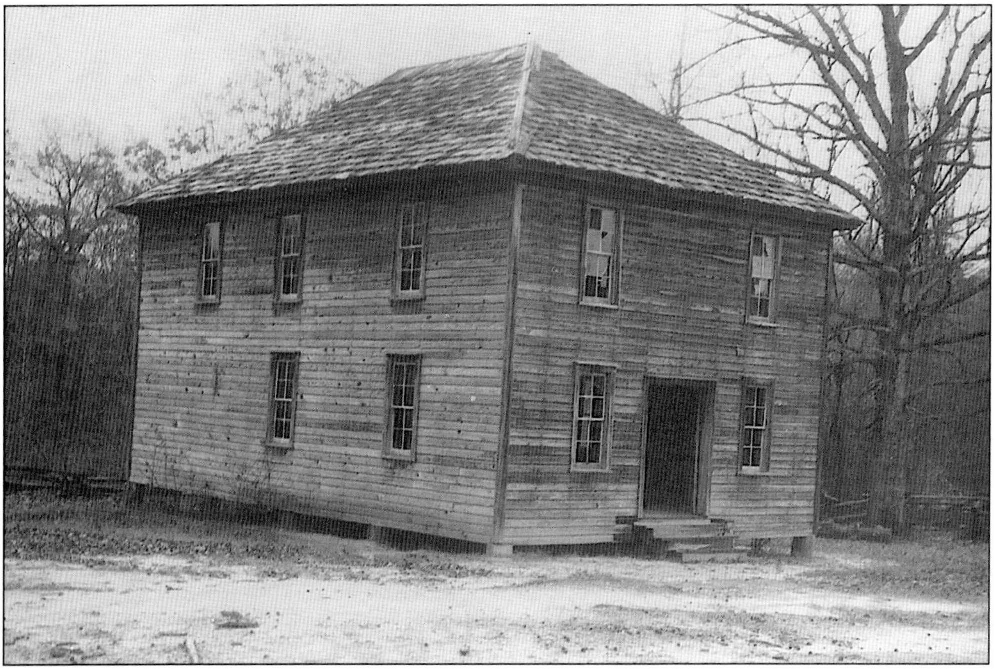

The Central Consolidated School for African-American students was located between Dubberly and Heflin. (Courtesy of Webster Parish School Board.)

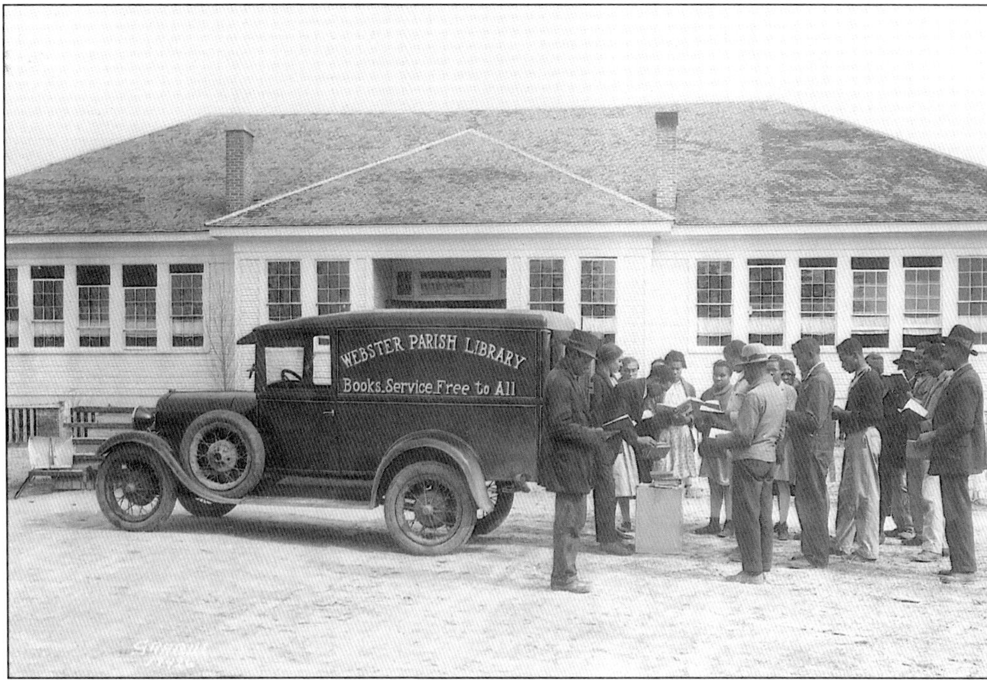

The new Central Consolidated School was built in the 1920s. Again, the delivery vehicle from the Webster Parish Library is seen delivering books for the library branch located in this school. (Courtesy of Webster Parish School Board.)

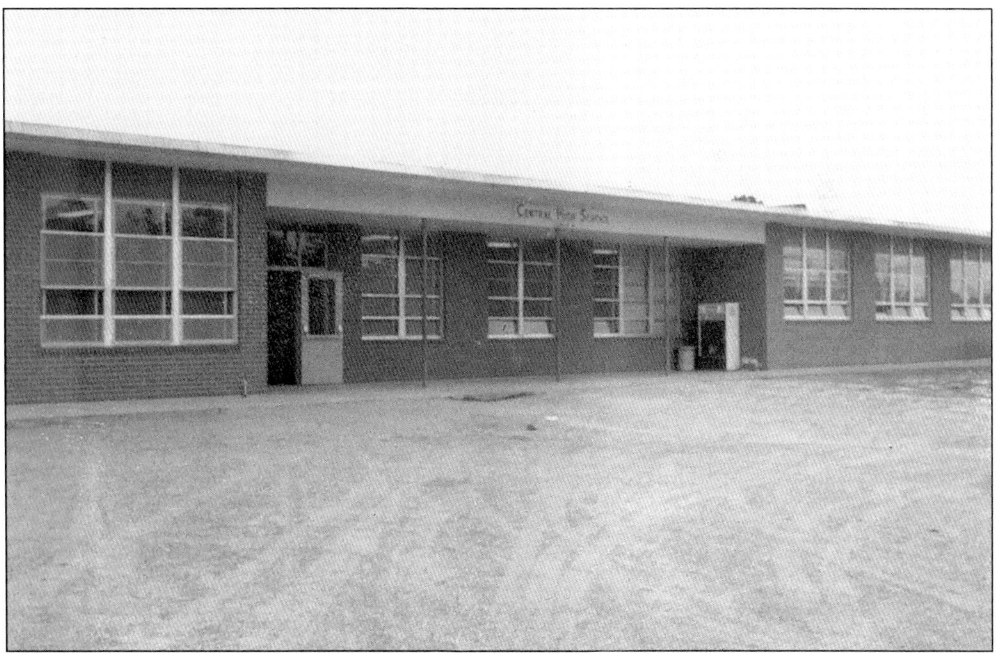

The current Central School is shown prior to 1974, while it was still Central High School. From 1974 until 2000, it served as the junior high school for students from the Sibley, Dubberly, and Heflin areas. It is being remodeled to serve as the elementary school for the students of the same districts beginning in the fall of 2000. (Courtesy of W.W. Williams Sr.)

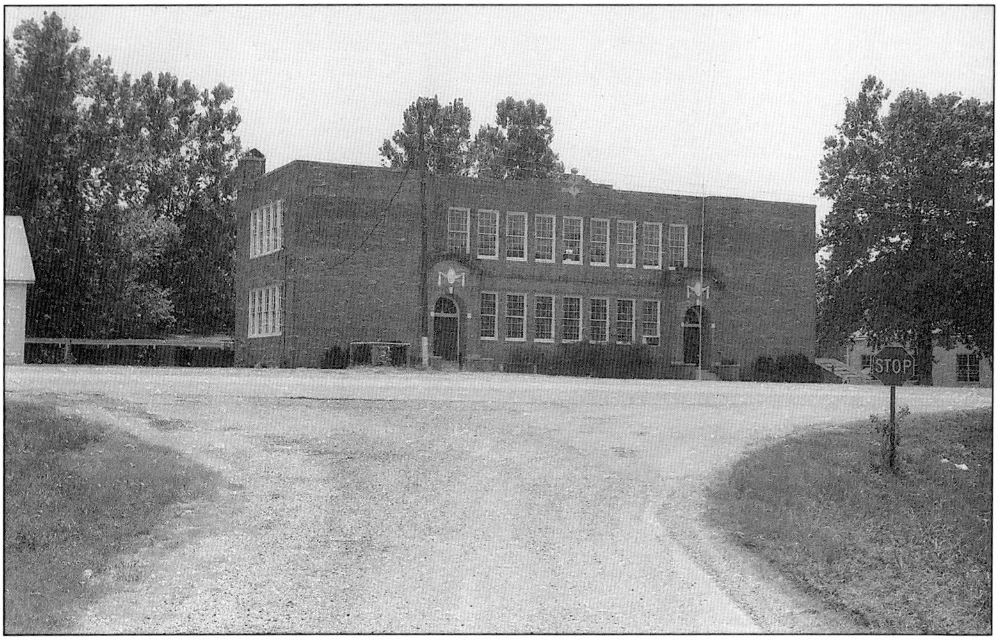

Dubberly High School is shown during the 1950s. This building was constructed during Richardson's consolidation program of the 1920s, and combined several small schools in the Dubberly area. It remained a K-12 school for the students of Dubberly until 1974. (Courtesy of W.W. Williams Sr.)

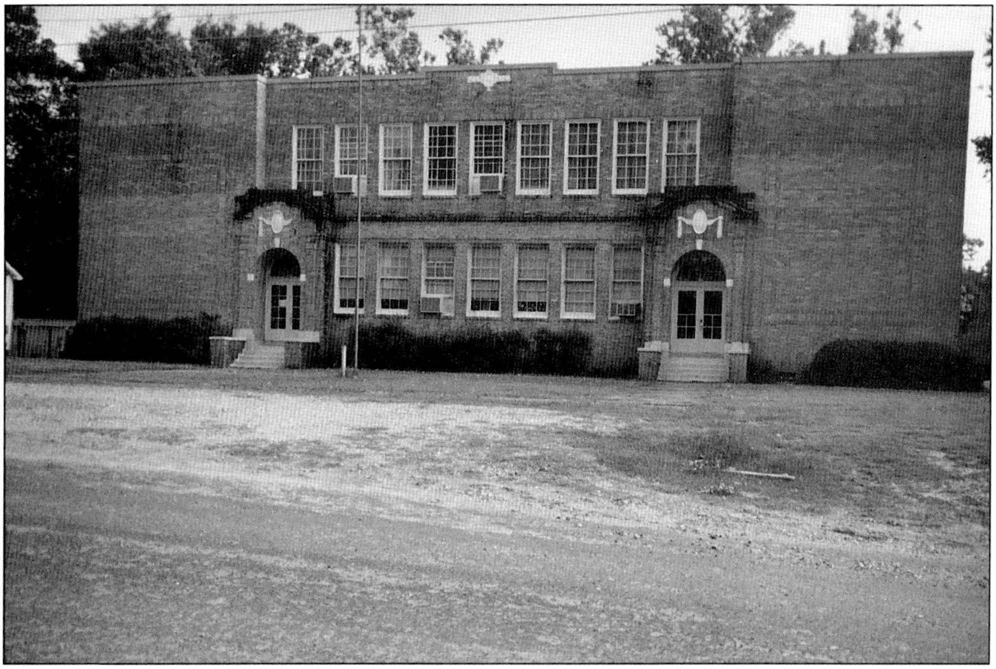

Dubberly Elementary School is shown during its last year of service, 1999–2000. Since 1974, the former K-12 school has housed elementary students from the eastern half of the Sibley, Heflin, and Dubberly areas. Beginning in the fall of 2000, these students will attend the new Central Elementary School and this building will be closed.

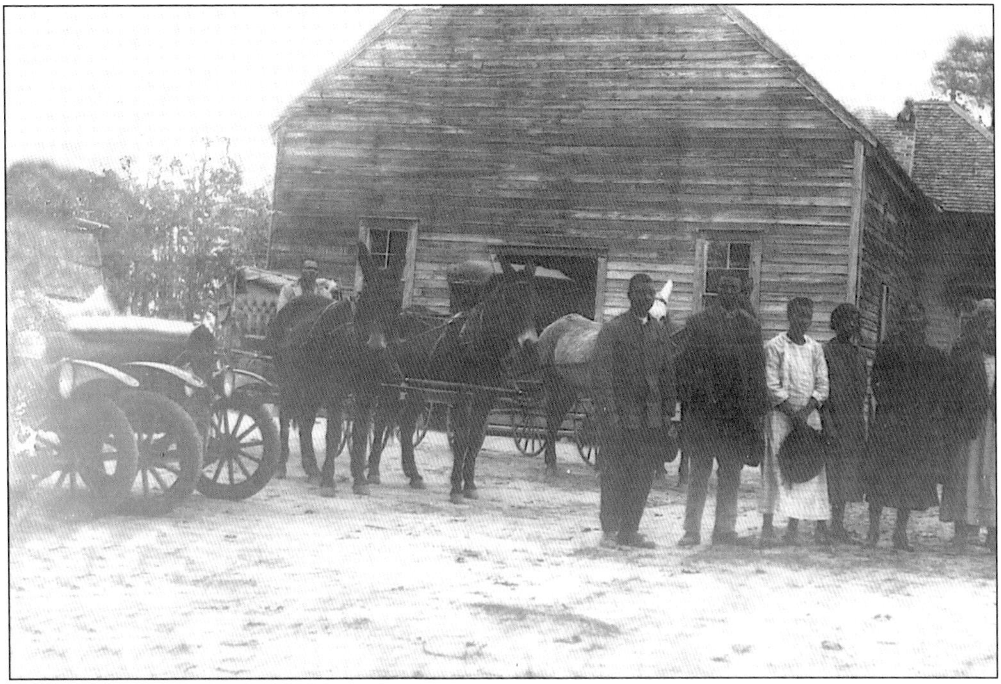

The St. John's School for African-American students near Heflin is pictured in the early years of the 20th century. (Courtesy of Webster Parish School Board.)

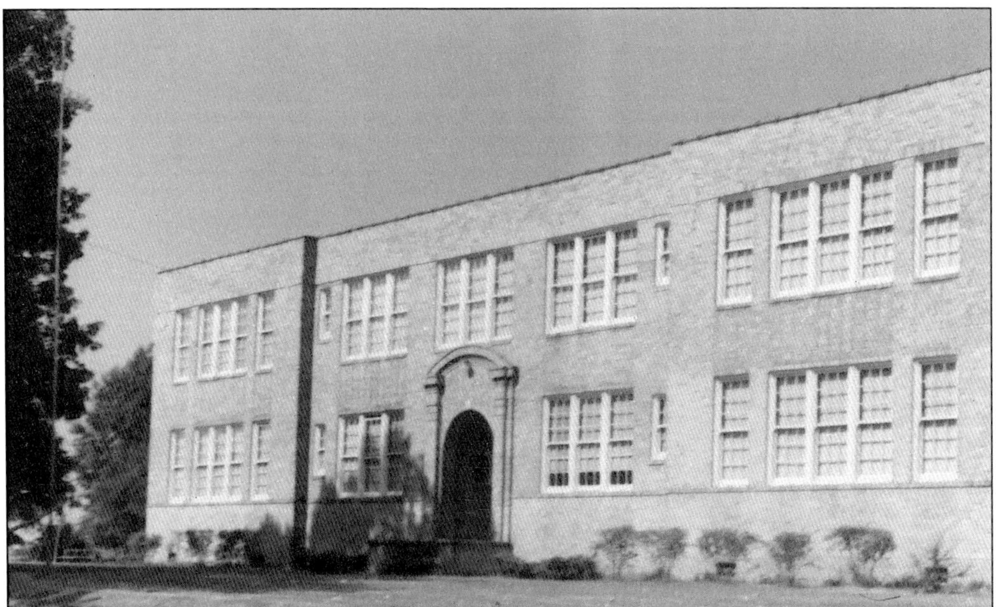

Heflin High School, built in the 1920s, is pictured during the 1950s. In 1974, this school was changed from a K-12 school for Heflin students to an elementary school for students from the western half of the Sibley, Dubberly, and Heflin areas. It will be closed in the fall of 2000 as the students will be attending the new Central Elementary School. (Courtesy of W.W. Williams Sr.)

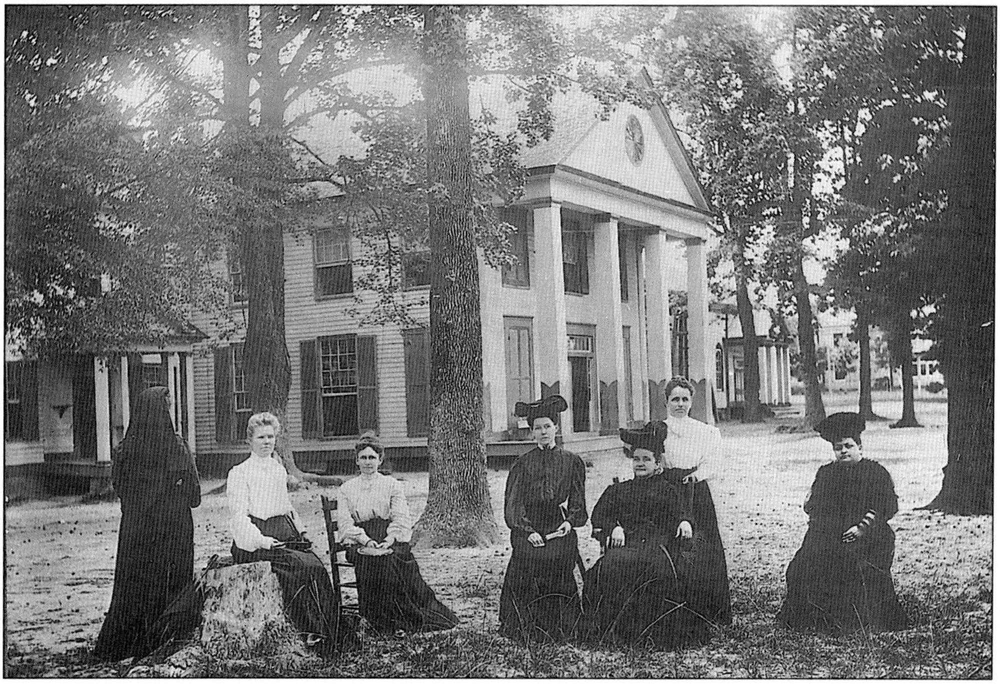

The 1875 graduates of the Minden Female College are shown as they gather for a reunion, probably in 1895 on the 20th anniversary of their graduation. Seven of the nine graduates of that year are shown with the main building of the college, erected in 1854, standing in the background. Today, Minden High School is located on the site of the female college. (Courtesy of Charles and Mary Rathbun.)

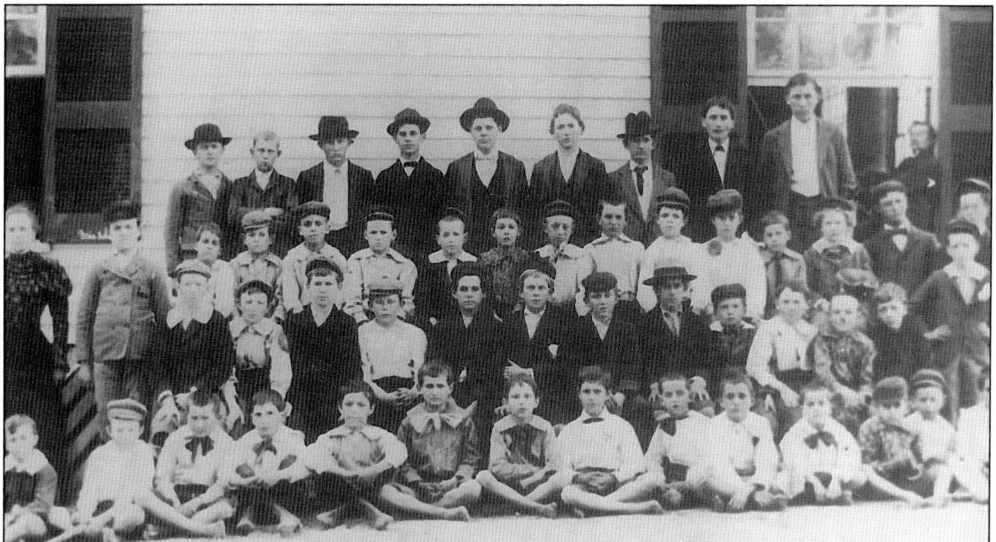

The students of the Minden Male Academy are pictured in 1895. The male academy and the female college both had their roots in the Minden Academy established in 1838. The male academy had moved and constructed its own building, shown in the background in 1850. The school would be consolidated into the new Minden Public School in 1898. Today, the old male academy campus is Academy Park in Minden. (Courtesy of Lillian Life Willis.)

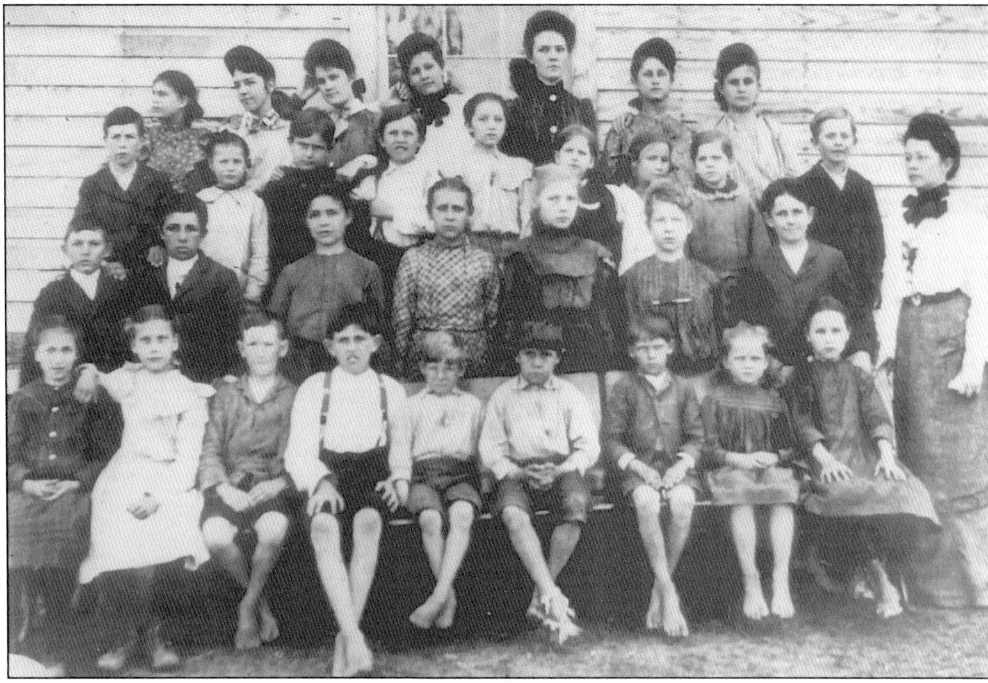

Students of the first Doyline School are shown outside their brand new school building in 1903. The teacher pictured at the right is Mary Lou Richardson, sister of E.S. Richardson. This school was later converted into the home of J.A. Cawthon. (Courtesy of Lee C. McIntyre.)

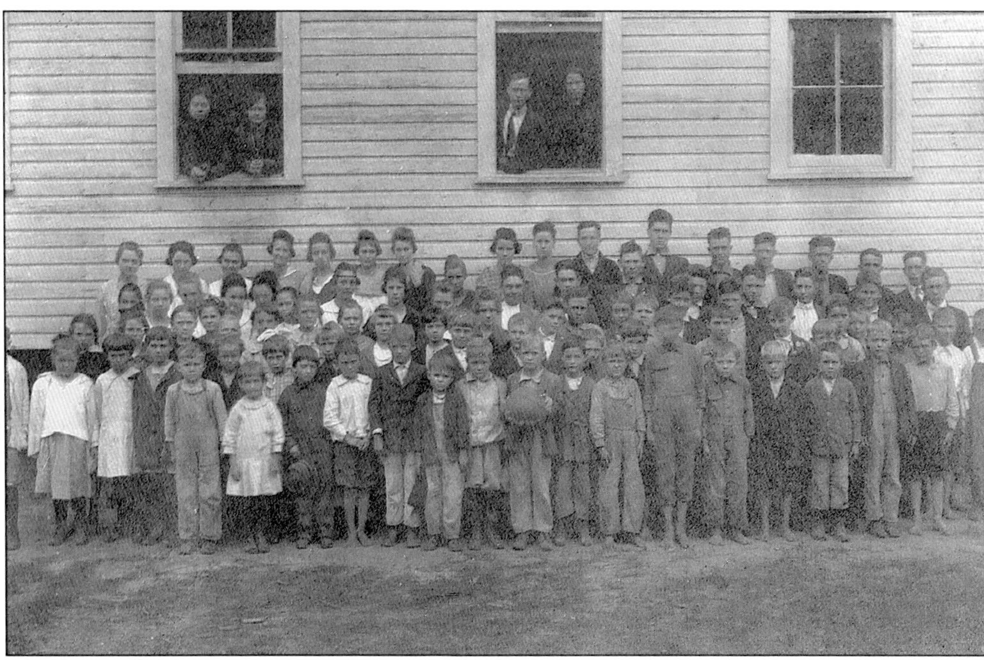

Evergreen School students are pictured outside (and inside) the school building, *c.* 1910. (Courtesy of R.O. Machen Jr.)

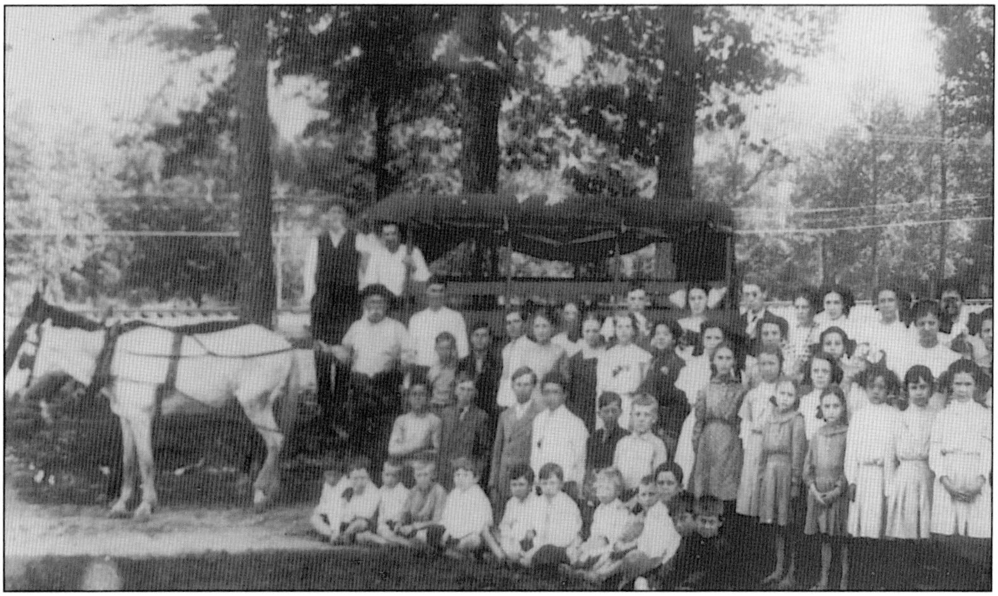

The forerunner of the "school trucks" and buses was the "school wagon." The Doyline school wagon, driven by Mr. Thompson, is shown with its regular passengers in 1914. (Courtesy of Lee C. McIntyre.)

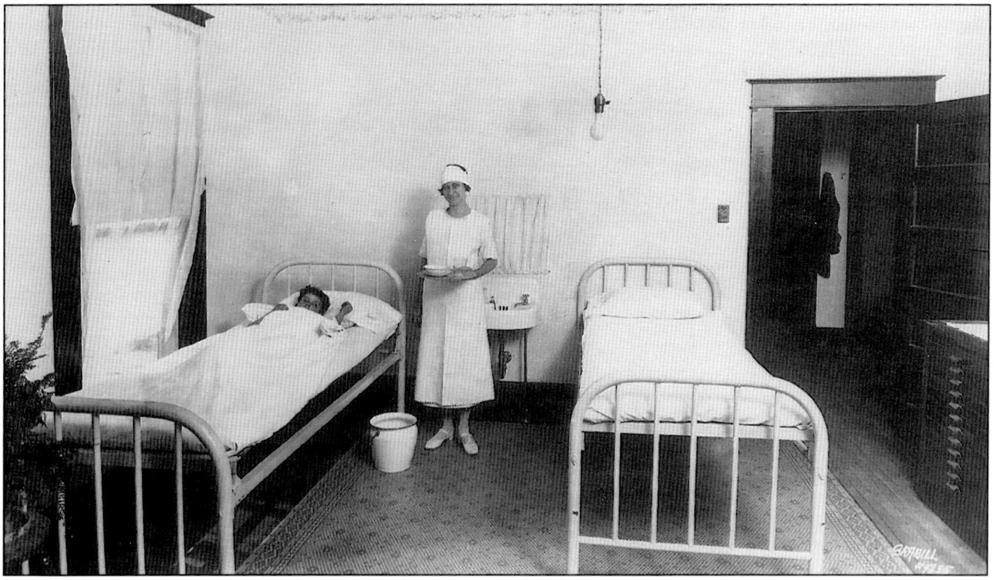

Pictured is one of the "sick rooms" or infirmaries built in each of the schools constructed by E.S. Richardson in the 1920s. Each school had a sick room, particularly for the rural students who came into town on the buses under the consolidation program and could not go home if they became ill. (Courtesy of Webster Parish School Board.)

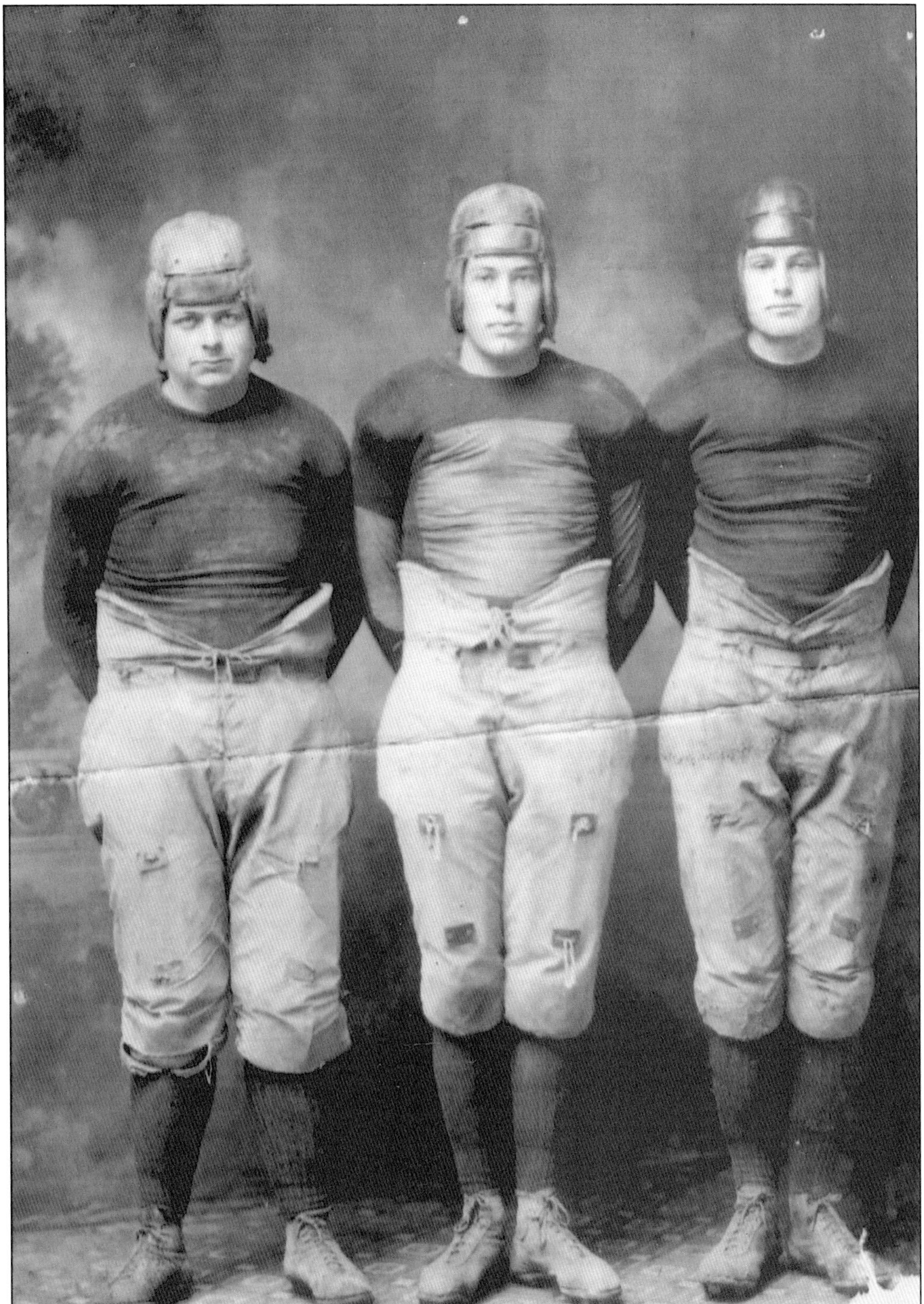

Three members of the Minden High School football team, shown c. 1920, are, from left to right, Ralph Tabor, Tom Tabor, and unidentified. In 1921, the Minden High Greenie football team was undefeated and unscored upon before traveling to New Orleans and losing the state championship game 6-0 to Warren Easton High School. (Courtesy of Virginia Fox.)

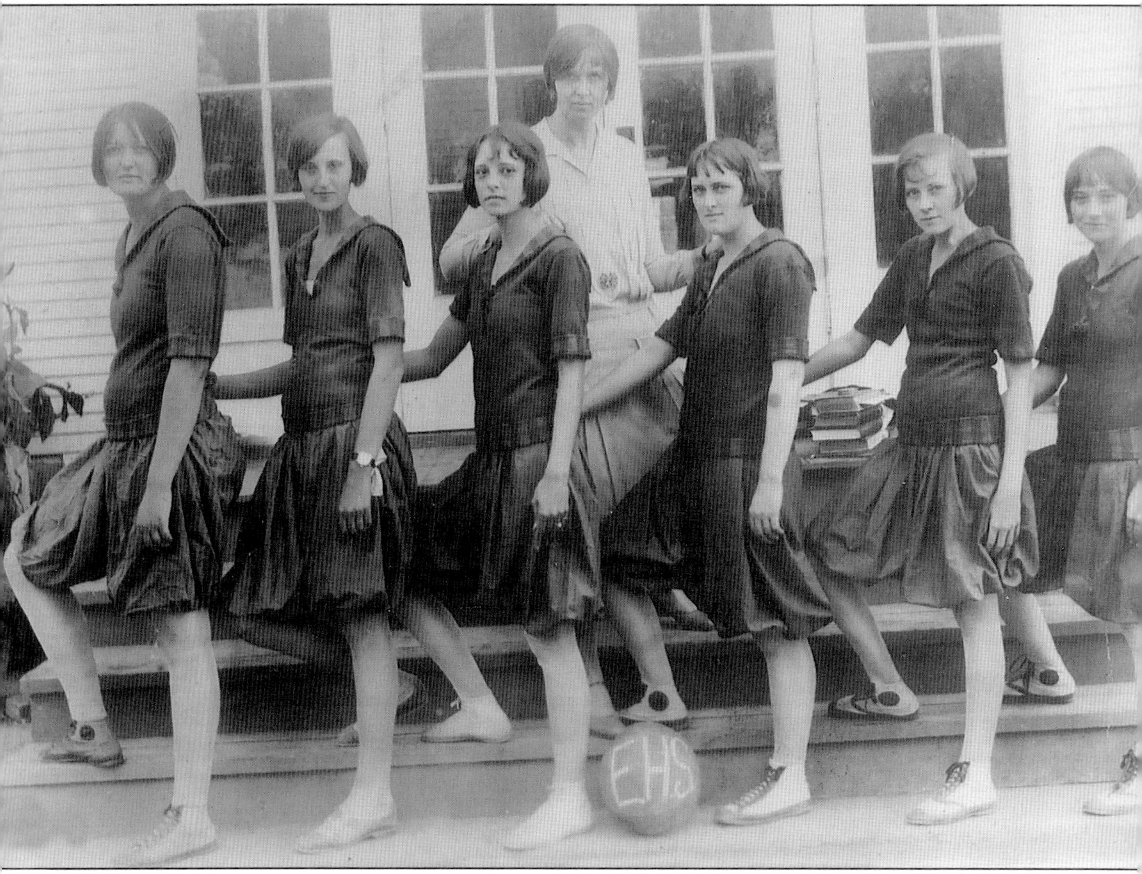

The Evergreen Lady Pups championship basketball team of 1925 are pictured with Mrs. C.M. Ingalls, coach. The players are, from left to right, Susie Miller, Eulah Martin, Juella Lewis, Estella Shaw, Johnnie Ingalls, and Lucy Lindsey. (Courtesy of Hazel Miller White.)

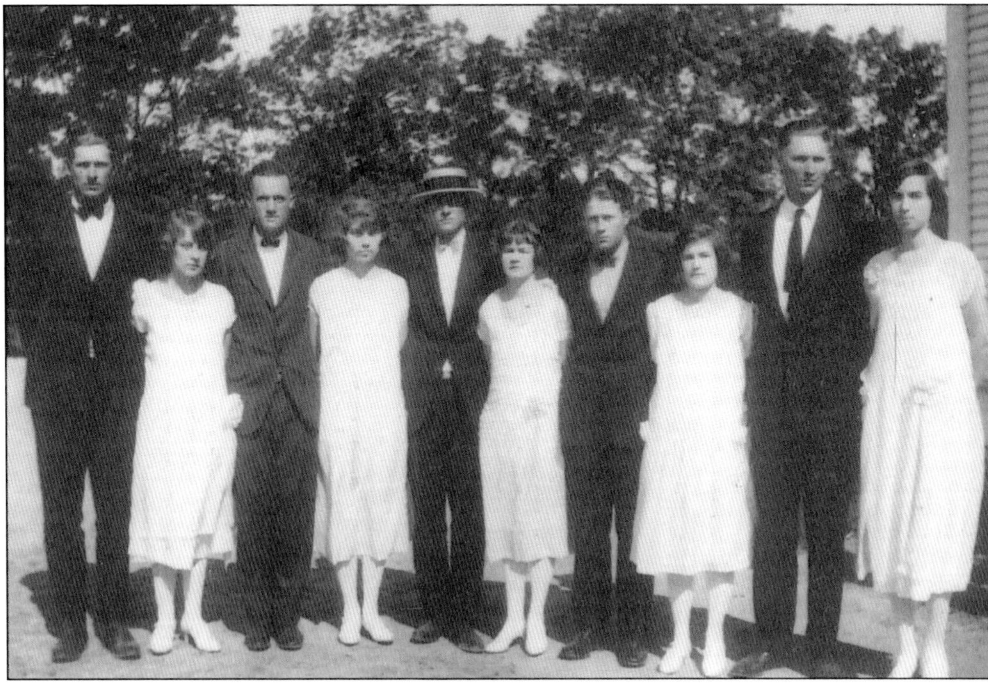

The 1925 graduating class of Evergreen High School included, from left to right, Bennie Miller, Estelle Anderson, Carl Etheridge, Rosamond Kirkley, Sam Heflin, Elva Sumner, Bill Martin, Coryce Miller, Jimmy Pruitt, and Estelle Smith. (Courtesy of Hazel Miller White.)

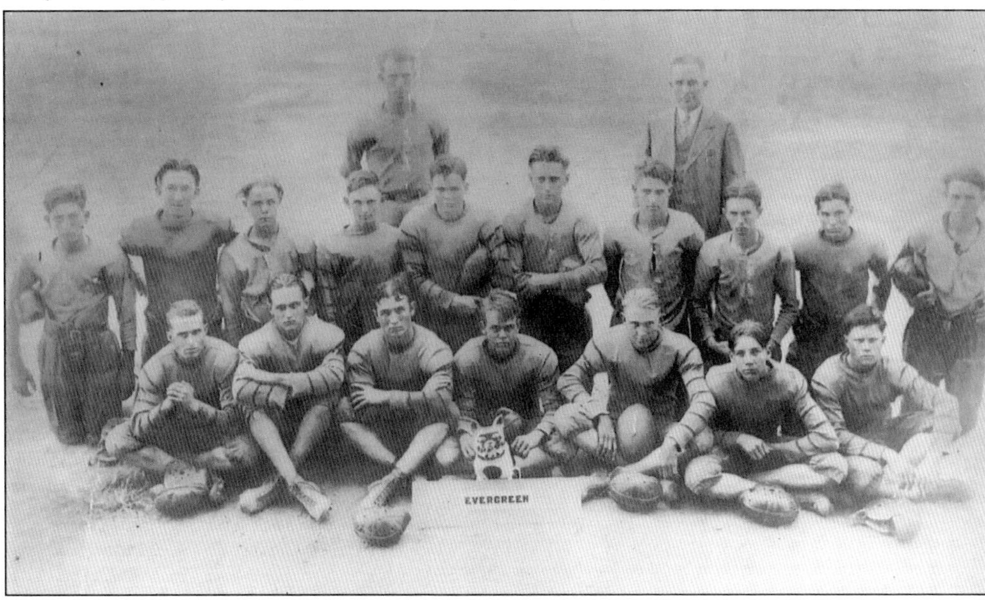

The Evergreen Bulldogs football team is pictured in the late 1920s. From left to right are the following: (front row) Jewel Horton, Etelle Shaw, Kenneth Martin, Jones Townsend, Herman Wright, Jack Kirkley, and Will C. Monk; (middle row) Laymon Benefield, Loyce Parker, Chester Childs, Leslie Childs, Neal Lee, Freddie Merritt, Buddy Martin, William Dunn, Floyd Smith, and Dayton Lee; (back row) R.O. Machen Sr., coach, and C.M. Ingalls, principal. (Courtesy of R.O. Machen Jr. and Hazel Miller White.)

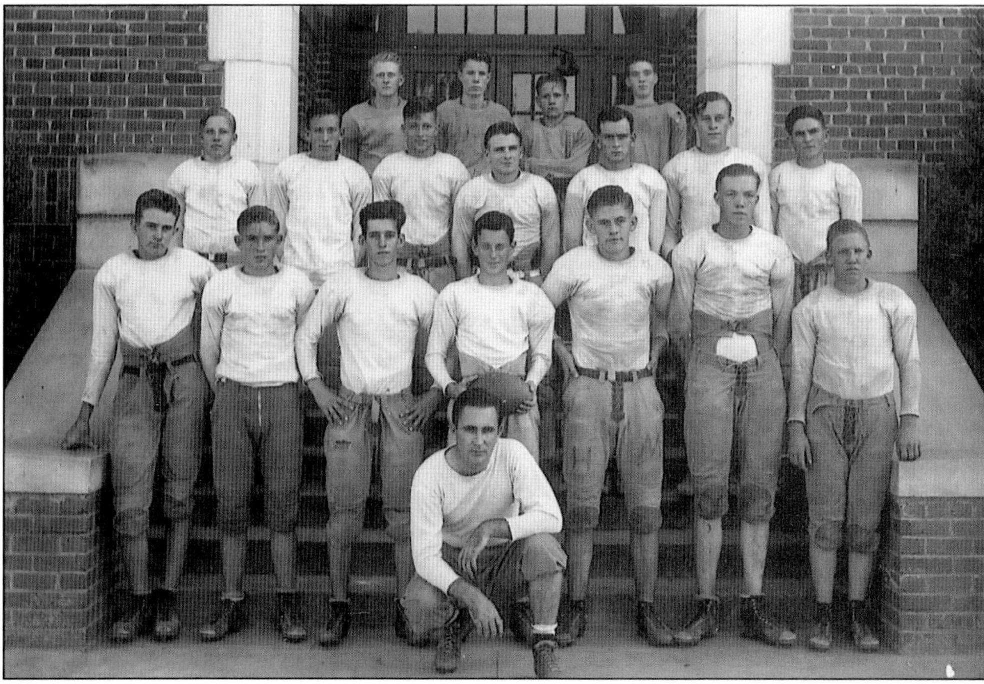

The Cotton Valley High School Wildcat football team is pictured in the late 1930s. (Courtesy of R.O. Machen Jr.)

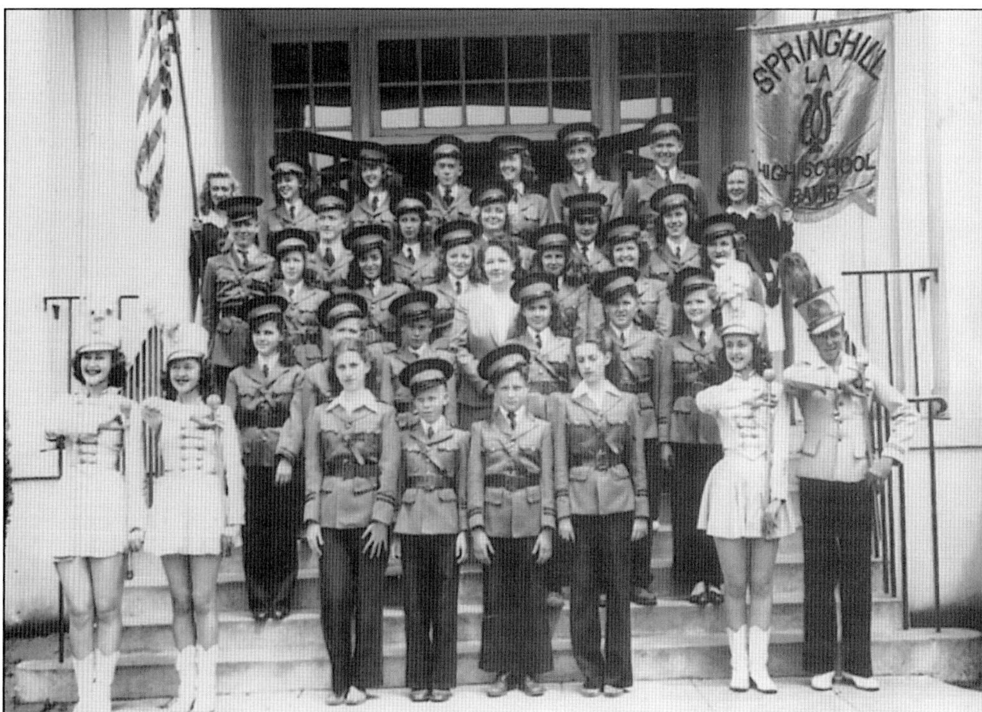

The Springhill High School band poses on the steps of the school in May 1946. (Courtesy of Dr. A.C. Higginbotham.)

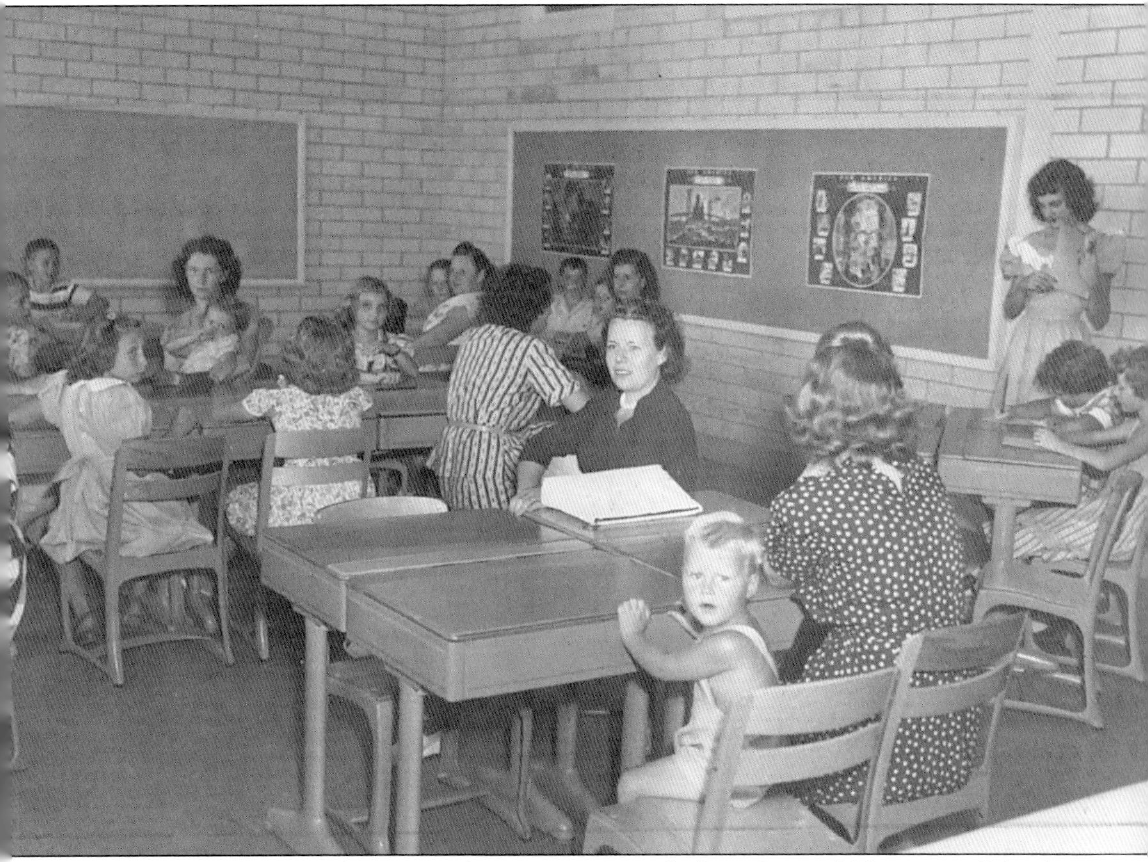

Mothers and students are shown in a classroom at Westside (later Stewart) Elementary School in Minden, shortly after the school opened in 1948. (Courtesy of W.W. Williams.)

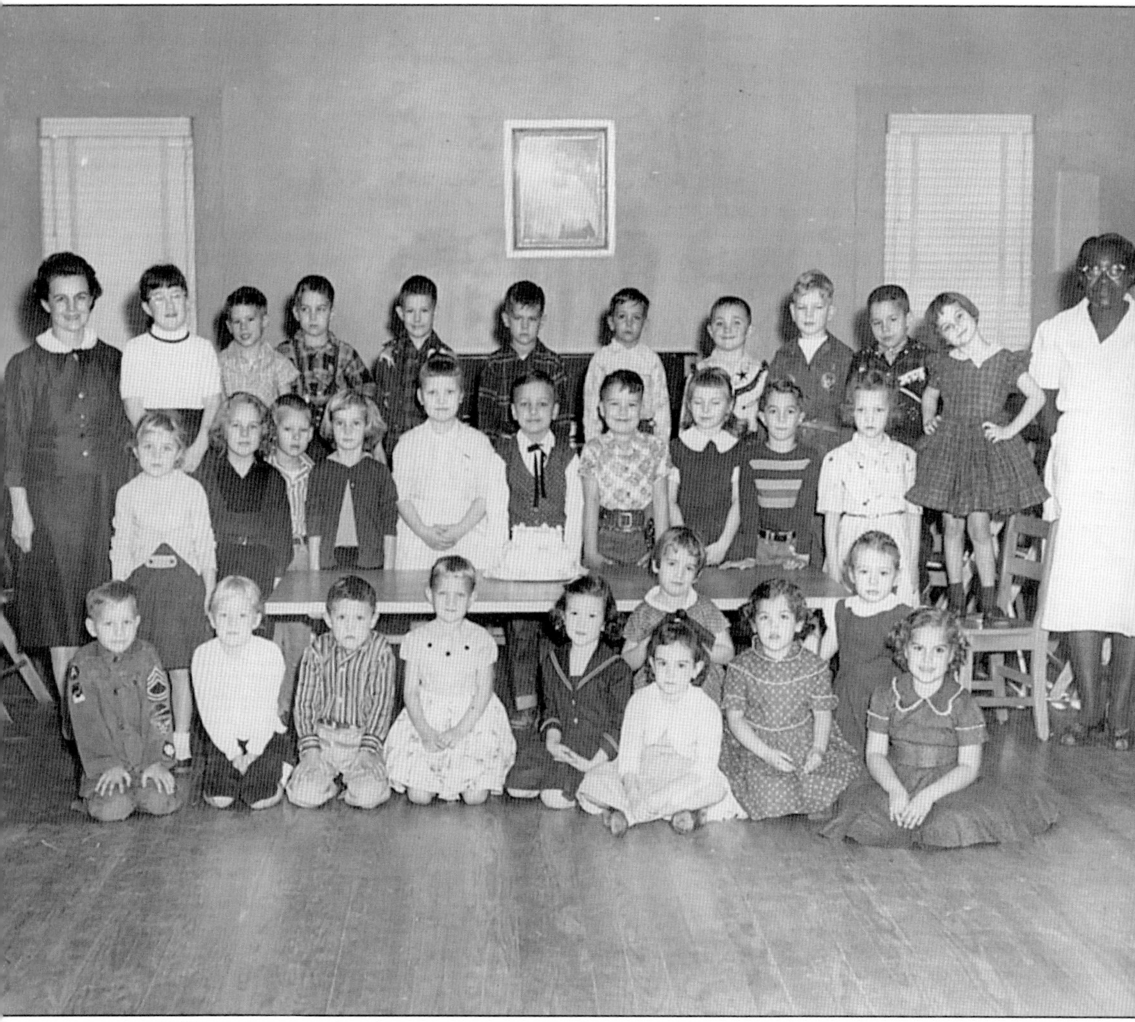

Mrs. Lillian Craton's kindergarten is pictured at St. John's Episcopal Church in about 1957. Mrs. Craton taught in the Webster Parish Schools for many years before opening a private kindergarten that later met in her home.

Four

South Webster

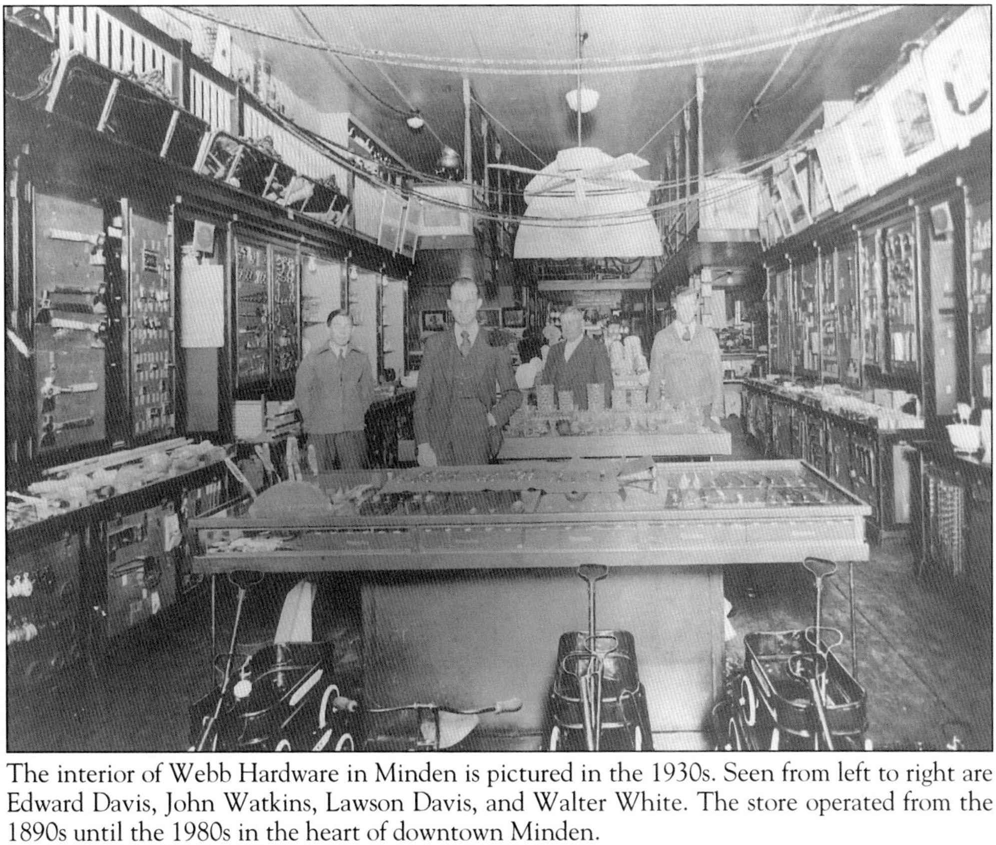

The interior of Webb Hardware in Minden is pictured in the 1930s. Seen from left to right are Edward Davis, John Watkins, Lawson Davis, and Walter White. The store operated from the 1890s until the 1980s in the heart of downtown Minden.

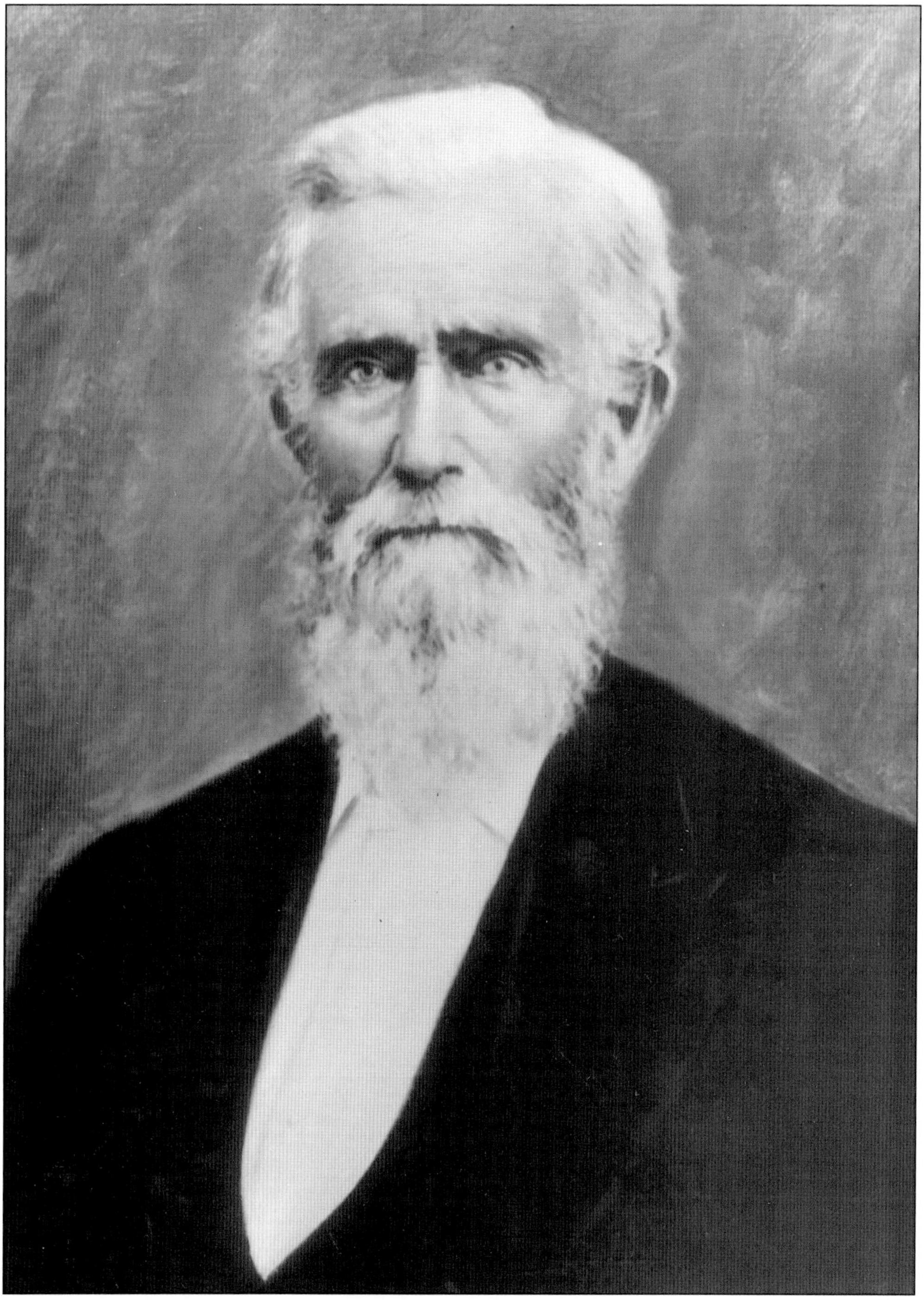

George Washington Baines, although never a resident of Minden, was the first pastor of the Minden Baptist Church from 1845 through 1850. While in Louisiana he spelled his name "Bains," adding the "e" when he moved to Texas, where he was president of Baylor University. His great-great-grandson was President Lyndon Baines Johnson, who visited the First Baptist Church during its 125th anniversary celebration in 1969. (Courtesy of Major DePingre.)

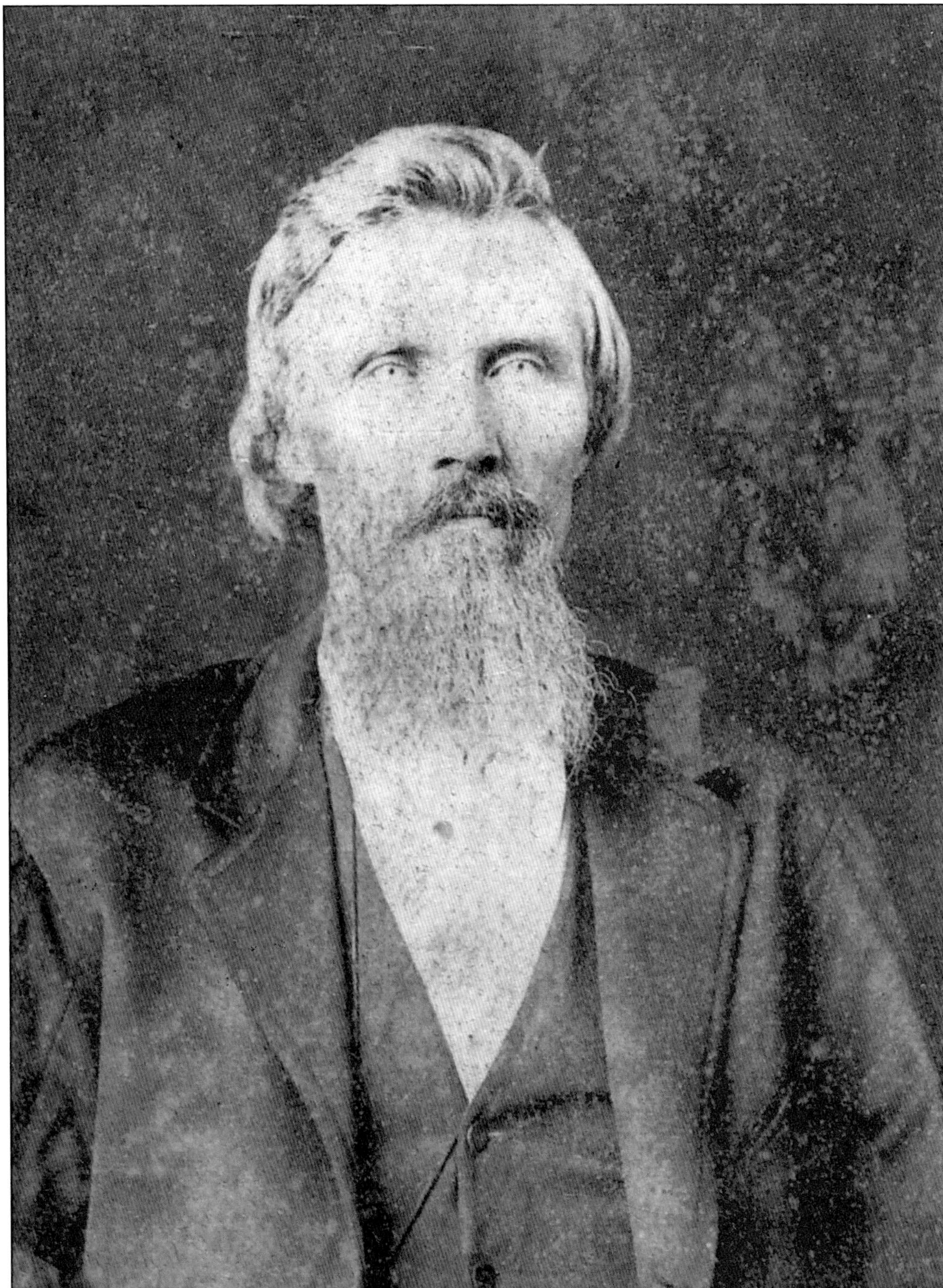

Dougald Stewart came to the Webster Parish area in the winter of 1850–51 along with his wife, Mary Elizabeth Culbertson. Stewart's descendants have been prominent in the life of Webster Parish since that time. They have been particularly influential in the areas of education and law. Several descendants of this pioneer settler have been pictured in other sections of this book. (Courtesy of Virginia Fox.)

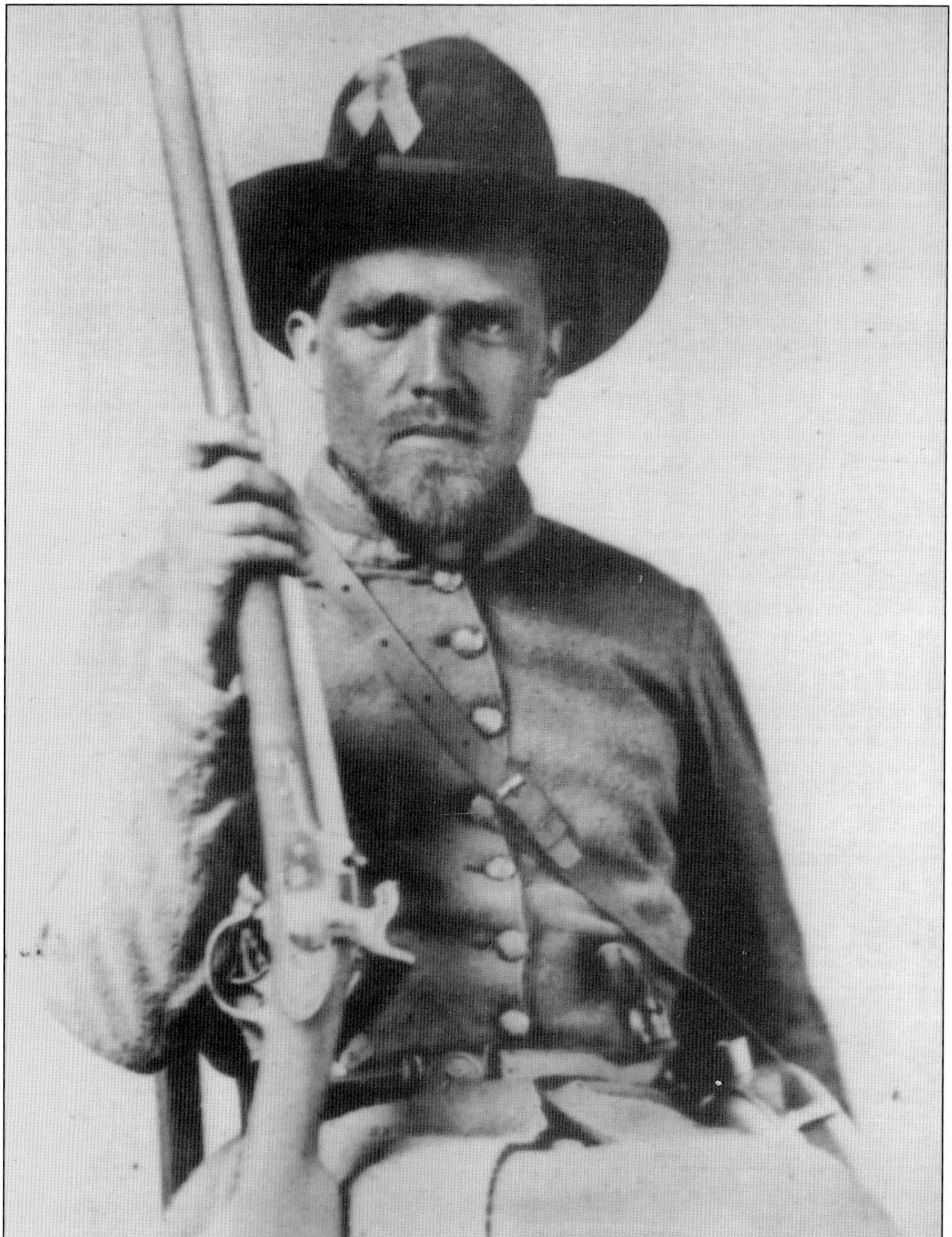

G.L.P. Wren, pictured earlier in this book as a state legislator, is seen here in the uniform of the Minden Blues, the best known unit from Webster Parish to serve in the Confederate Army. Wren had come to Webster Parish in 1848. During the Civil War he fought with the Army of Northern Virginia in most of the important battles of the war, including Bull Run and Gettysburg. Twice captured, he spent time in the Union prison camp at Fort Delaware. After the war he taught school at Pine Grove, north of Minden. In 1869 he married Ellen Carr. The couple had eight children, and their descendants are still prominent in Webster Parish today. (Courtesy of Marcus D. Wren Jr.)

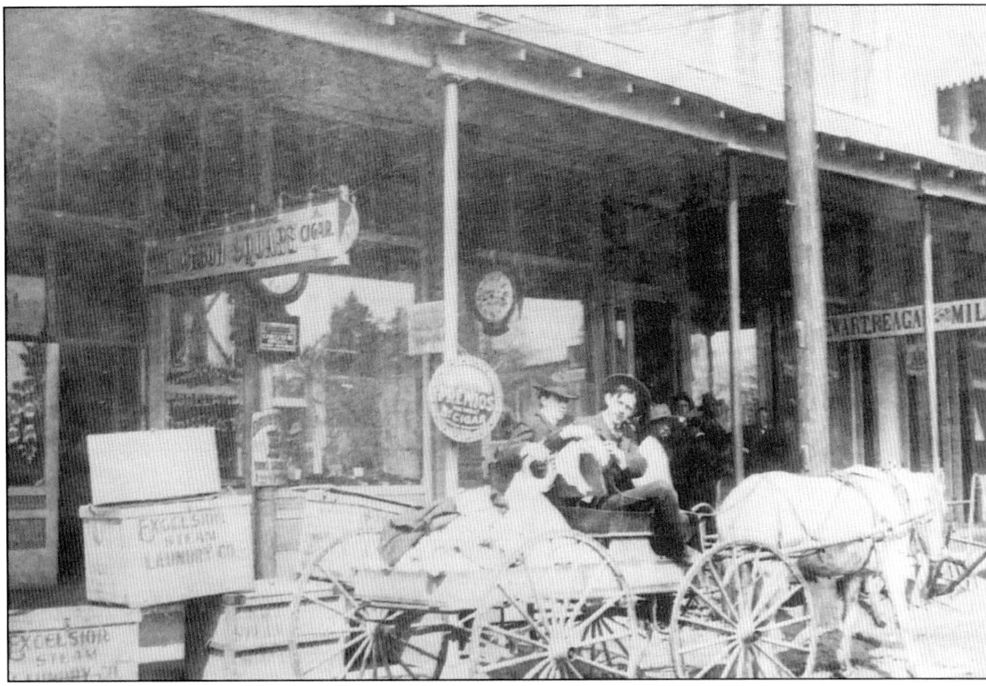

A wagon from the Excelsior Steam Laundry of Shreveport picks up a load of laundry in downtown Minden during the late 1880s. (Courtesy of Major DePingre.)

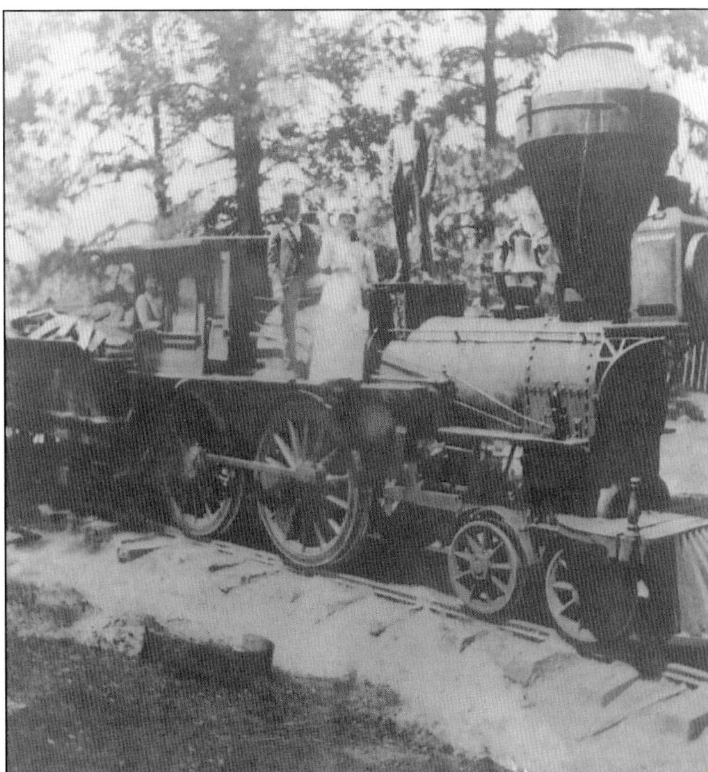

The first locomotive came to Minden in 1885. Minden had been bypassed by the main east-to-west line of the Vicksburg, Shreveport and Pacific Railroad, which ran to the south through Lanesville. F.H. Drake constructed the Minden Tap Railroad, which connected Minden to the main line by 1885. (Courtesy of Major DePingre.)

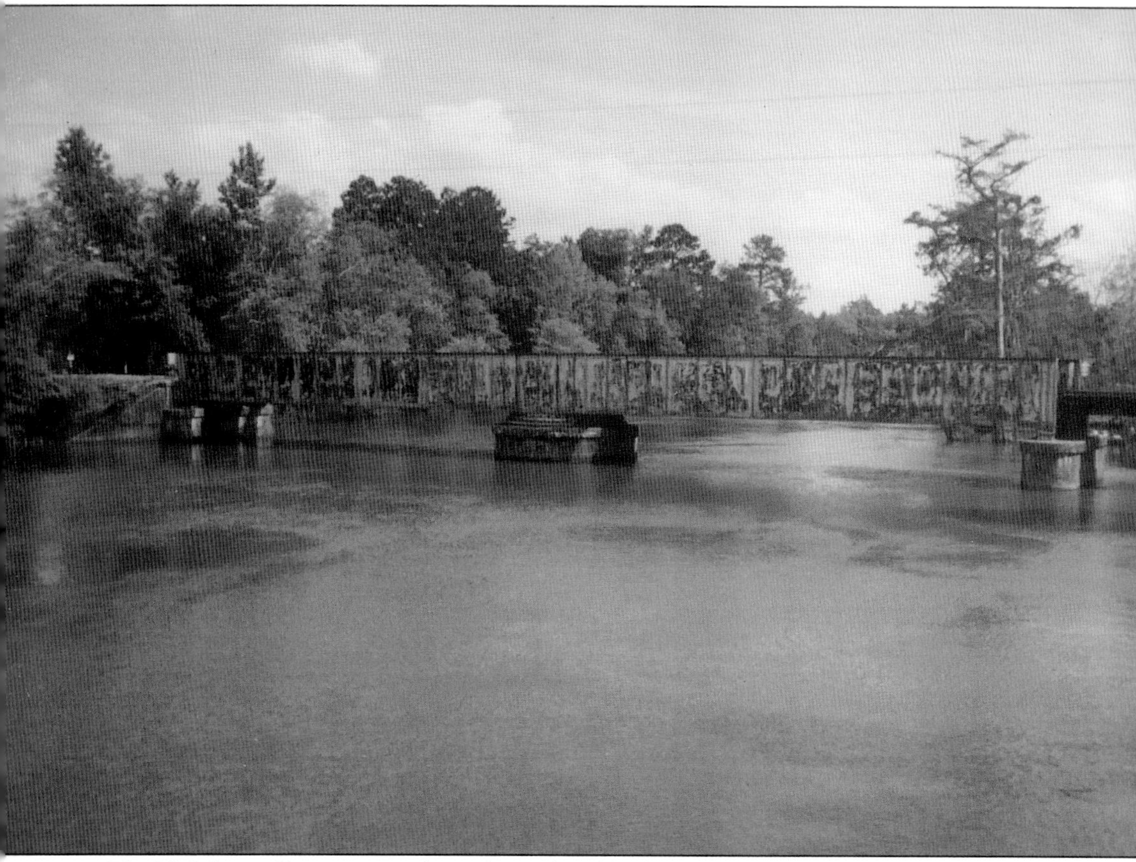

The Vicksburg, Shreveport and Pacific Railroad bridge crossed Bayou Dorcheat between Sibley and Dubberly. Still in use today, the bridge was constructed in 1884, when the railroad across North Louisiana was completed. Originally designed with a center turntable to allow the bridge to pivot and let steamboats pass, the bridge was last opened for a boat to pass in the 1890s.

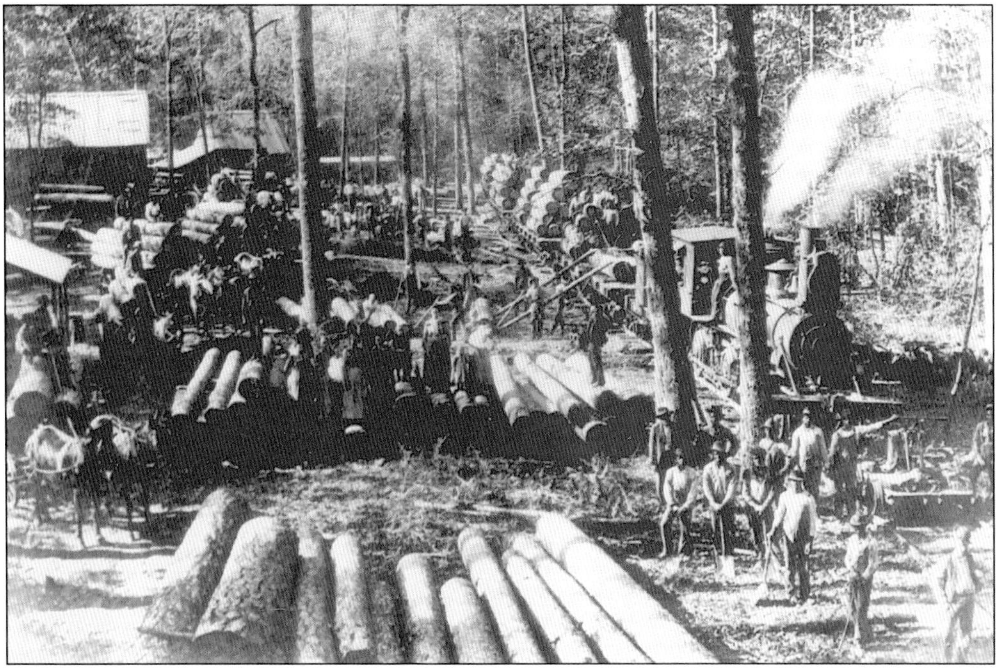

The Drake Logging Camp along the Minden Tap Railroad is pictured in about 1904. By this time, the Tap Railroad had been acquired by William Buchanan's Louisiana and Arkansas Railroad and had become part of that system's north-to-south rail line. (Courtesy of Major DePingre.)

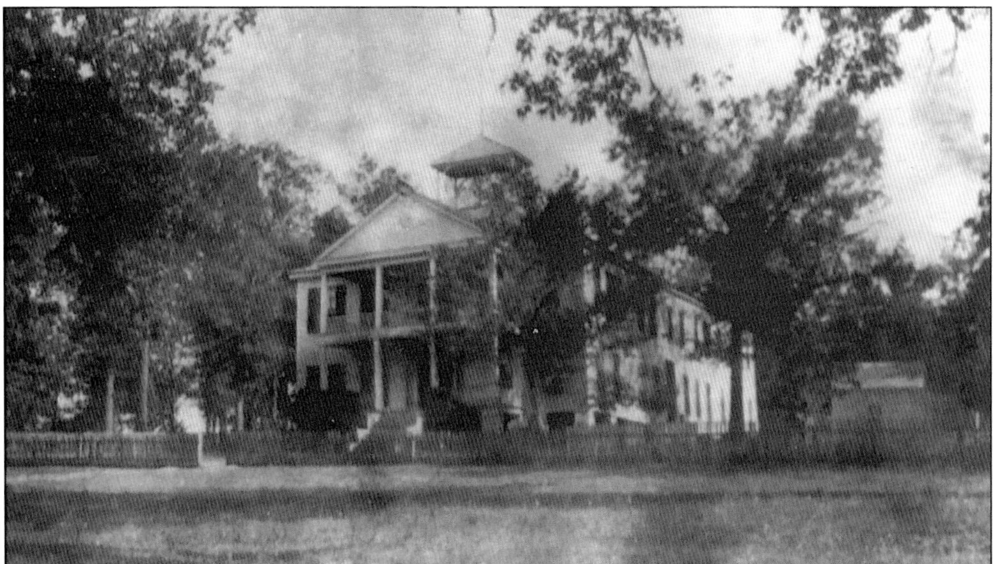

The Long Springs Resort Hotel, located north of Minden along the L&A Railroad tracks, is seen in the mid-1890s. The resort Sulfur Springs, located in the area had been well known for many years. The extension of railroad tracks created easier access to the site, and a boom in business that allowed the development of the resort hotel. The boom was short lived and the hotel was turned into a residence by the early 1900s; it burned in the 1920s. (Courtesy of Major DePingre.)

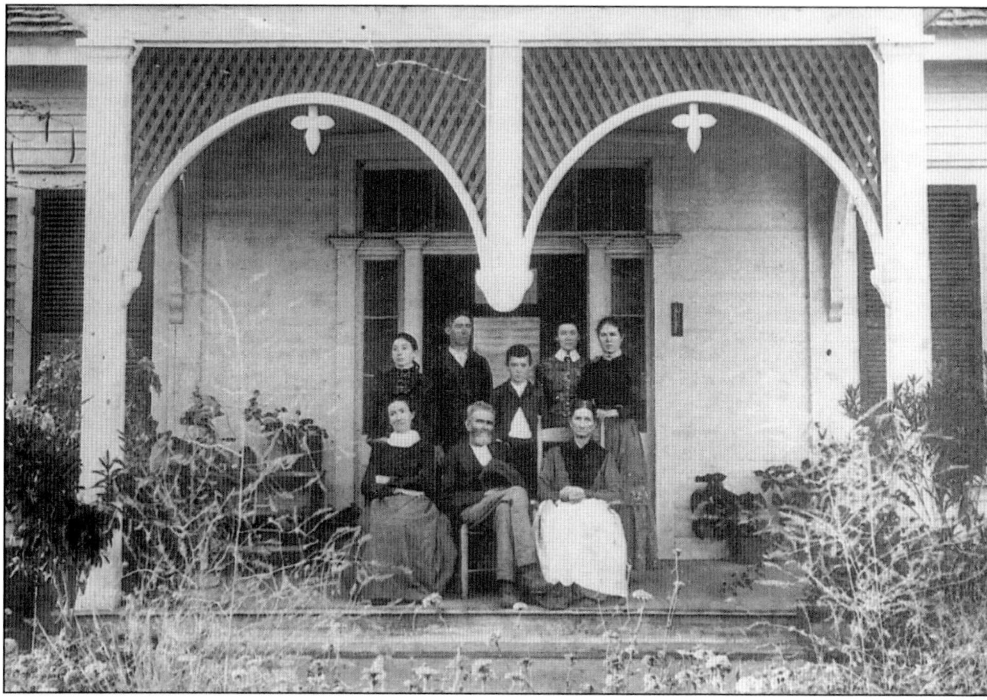

The family of John Sidney Killen, prominent farmer, Baptist layman, and legislator, is pictured on the front porch of the family home in about 1900. The Killen home, which was built about 1880, still stands today on U.S. Highway 80 West in Minden. Killen had a huge farm that produced many unique varieties of fruit and other crops. He earned recognition across the South as a innovator in crop development. (Courtesy of George Turner.)

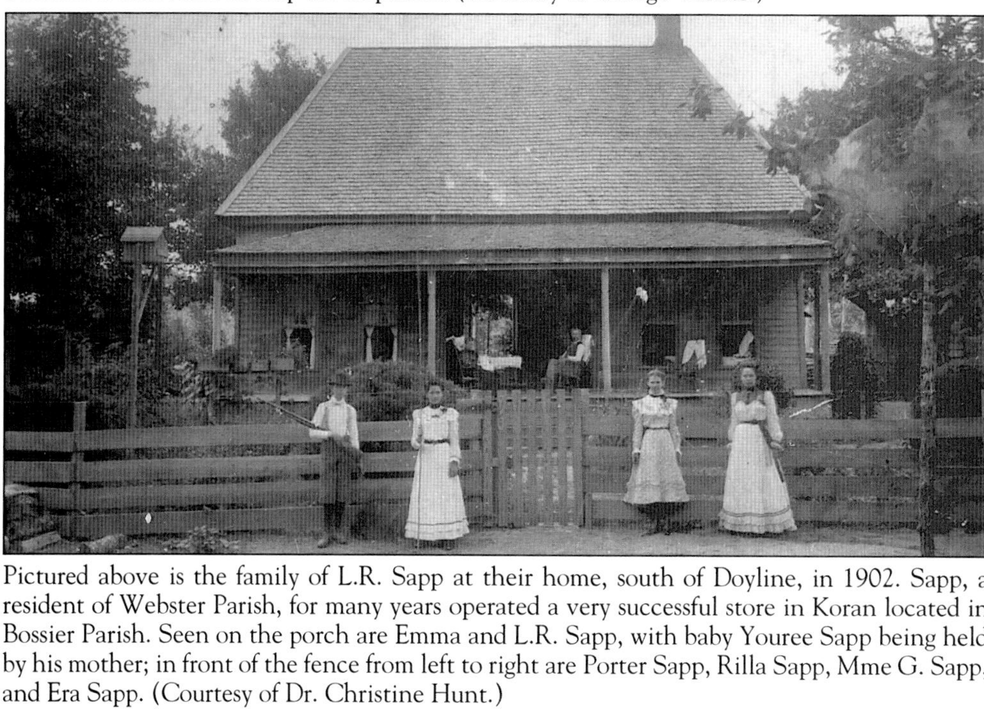

Pictured above is the family of L.R. Sapp at their home, south of Doyline, in 1902. Sapp, a resident of Webster Parish, for many years operated a very successful store in Koran located in Bossier Parish. Seen on the porch are Emma and L.R. Sapp, with baby Youree Sapp being held by his mother; in front of the fence from left to right are Porter Sapp, Rilla Sapp, Mme G. Sapp, and Era Sapp. (Courtesy of Dr. Christine Hunt.)

R.L. Sapp is pictured about 1910. (Courtesy of Dr. Christine Hunt.)

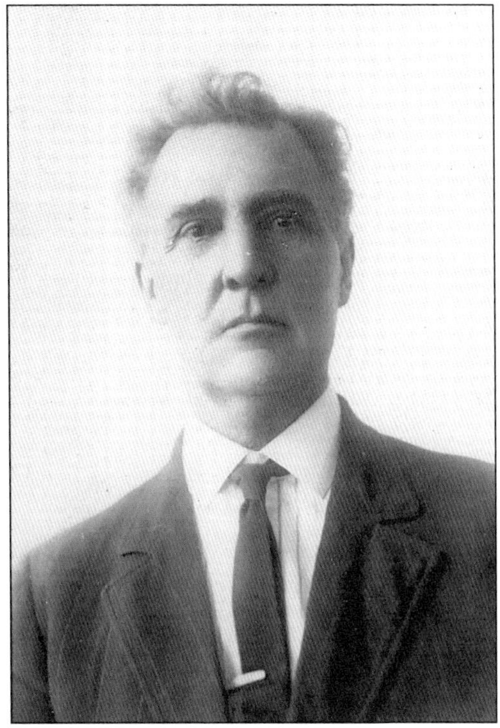

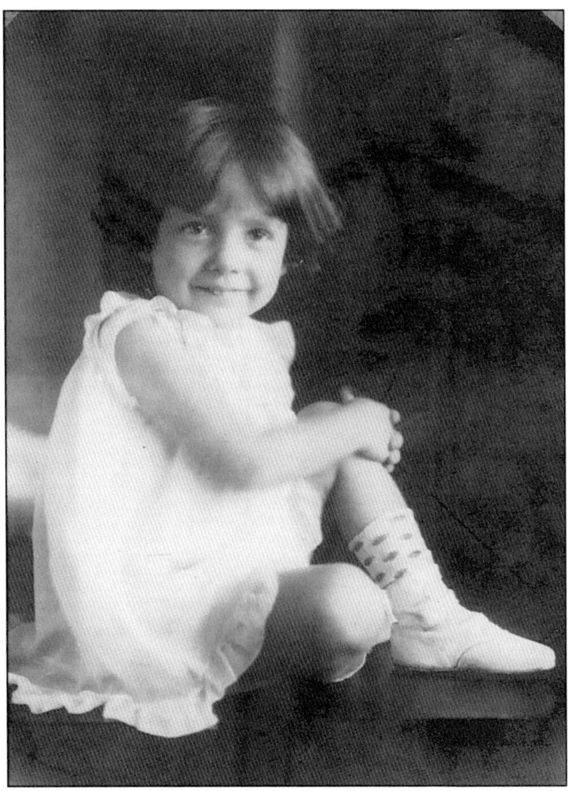

Christine Sapp, daughter of Youree Sapp and granddaughter of R.L. Sapp, is pictured about 1930. Christine later married and became Dr. Christine Hunt. She served many years as a teacher in the Webster Parish schools, and retired as principal of E.S. Richardson Elementary School. (Courtesy of Dr. Christine Hunt.)

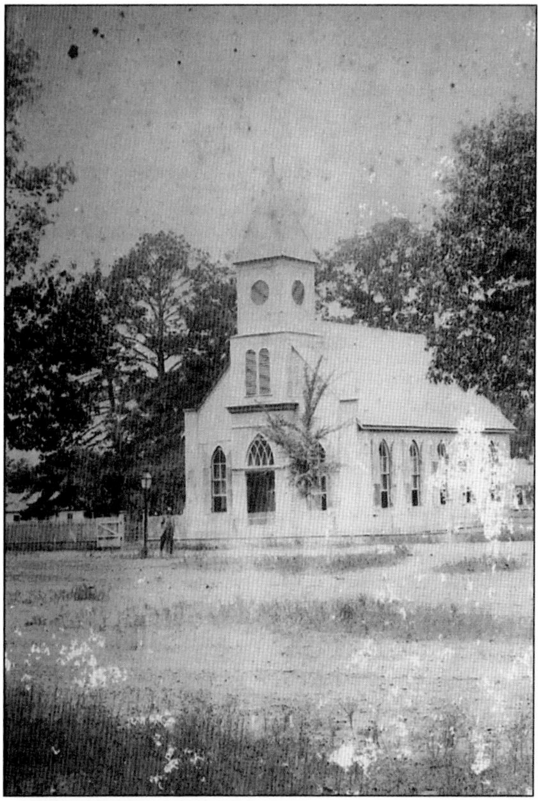

Minden Presbyterian Church is shown about 1900. The church was constructed on property donated by Hervey Drake. This building was used until 1924, when the church facility currently in use was built. (Courtesy of Major DePingre.)

The Yellow Pine Christian Church, built around 1902, has been placed on the National Register of Historic Places. Originally built as a "union" church for all residents of the lumber boom town of Yellow Pine, the church affiliated with the Christian Church in the late 1940s.

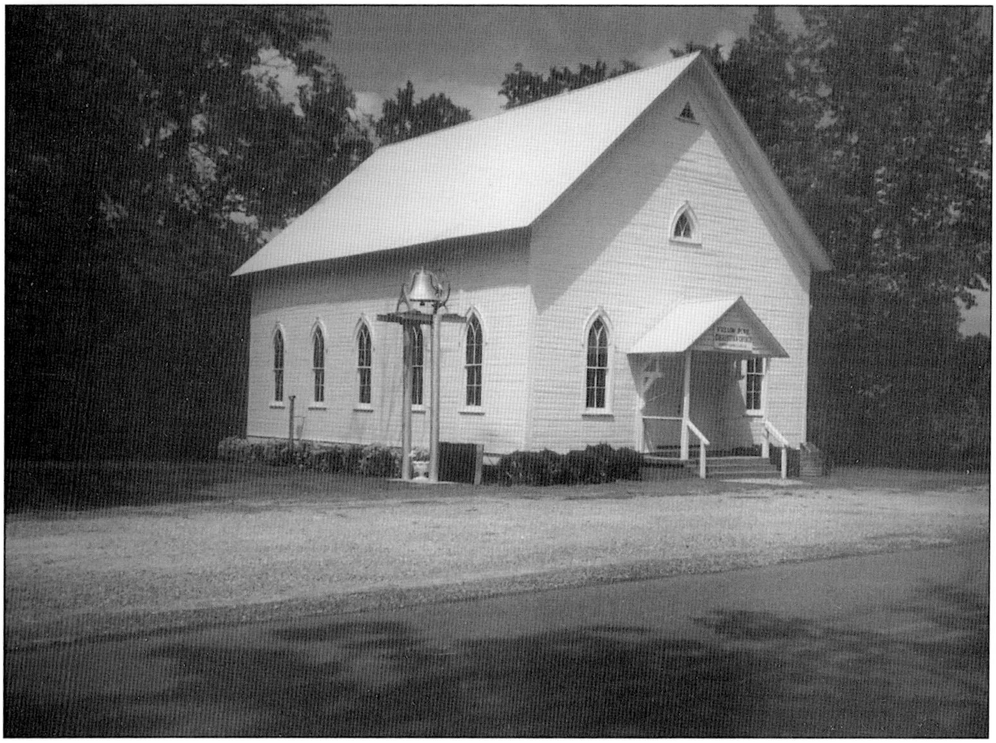

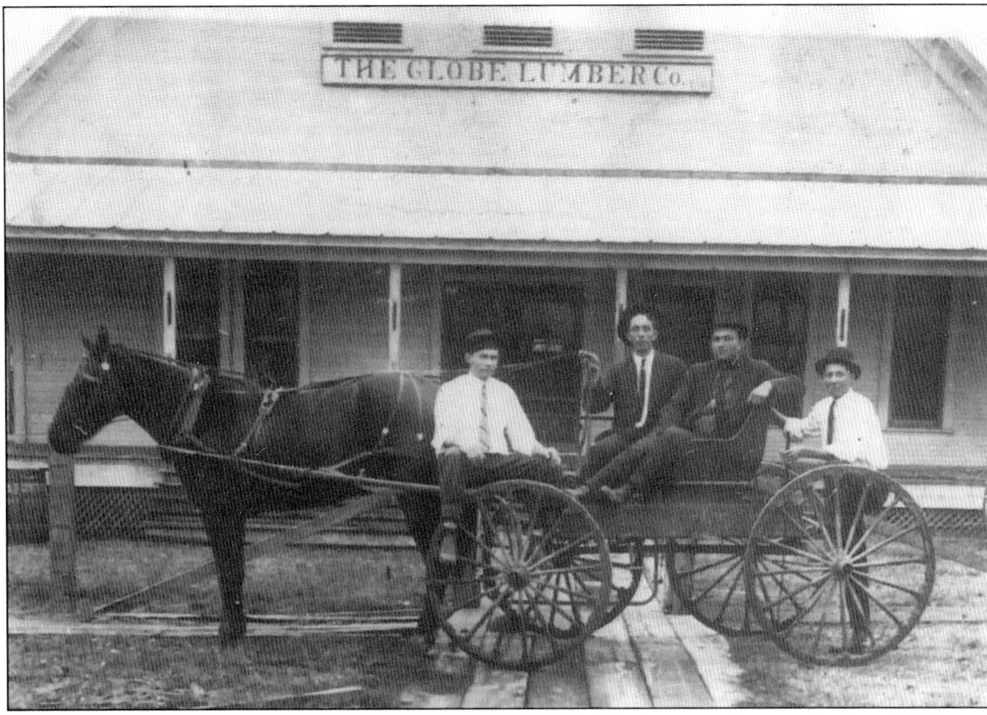

The community of Yellow Pine enjoyed an enormous growth spurt during the late 1890s and early 1900s, when the Globe Lumber Company opened a huge lumber mill in the area. The town eventually boasted more than 3,000 residents and was a thriving community. Pictured here are several men in front of the headquarters of the lumber company in about 1908. (Courtesy of Opal Corbin.)

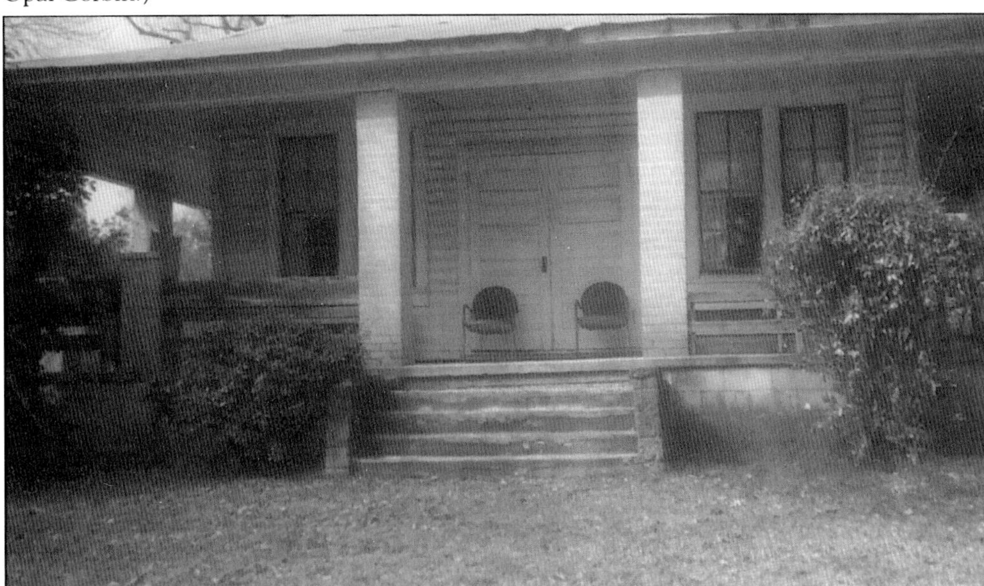

The boom at Yellow Pine was followed by as nearly as rapid of a decline after the Globe Lumber Company closed. Little remains today of the town, except the church and this home of the McKinney family, which was the town's school. (Courtesy of Opal Corbin.)

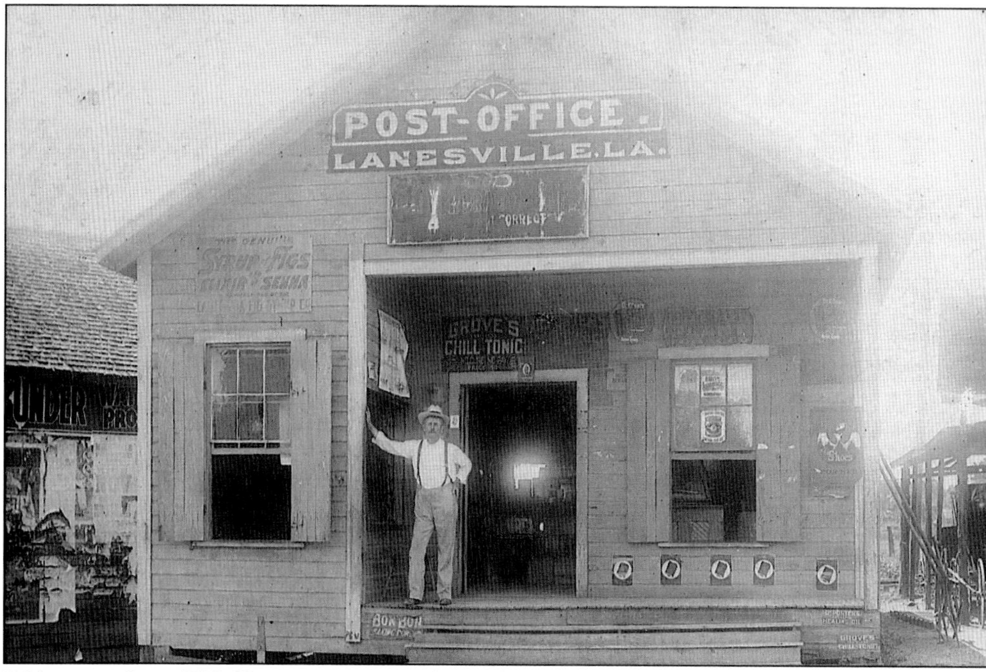

Sibley merchant E.E. Kennon is pictured standing in the doorway of the post office prior to 1912. Notice the sign designating the structure as the Lanesville Post Office. The community had been named after the Lane family, which first settled in the area prior to the Civil War. (Courtesy of Mary Nell Slater Rhea.)

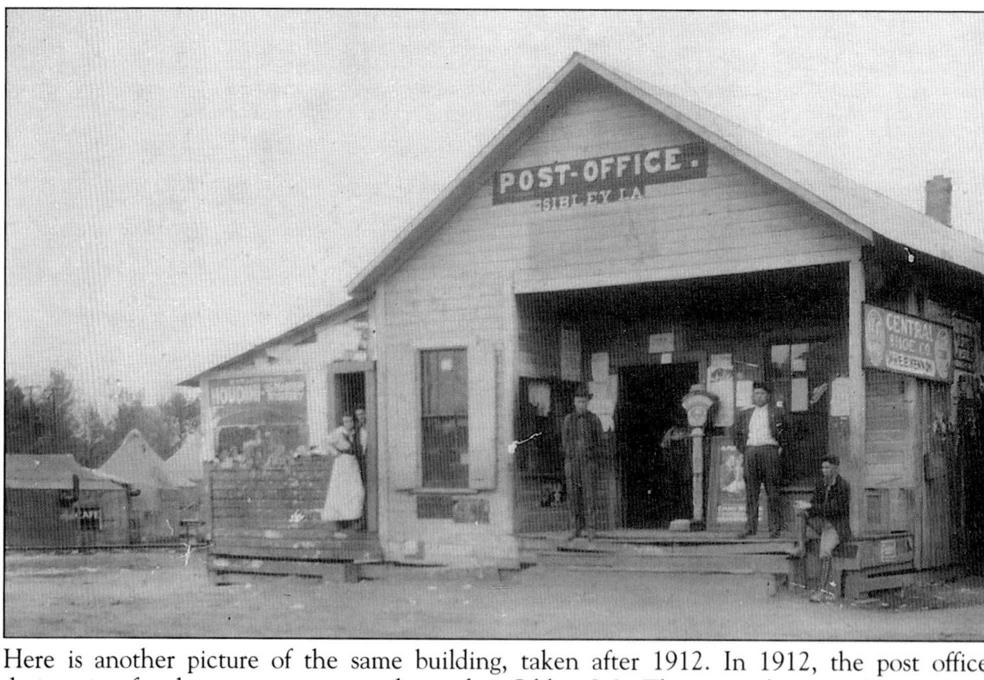

Here is another picture of the same building, taken after 1912. In 1912, the post office designation for the community was changed to Sibley, LA. This name became the common usage for the town, even though the official name was not changed on state records until the late 1950s. (Courtesy of Mary Nell Slater Kennon.)

Dr. R.W. Smith practiced medicine for many years in the Dubberly area. His son was Dr. R.E. Smith of Minden and his son-in-law was Dr. Paul Crutsinger of Minden. (Courtesy of Quay Crutsinger Griffith.)

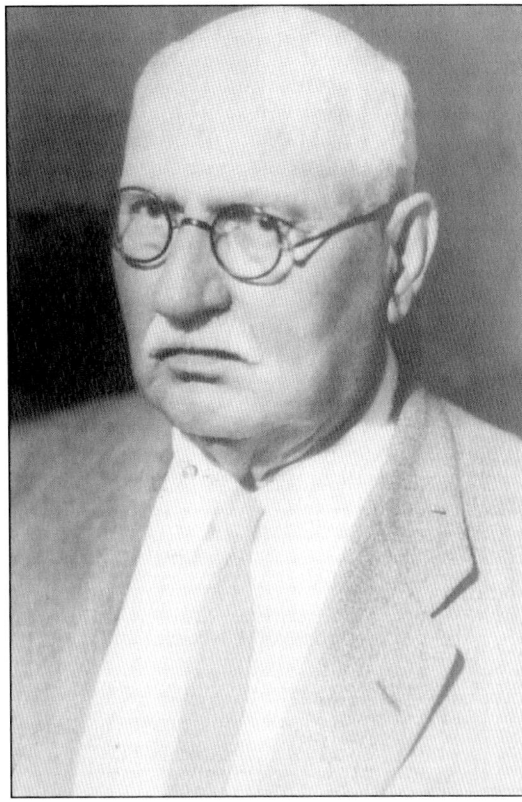

The home of Dr. R.W. Smith in Dubberly is shown in the 1890s. (Courtesy of Quay Crutsinger Griffith.)

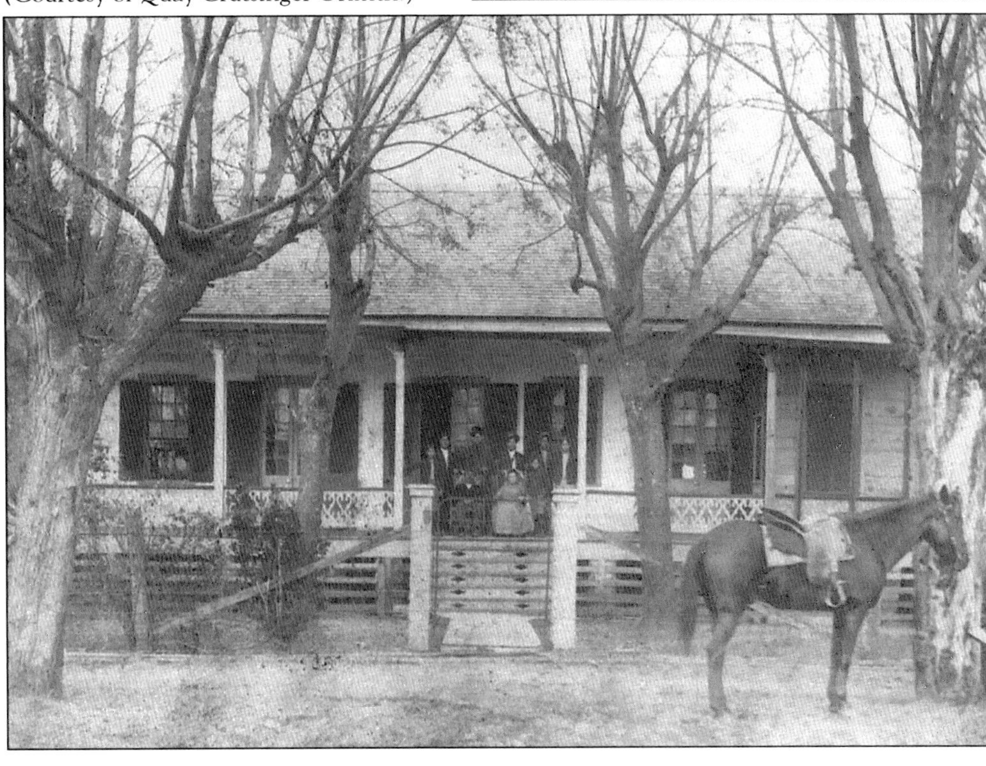

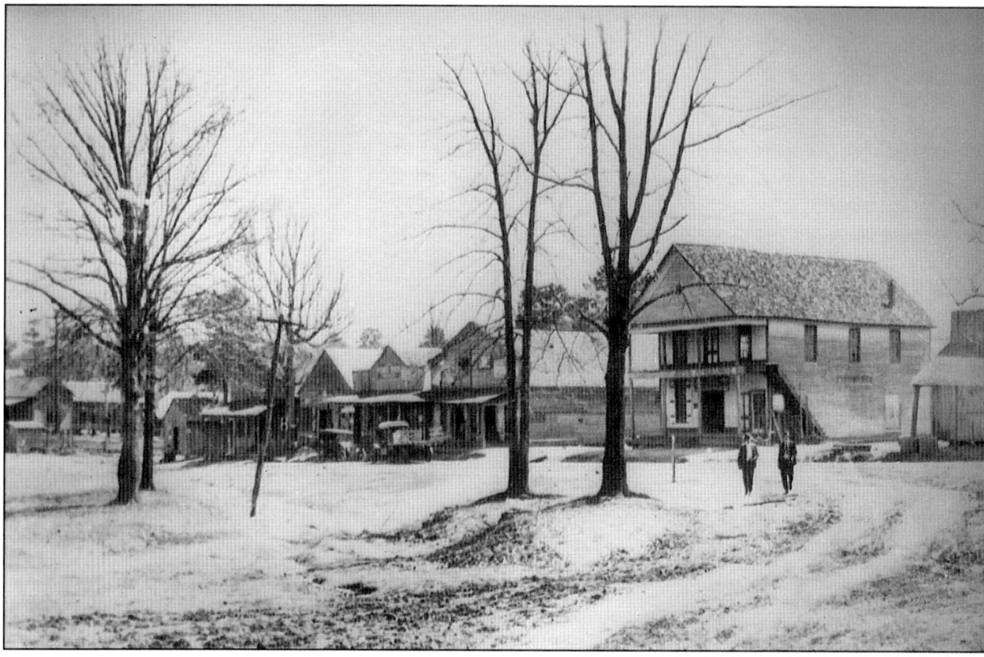

Downtown Dubberly is pictured before it was destroyed by a fire in the early 1920s. This picture was taken around 1915. Shown from left to right are the M.T. Worsham Barber Shop, the Bessie Batton House, the T.C. Connell Store, the J.C. Worsham Store, the M.H. Boyet Store, the W.W. McCoy Store, the Dan Parham Saloon, and the Pat McCrary Store. (Courtesy of Joe Butler and Carolyn Walraven.)

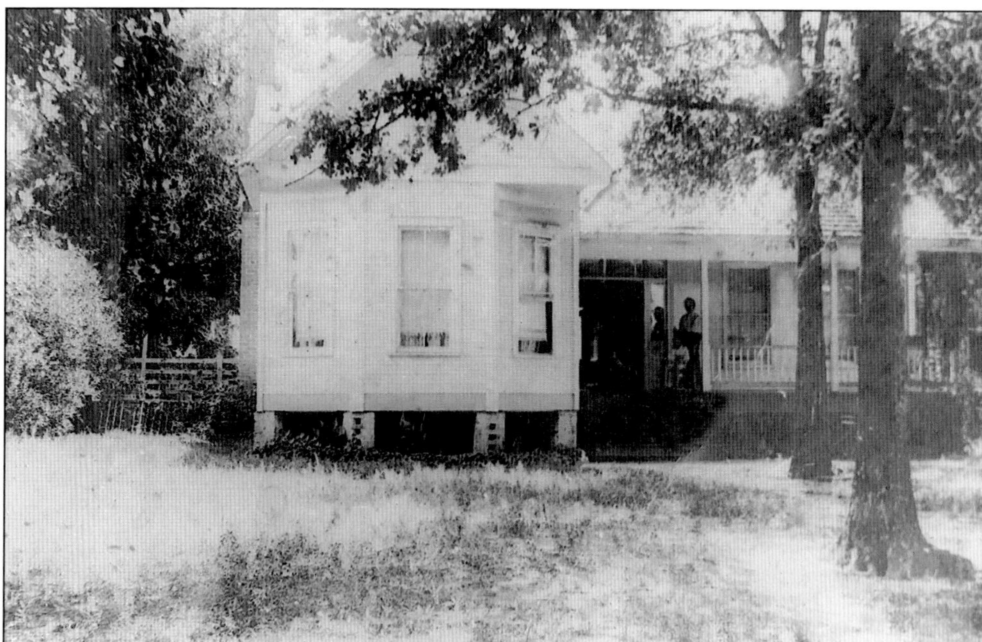

Pictured is the home of W.G. Stewart, north of Minden. Mr. Stewart was a son of Dougald Stewart, pictured earlier in the chapter. W.G. Stewart was pictured in the chapter on education for his service as president of the Webster Parish School Board. (Courtesy of Virginia Fox.)

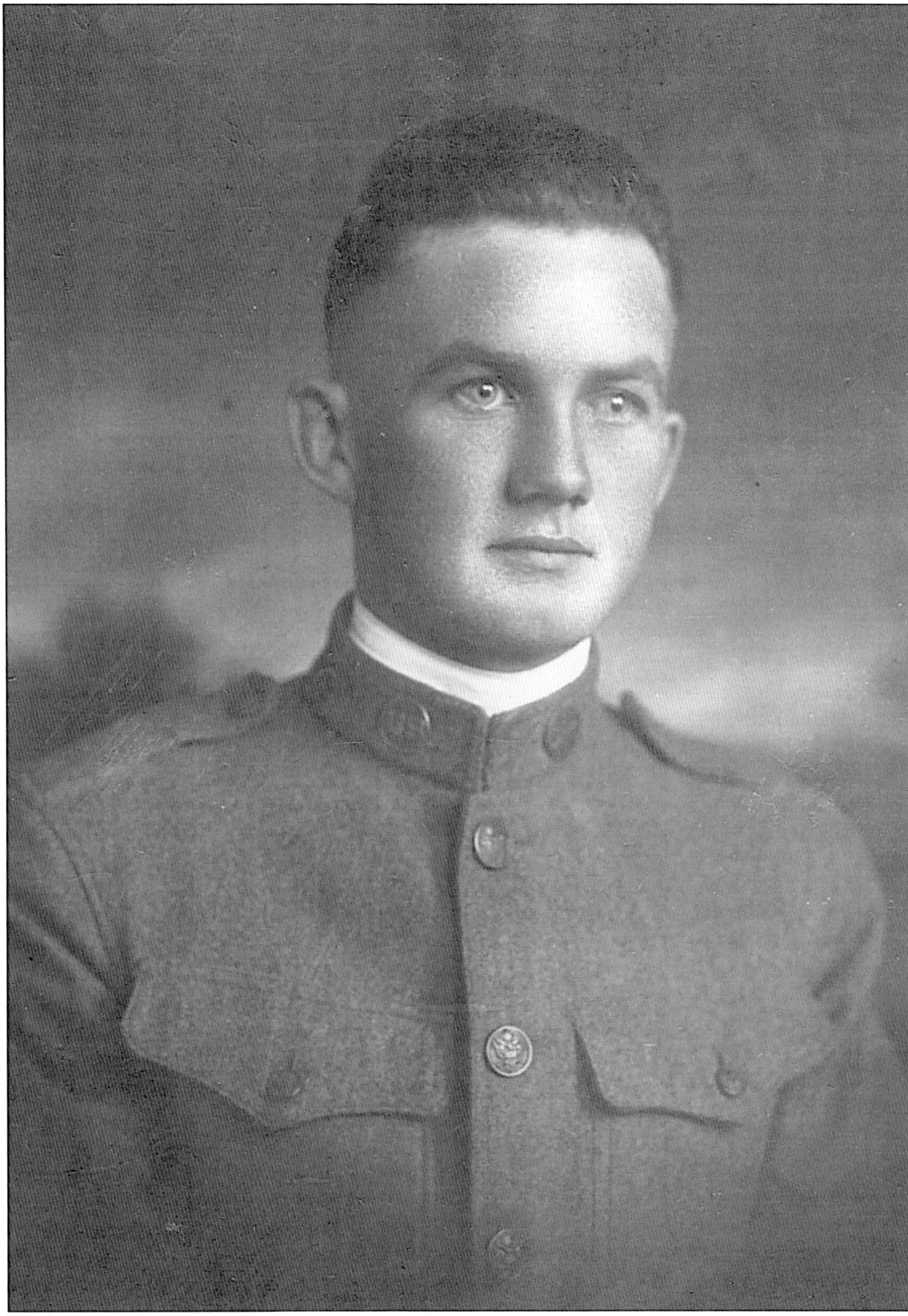

James Stewart, son of W.G. Stewart, is pictured in his World War I uniform. He became a prominent farmer in Webster Parish and raised his family in the home built by his father. Today, one of his daughters still lives in the home. Another daughter married the grandson of G.L.P. Wren, uniting those two prominent Webster Parish families. (Courtesy of Virginia Fox.)

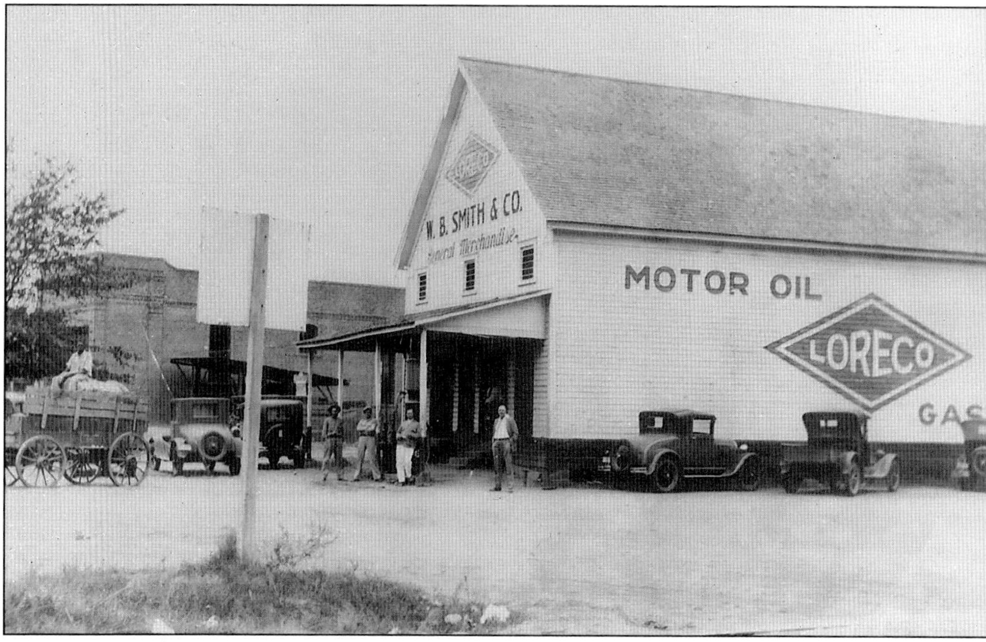

The W.B. Smith & Co. store in downtown Heflin is seen in the early 1920s. Notice the mixture of early automobiles used by some customers of the store, which featured gasoline pumps, while others are still using wagons to come to town. In the background is the Bank of Heflin, which was built but never opened, and has been used as a barn for many years. (Courtesy of Vernita and Lloyd Beatty.)

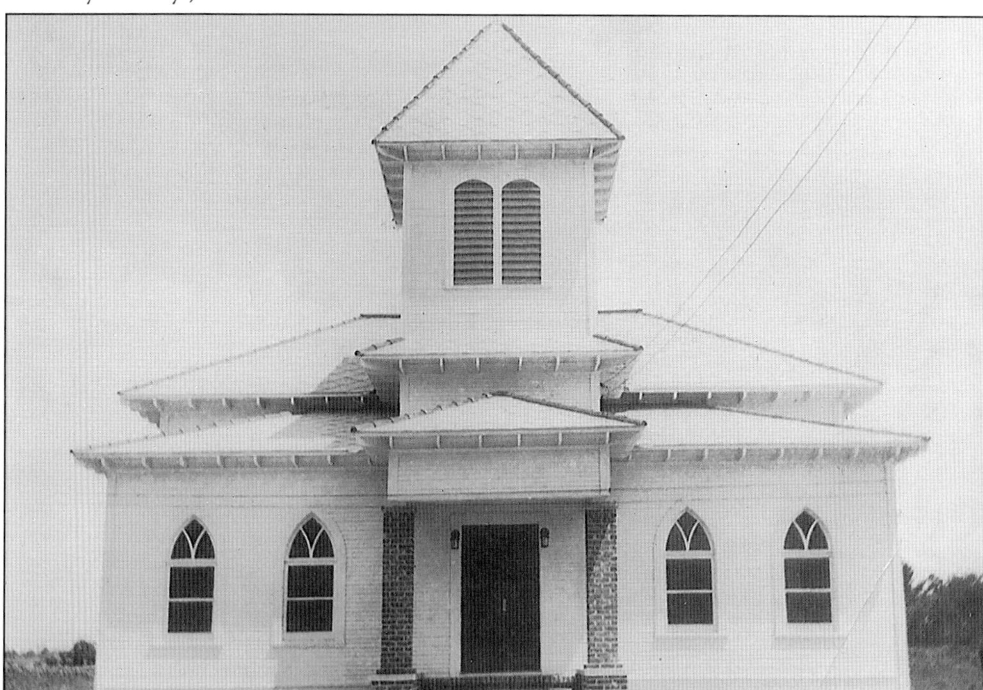

The Heflin Methodist Church is shown shortly after its completion. The church building is still in use today. (Courtesy of Vernita and Lloyd Beatty.)

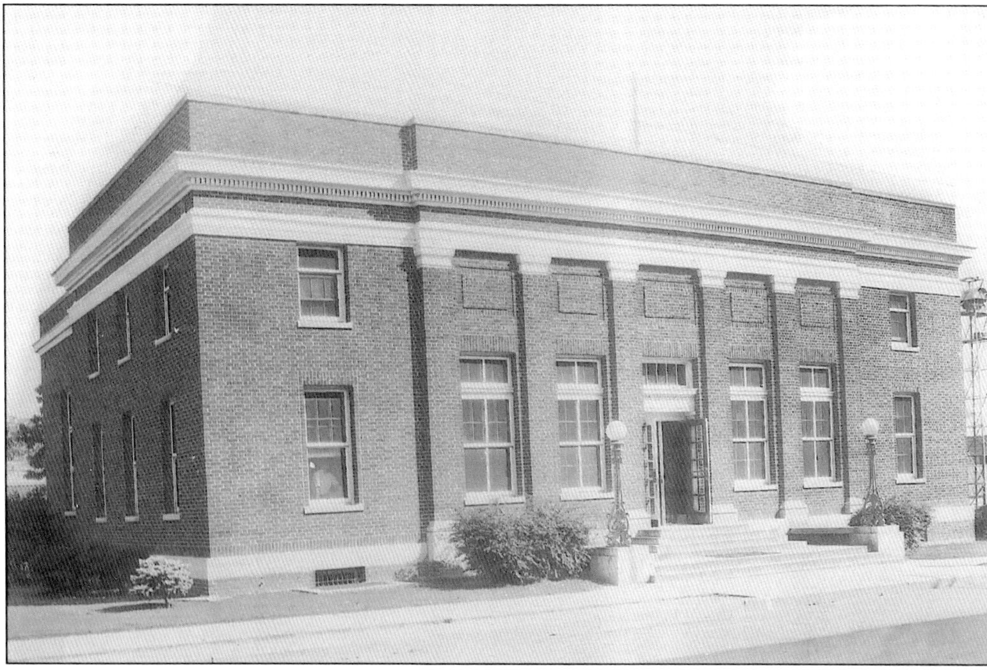

The United States Post Office on the corner of East Union and Main in downtown Minden was used from 1916 until 1960. It is shown here during the 1920s. Prior to the construction of this post office, part of the land had been the site of the first Webster Parish Courthouse, built in 1872. Today, Hibernia National Bank is located on the site. (Courtesy of Lillian Life Willis.)

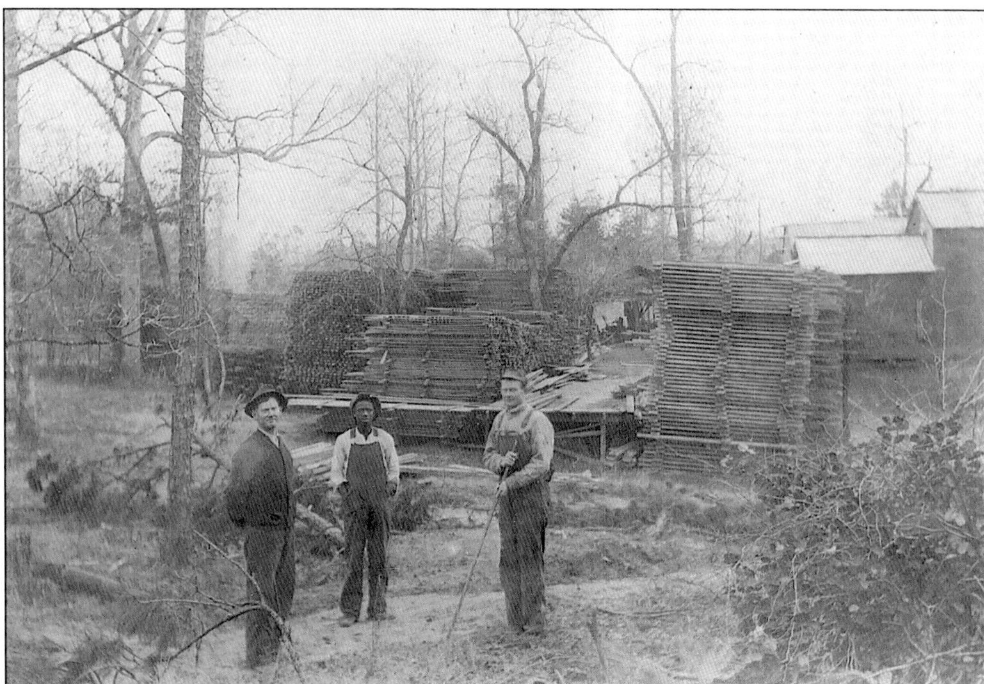

Pictured at the Turner Brothers Lumber Company in the 1920s are, from left to right, Phares Turner, Tom Woods, and J.K. Turner Sr. (Courtesy of George Turner.)

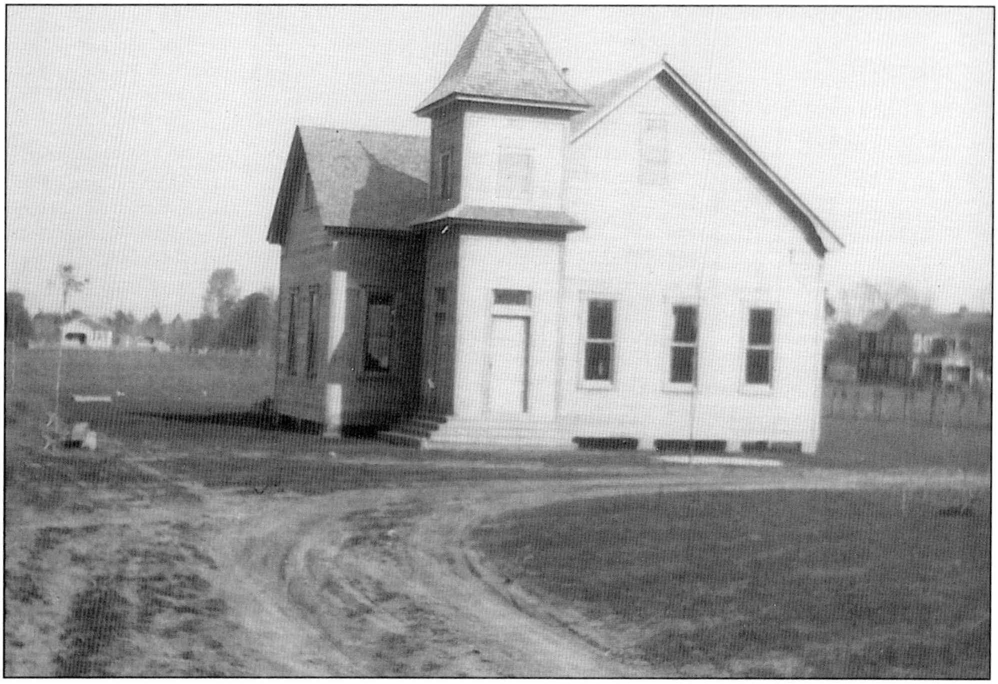

This building was the first home of the First Baptist Church of Doyline, constructed in 1924. (Courtesy of Lee C. McIntyre.)

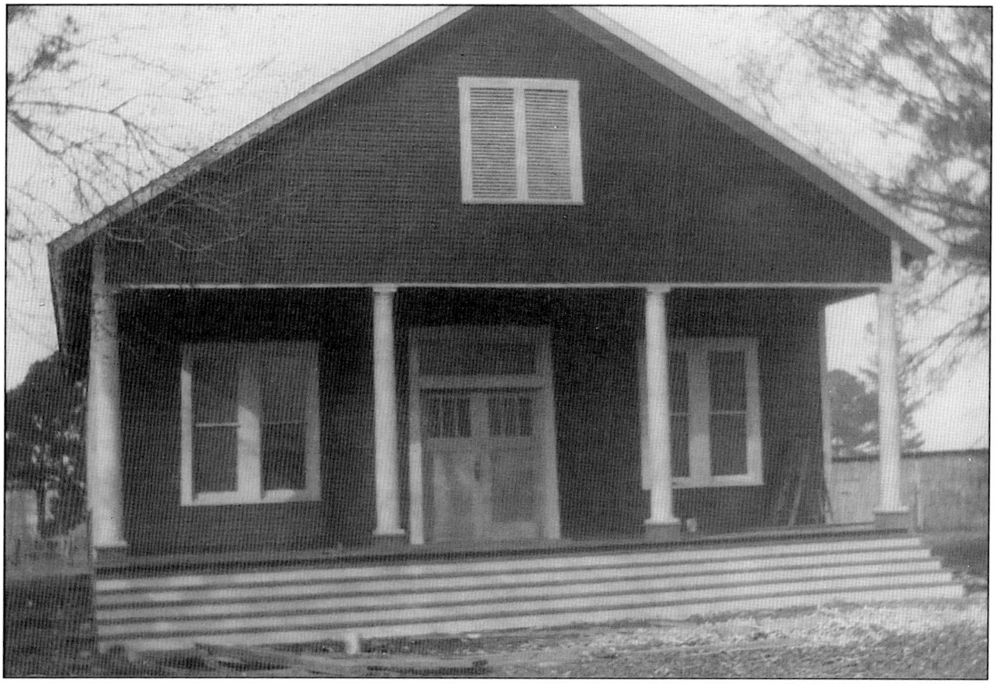

The third home of the Doyline Methodist Church was first used in 1926. (Courtesy of Lee C. McIntyre.)

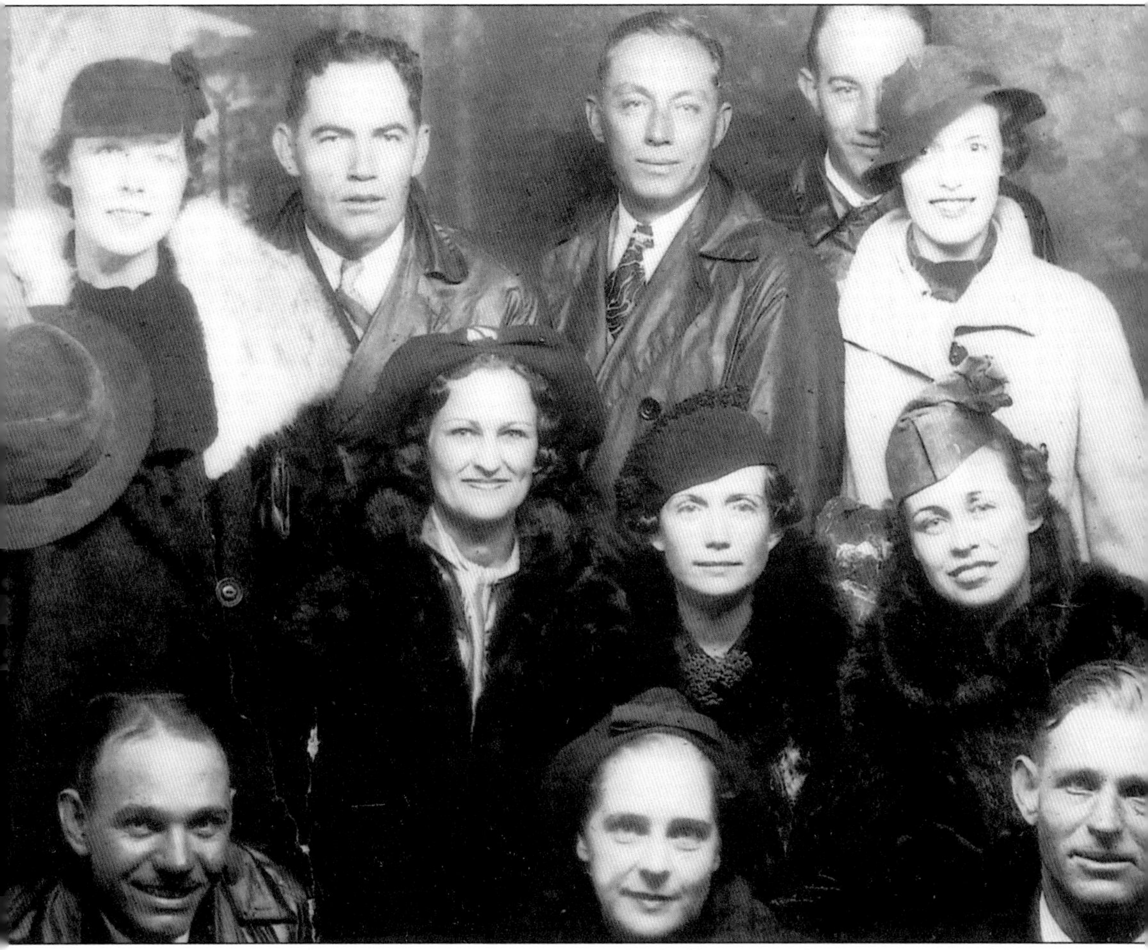

A group of Minden residents prepare to attend a LSU football game in the 1930s. Pictured from left to right are the following: (front row) Dr. Carroll Summer (parish health officer), Dorothy Bridges, and H.L. Bridges; (middle row) Jewel Taylor, Dorothy White, and Marie Watkins; (back row) Fairy Drake, Sam White, James Taylor, Rob Watkins, and Georgia Summer. (Courtesy of Luther and Claire Drake Moore.)

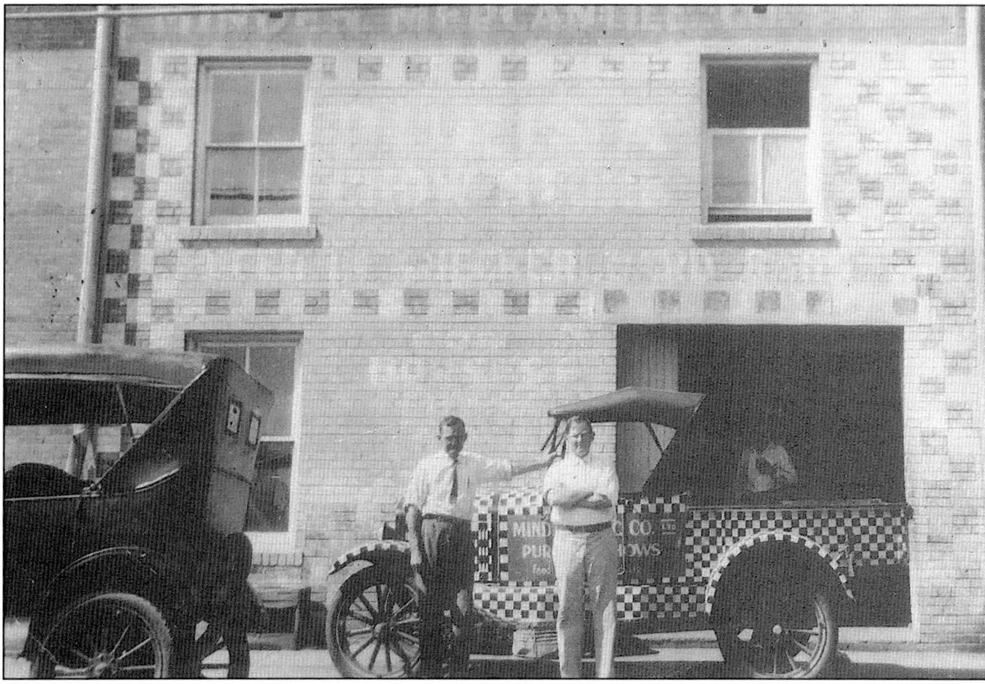

The loading entrance of Minden Mercantile is seen on "back street" in Minden in the early 1920s. They were the local Purina dealer; notice the checkerboard square design on the delivery vehicle. Pictured are a Mr. Pevy and Sidney Turner, one of the owners of the firm. (Courtesy of Ruth Turner Stinnett.)

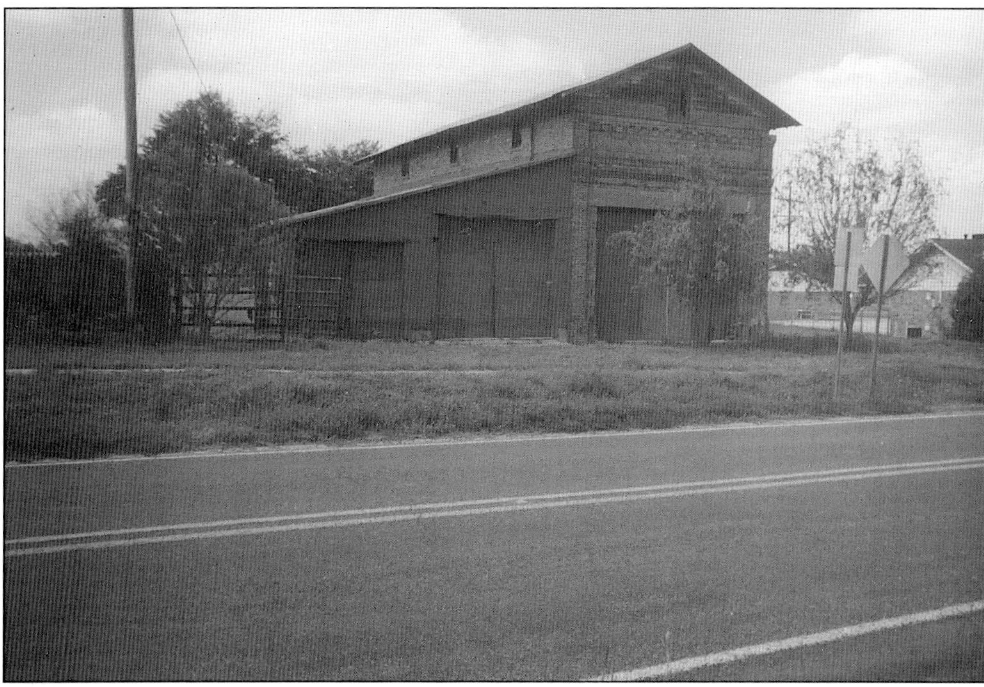

The never-used Bank of Heflin is seen as it looks today, after more than half a century of use as a barn.

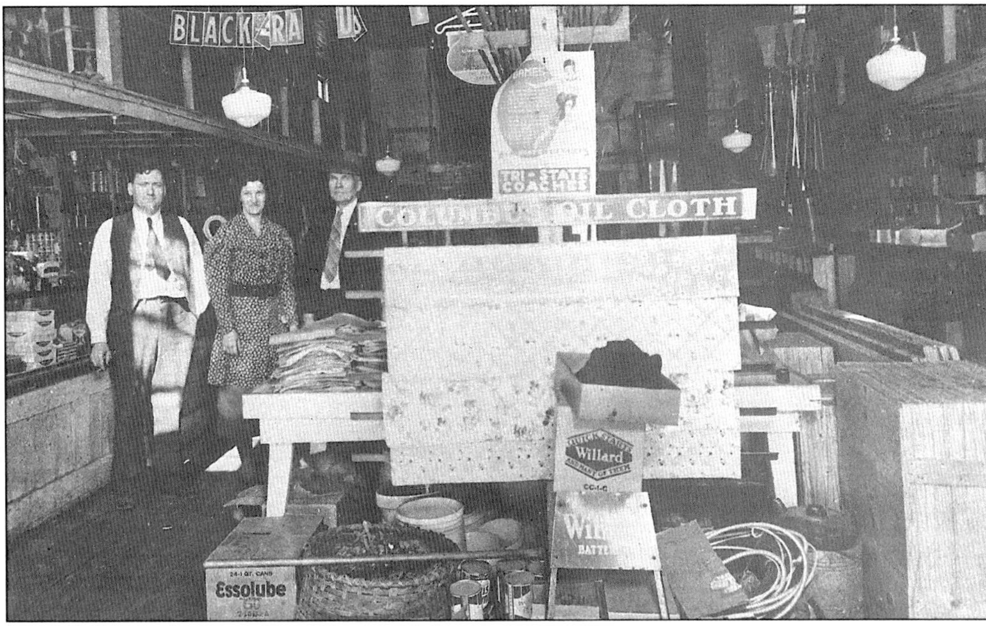

This interior view of the H.H. Johnson store at McIntyre was taken in 1934. The community of McIntyre, west of Minden, had been called Melrose until the railroad came through the area in 1898. There was already a Melrose on the line, so the residents chose to rename the community after the McIntrye family, which was among the earliest settlers. (Courtesy of Major DePingre.)

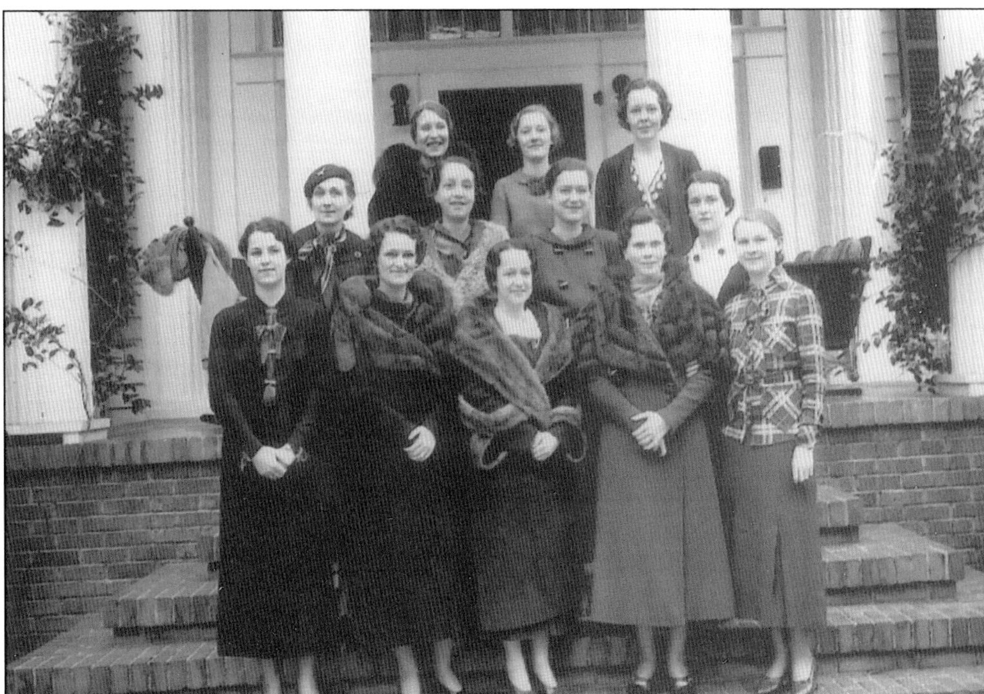

The first officers of the Minden Junior Service League are pictured on the steps of the A.E. Drake home in the 1930s. (Courtesy of Luther and Claire Drake Moore.)

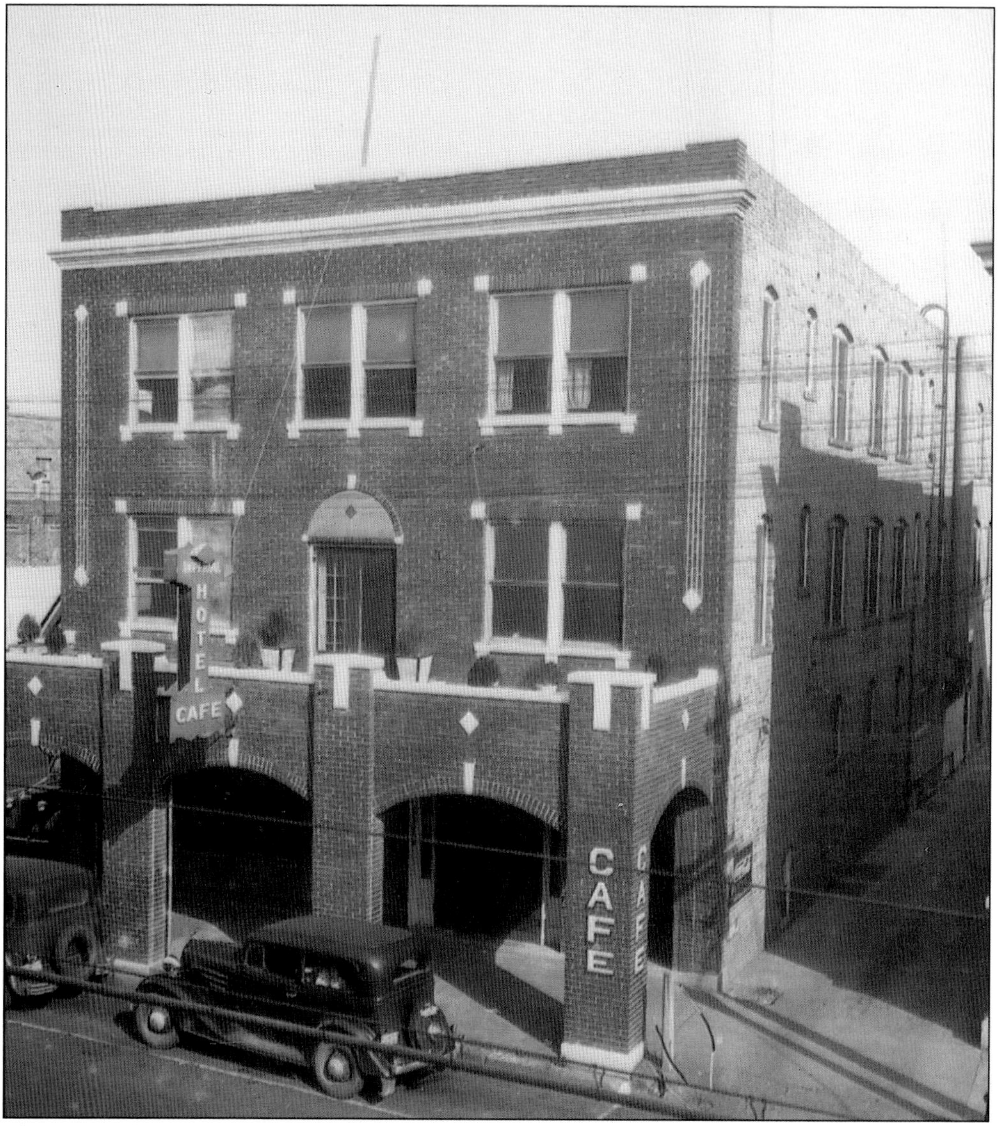

The Imperial Hotel in downtown Minden is pictured during the early 1930s. For many years the dining room of this hotel was the meeting place for many civic clubs and banquets in Minden. The hotel portion of the building has been abandoned for years, but two storefront business operate out of the structure today. (Courtesy of Major DePingre.)

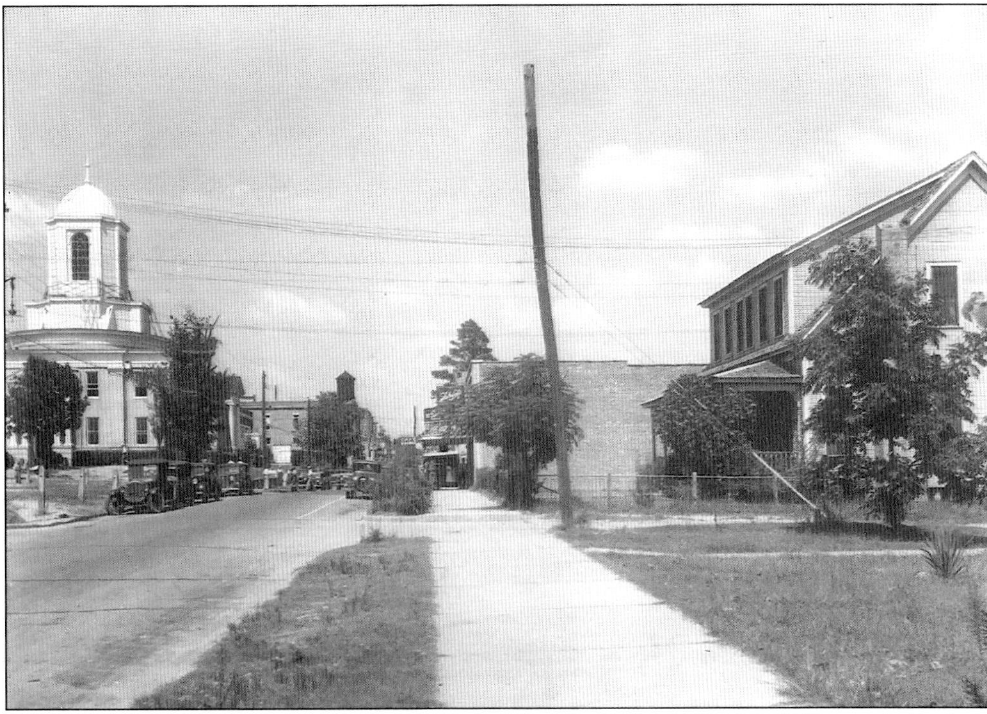

South Broadway (Back) Street in Minden is seen during the 1930s, complete with hitching posts and Model T Fords. The 1905 Webster Parish Courthouse is seen at left, after its 1933 remodeling when the clock was removed from the dome after having been out of service for more than a decade. The house in the foreground is Mrs. Owen's boardinghouse, which stood on the corner of Pine and South Broadway. (Courtesy of Major DePingre.)

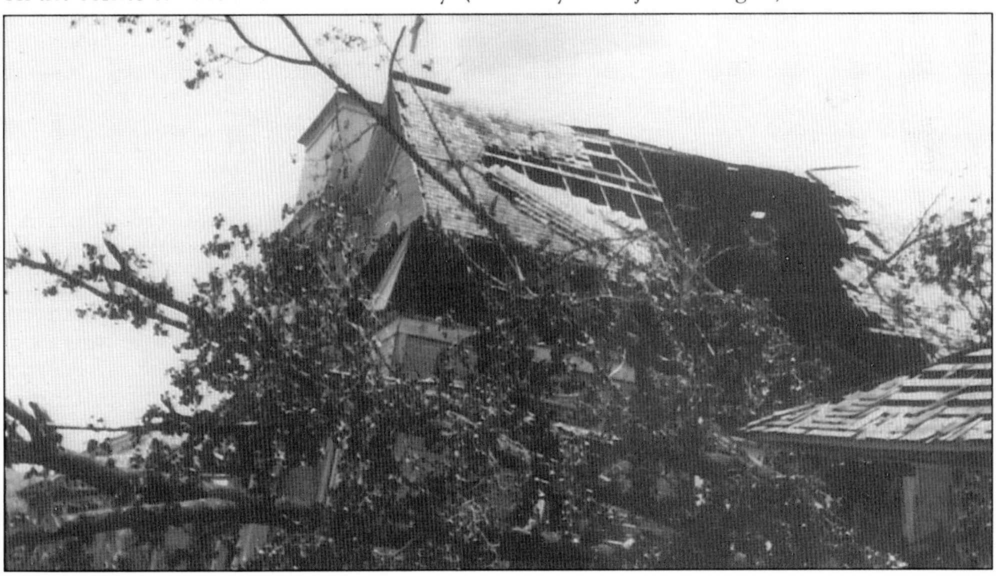

St. Anne's Catholic Church is shown after being destroyed by the May 1, 1933 tornado that struck Minden. In the right foreground of the picture is the edge of the roof of the building constructed in 1846 as the first home of the Minden Baptist Church. That structure was not as severely damaged by the tornado. (Courtesy of Major DePingre.)

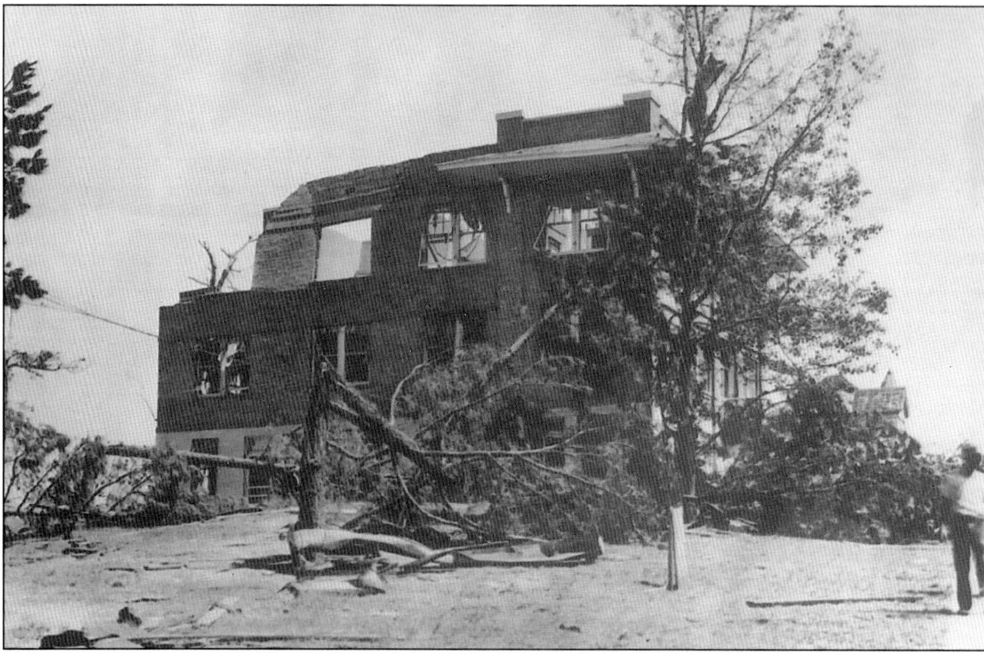

An image of the shell of the office building of the Louisiana and Arkansas Railroad is seen after it was wrecked by the 1933 tornado. This building was rebuilt and continued to be used by the railroad, later becoming home to a meat storage facility. (Courtesy of Major DePingre.)

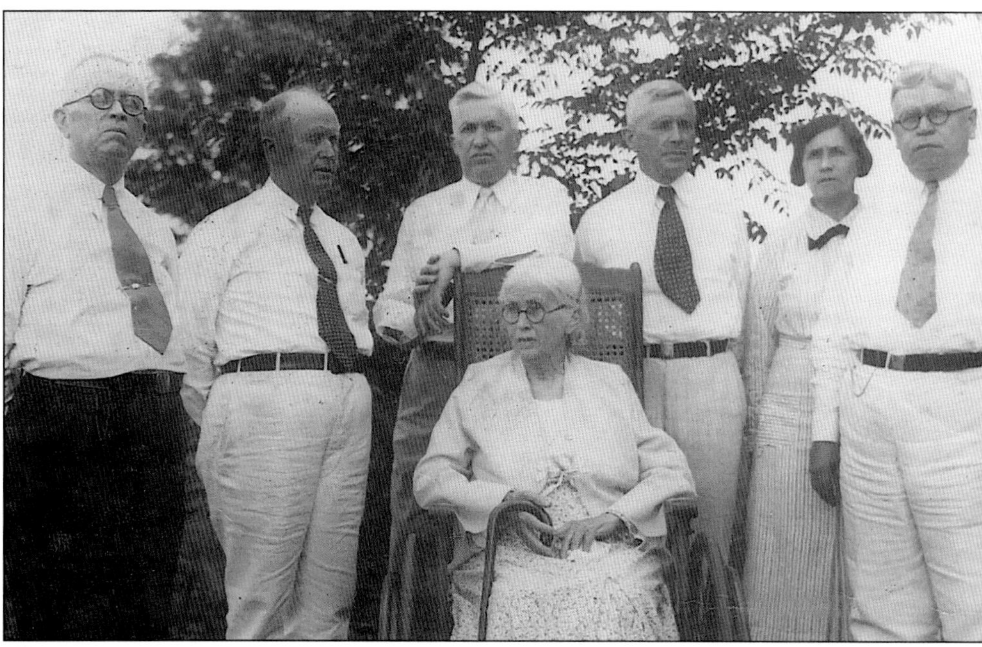

Ellen Carr Wren is shown on her 90th birthday in 1936. Mrs. Wren married G.L.P. Wren (pictured earlier in this book) in 1869, and the couple had five sons and one daughter. Shown above are Mrs. Carr with her children, Lovick, Floyd, Herbert, Marcus, Ava, and Atticus. (Courtesy of Marcus D. Wren Jr.)

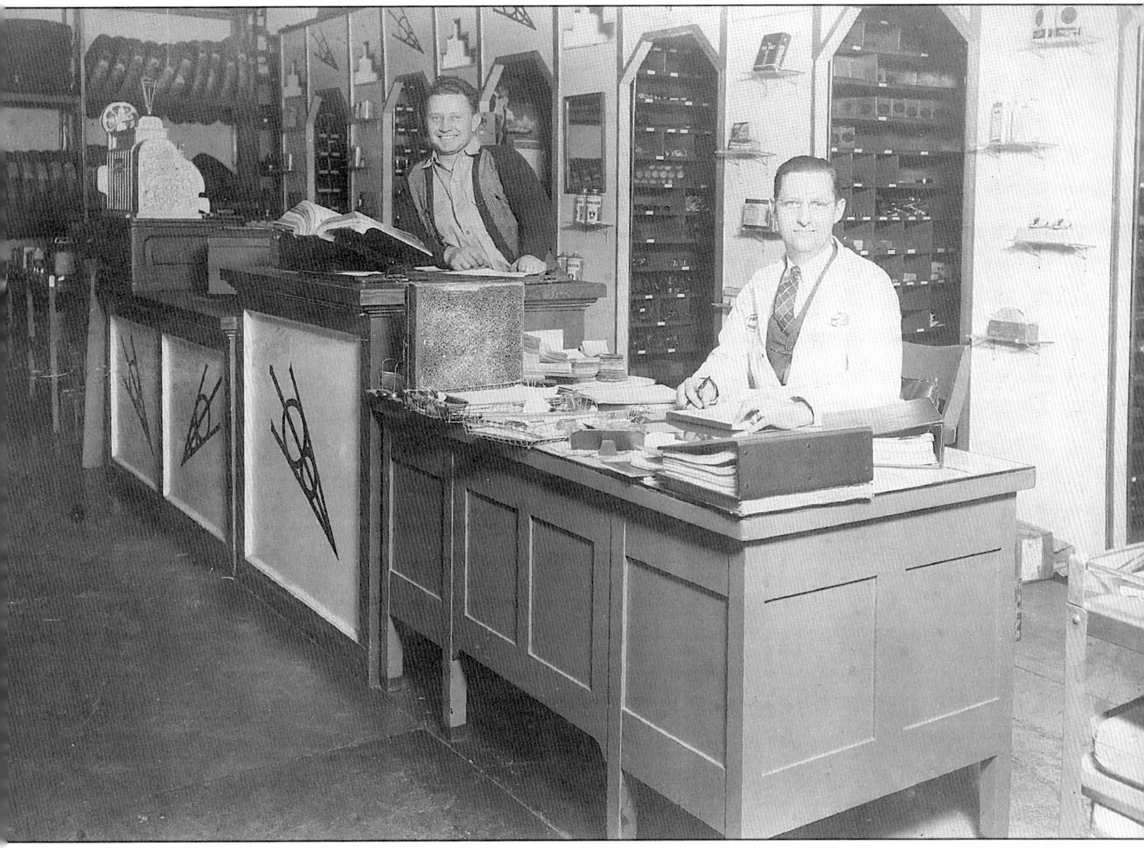

The parts department of Andress Motors Company in Minden is seen in the late 1930s. Seated is parts manager Conrad S. Adkins, with partsman J.C. Agan Jr. standing behind the counter.

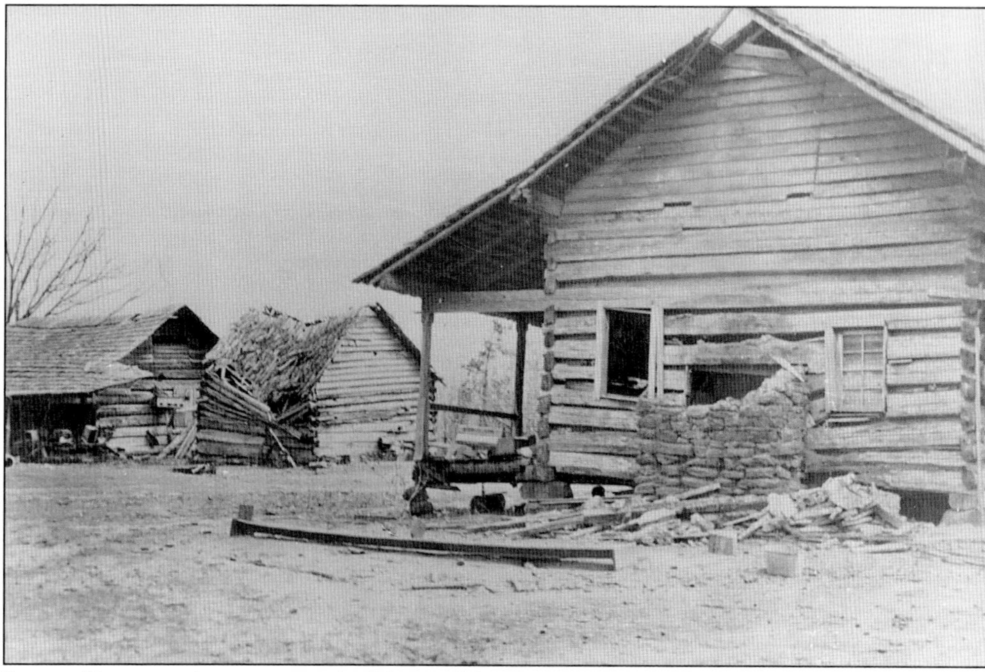

Pictured here are the remaining buildings of the Germantown Colony before restoration in the late 1930s. The utopian community ceased operations in 1871, and nearly all the structures were lost before efforts to save the remaining buildings began in the early 1940s.

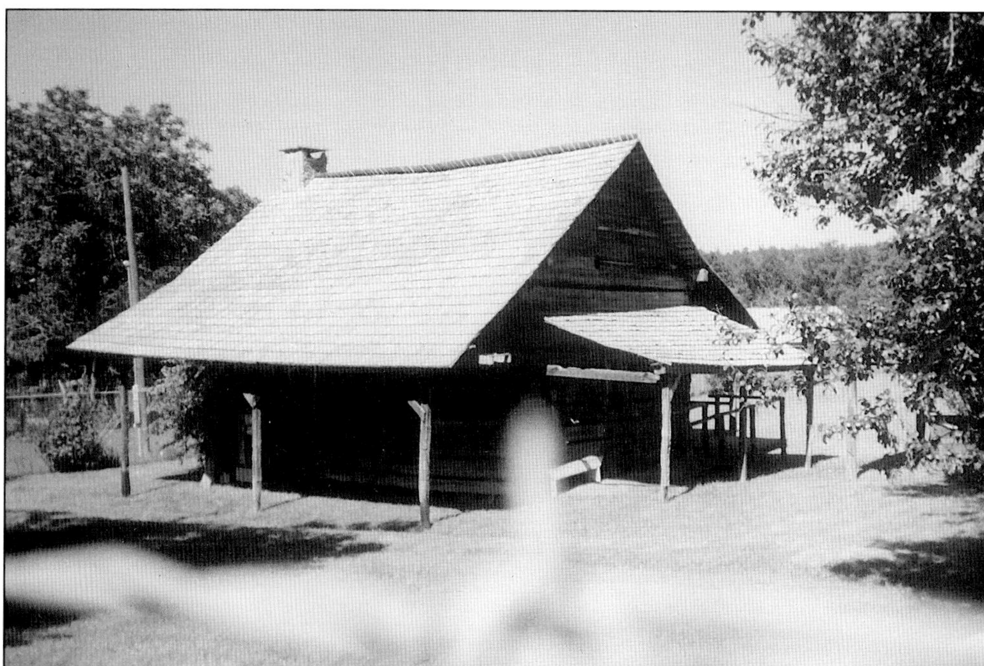

The restored Countess' Cabin is pictured at the Germantown Colony Museum, located north of Minden. The museum was established in 1975 and is under the control of the Webster Parish Police Jury.

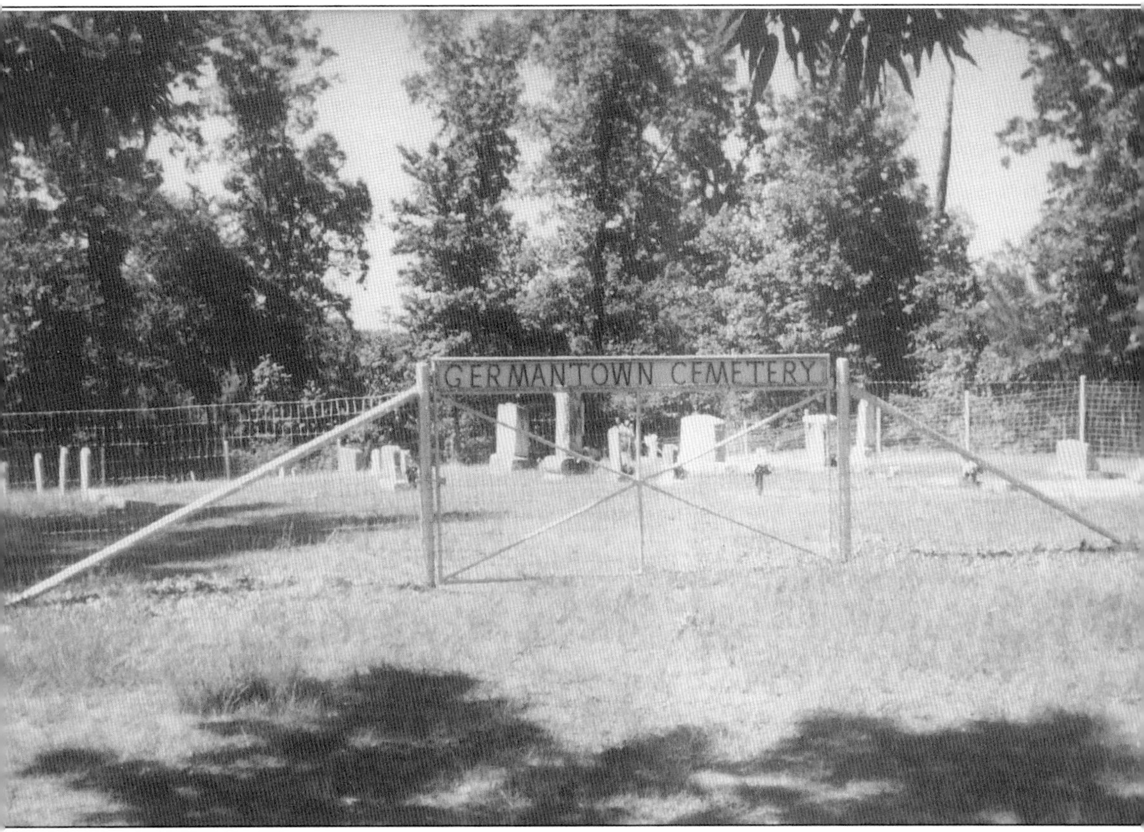

The Germantown Cemetery, which is privately held and not part of the museum, contains the graves of many of the descendants of the original colonists who came to this site in 1835.

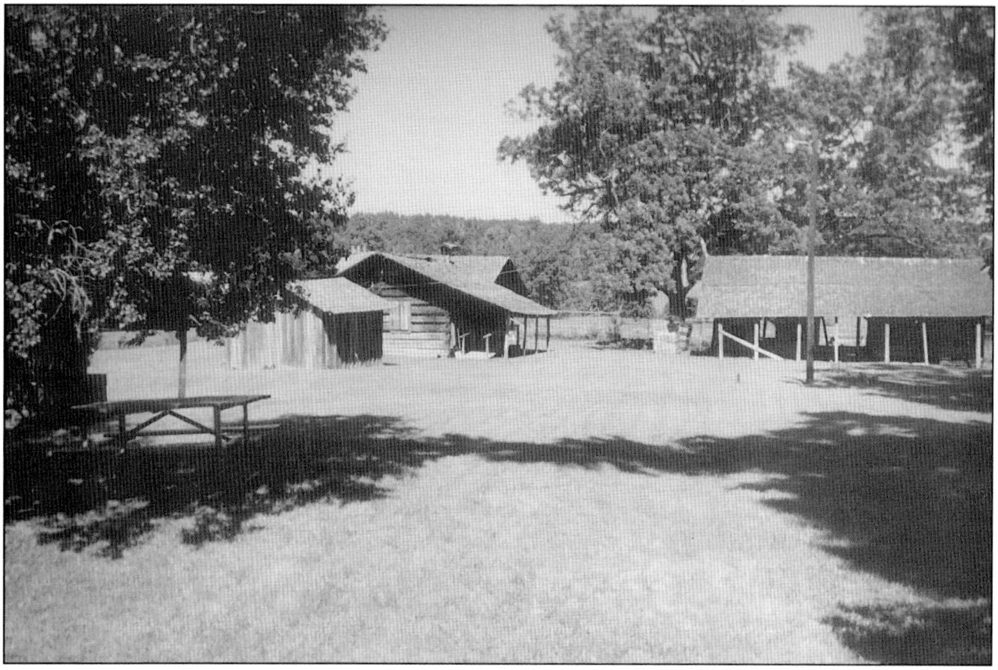

Another view shows the buildings of the Germantown Colony Museum. The buildings contain many artifacts left by original settlers, and the various tools and other items give an interesting picture of daily life in this unique experiment in communal living.

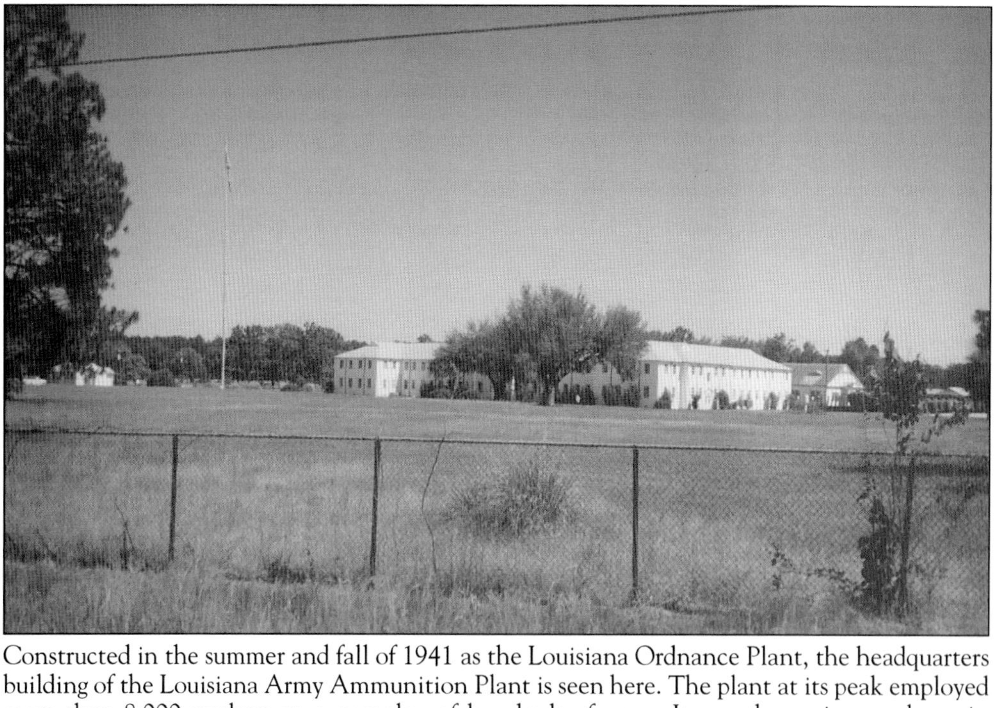

Constructed in the summer and fall of 1941 as the Louisiana Ordnance Plant, the headquarters building of the Louisiana Army Ammunition Plant is seen here. The plant at its peak employed more than 8,000 workers on a complex of hundreds of acres. It was the major employer in Webster Parish for many years. The plant was finally closed and today parts of its facilities are used by the National Guard while another section is being remodeled to house a parish prison.

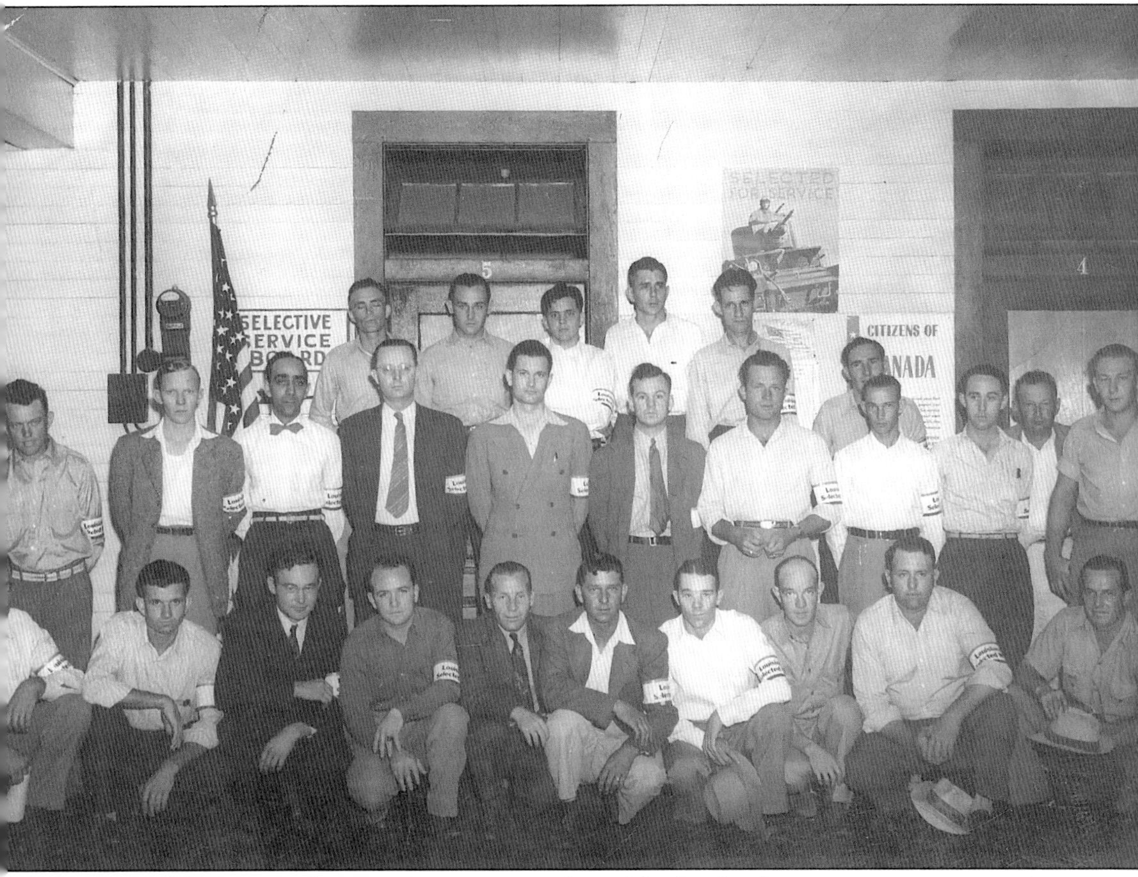

A group of draftees are shown as they prepare to leave Minden for their training assignments in 1942. This picture was taken outside the Selective Service Office in the Miller Building, which still stands on the corner of Main and Union in downtown Minden.

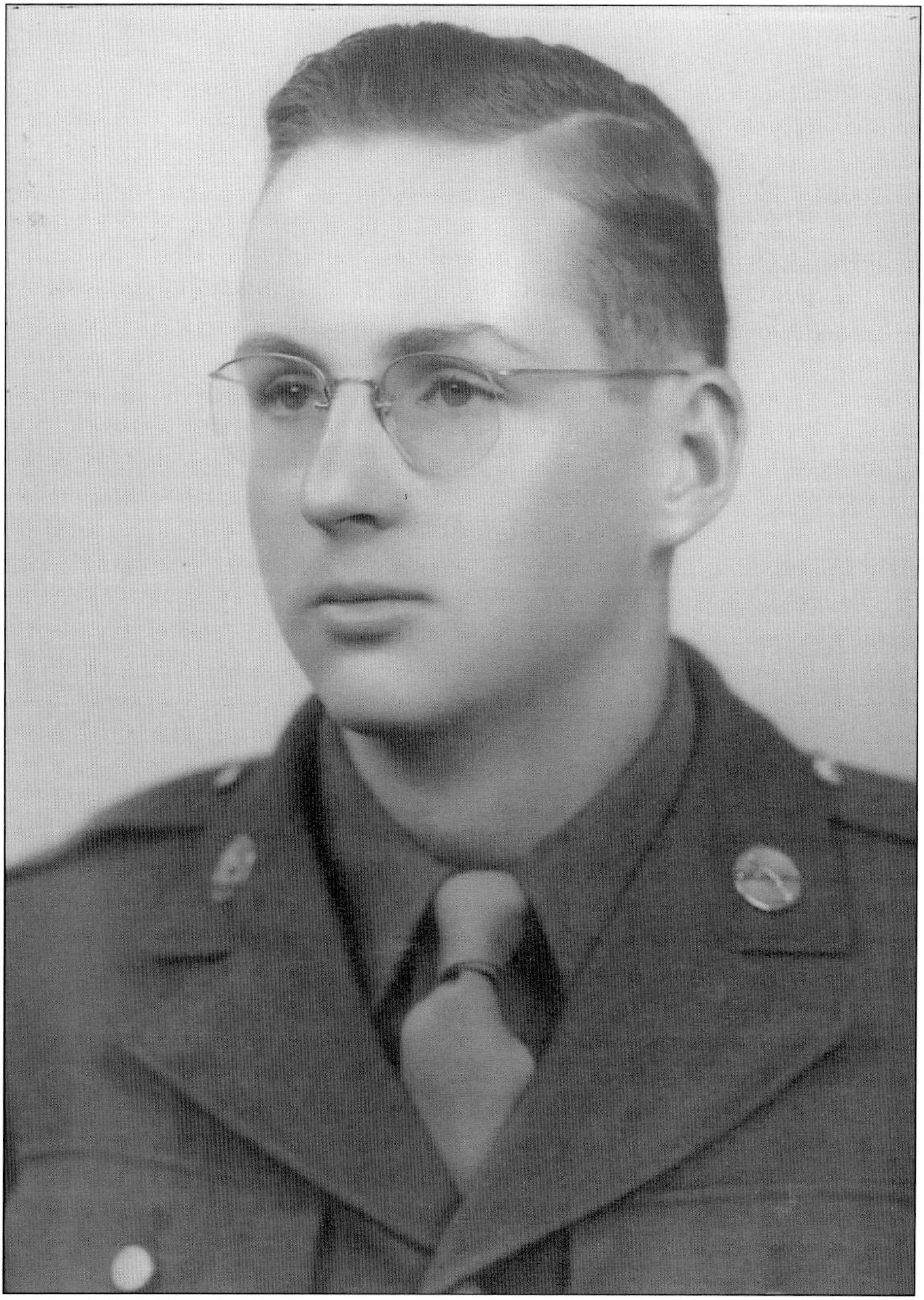

Private Aubrey E. Drake Jr. was an eager 18-year-old son of a prominent Minden family that turned down the chance to go to Officer's Training School in order to to fight for his country. He enlisted in early 1945 and was killed during the last few weeks of the war in April 1945. He was buried in Belgium and his family was unable for a time to find the location of his grave. (Courtesy of Luther and Claire Drake Moore.)

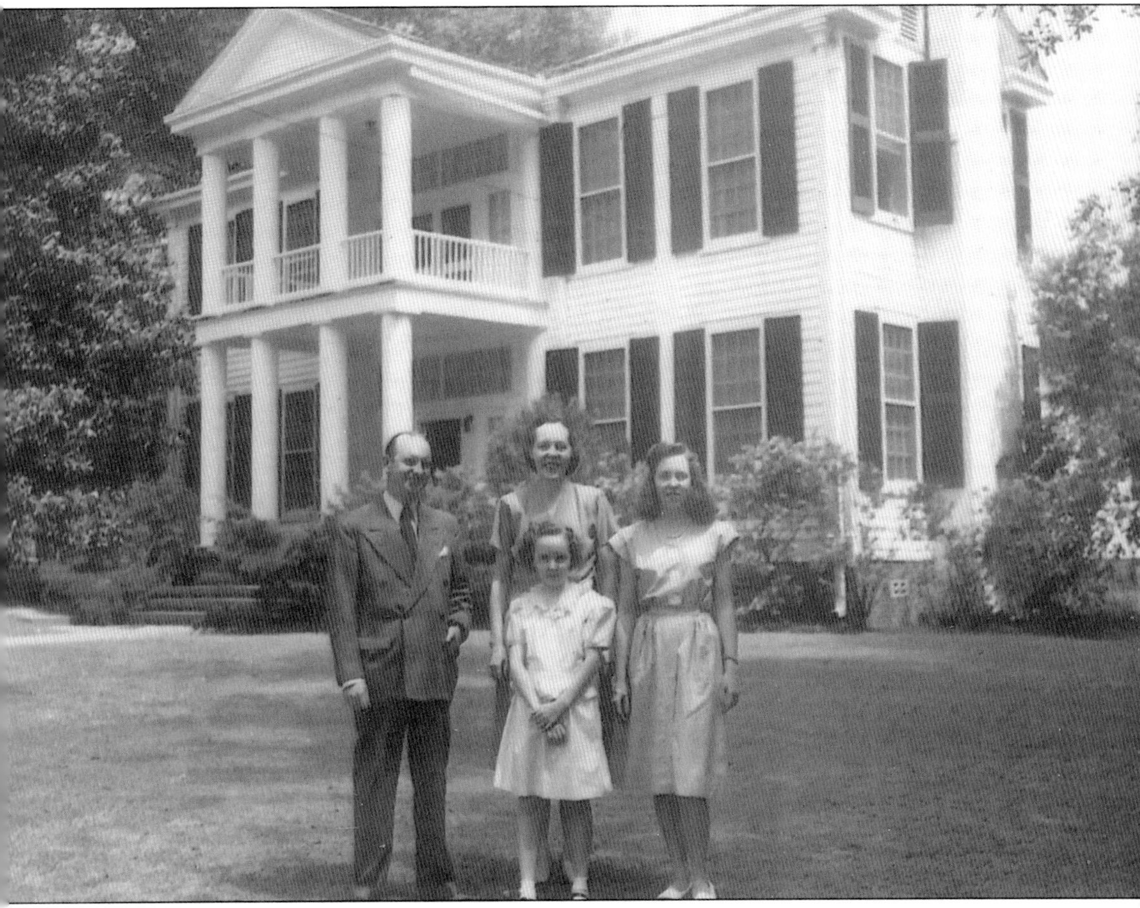

Eventually the Drake family found a Belgian family that located the grave of their son and promised to keep up the grave. This is the picture the Drake family sent to the family in Belgium. Pictured are from left to right are Aubrey Drake Sr., Fairy Drake, Sybil Drake, and, in front, Claire Drake. (Courtesy of Luther and Claire Drake Moore.)

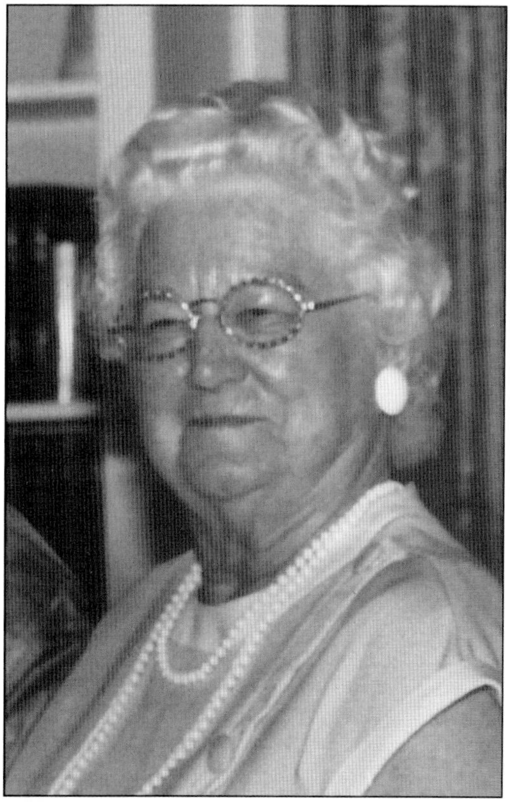

Mrs. Roy Miller Inabnett is the daughter of Mr. Joe Miller, a prominent Minden merchant from the early 1870s until his death in the early 1950s. Mrs. Inabnett has been a civic leader in Minden for years, particularly active in the First Methodist Church, historical organizations, and the Minden Garden Club that her mother, Roy Scales Miller, helped found. (Courtesy of Minden *Press-Herald*.)

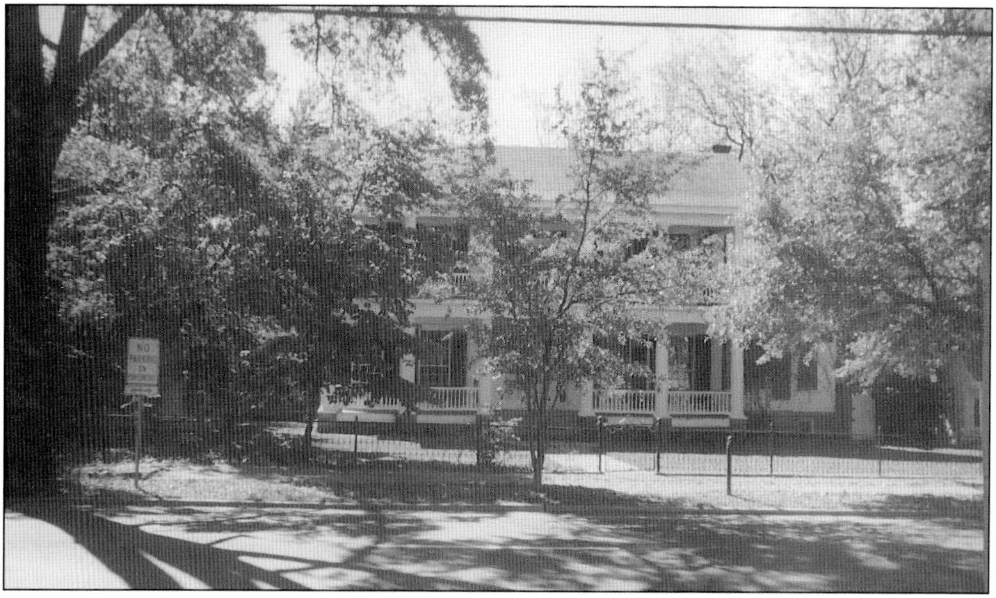

The Miller-Inabnett home is located behind the Webster Parish Courthouse in downtown Minden. Occupied today by Mrs. Roy Inabnett, the home has been in the Miller family since the 1890s. It was originally started by Lucy Brodnax Kennon in the early 1850s, but she died before the home was completed and the home was first occupied by her son-in-law, William Hardy, around 1855.

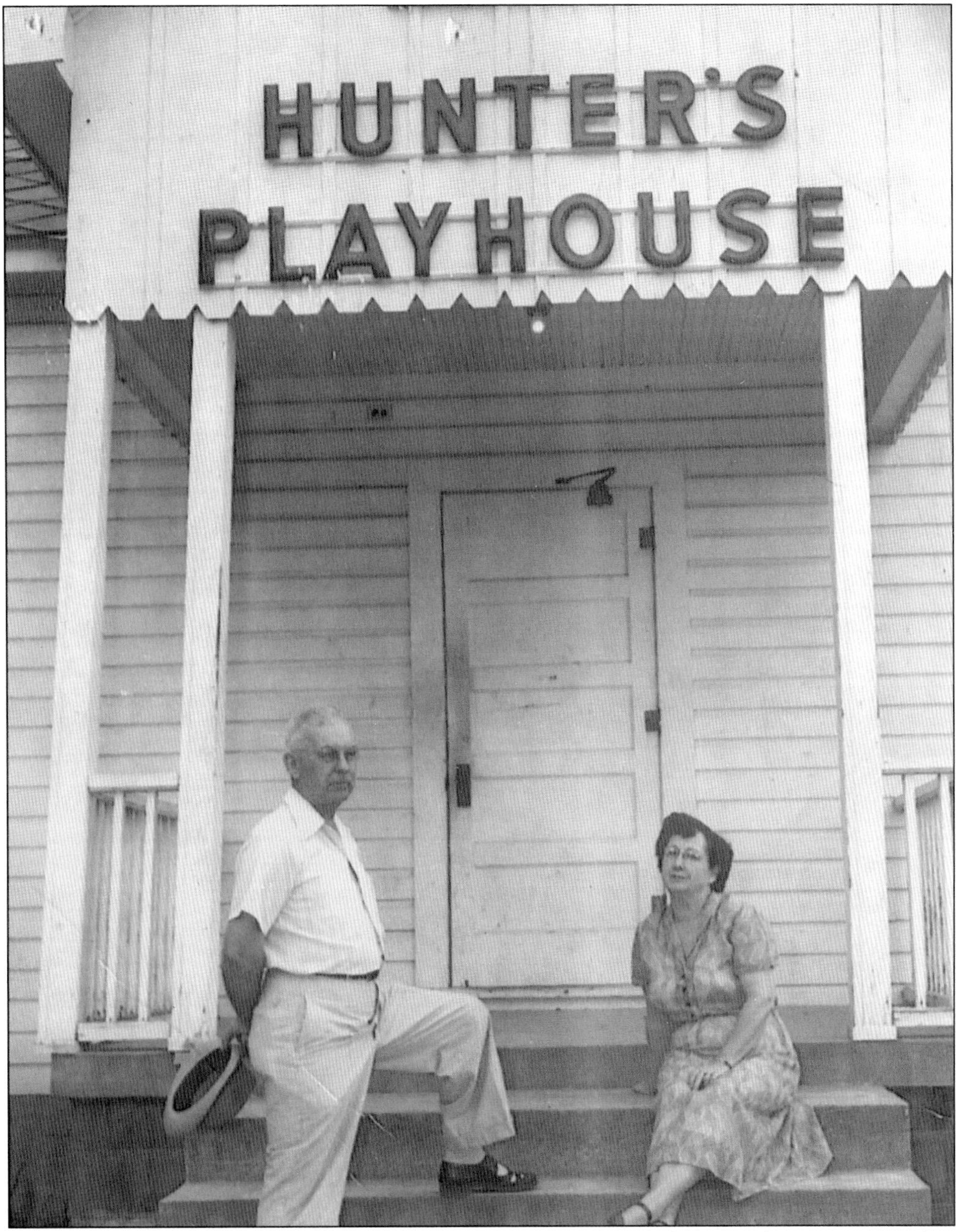

Hunter's Playhouse was the gathering spot for Minden teenagers for several generations. They could be assured of having a good time while still having adult supervision. Shown on the steps are Larry and Gladys Hunter, who operated the playhouse and a complete recreation facility for the youth of Minden before any city facilities were created. Mr. Hunter owned the local Coca-Cola Bottling company, founded by his father, and sponsored local youth and semi-professional baseball teams. Mrs. Hunter worked in all areas of the Hunter's program and also served on the Webster Parish School Board. Without the generosity of the Hunters, recreation would have been denied to Minden youth and the city recreation program might not have been created for many years. (Courtesy of Ben Hunter.)

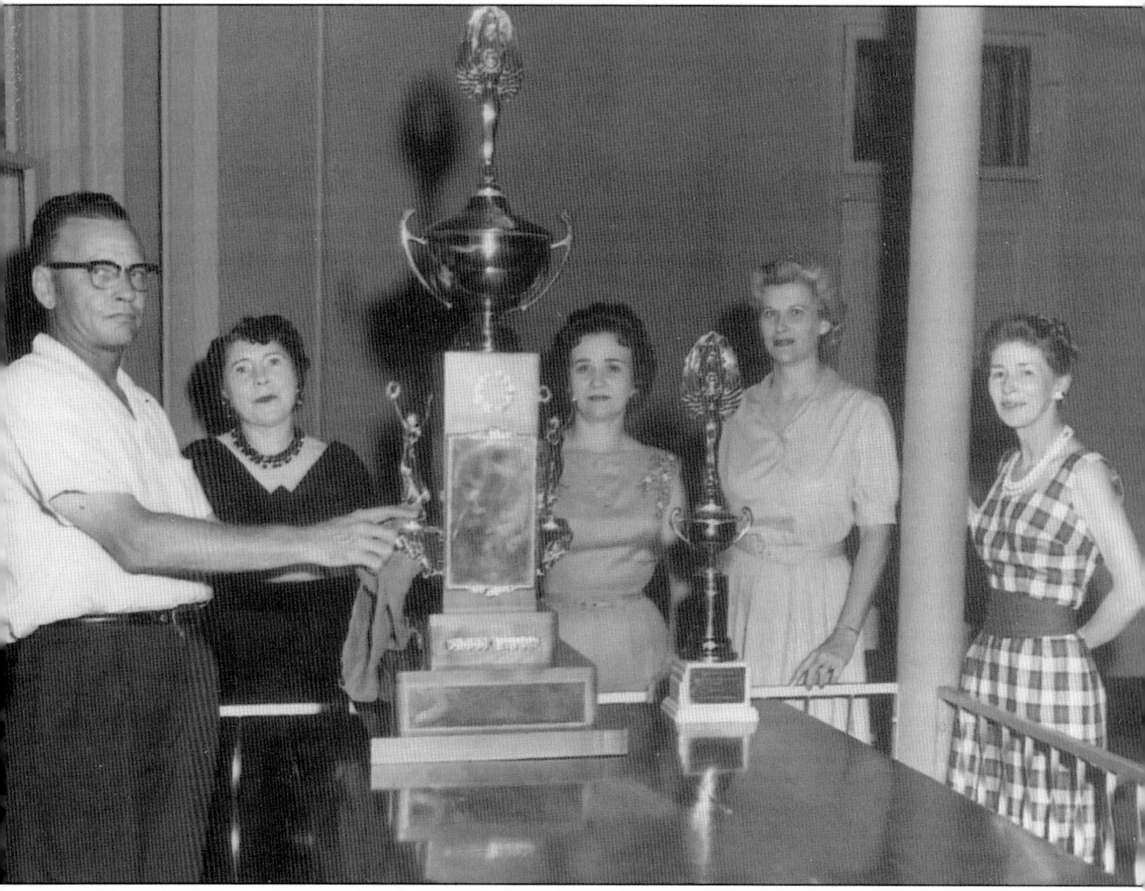

Minden receives a trophy designating it the "Cleanest City in Louisiana" for 1960. Shown accepting the trophy is Mayor Frank Norman, while in the background are civic volunteers, from left to right, Mrs. D.W. Stewart, Mrs. Carter Norman, Mrs. S.B. Samuel, and Mrs. Paul Campbell. (Courtesy of Major DePingre.)

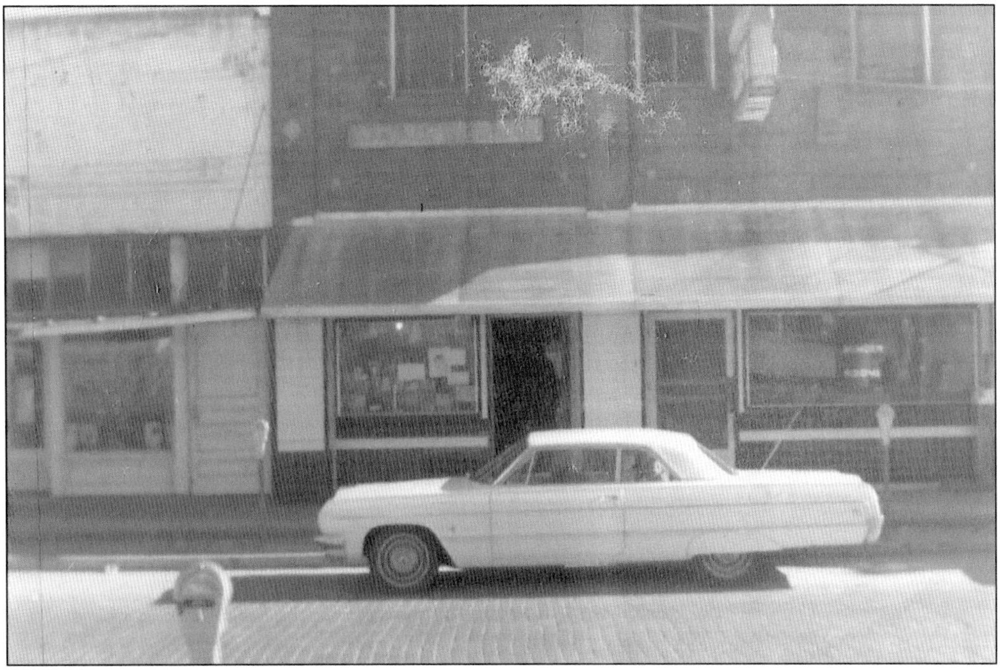

A picture of Warren's Drug Store on South Broadway was taken shortly before the row of stores were destroyed to make room for the Minden Civic Center in 1969. (Courtesy of the B.T. Warren family.)

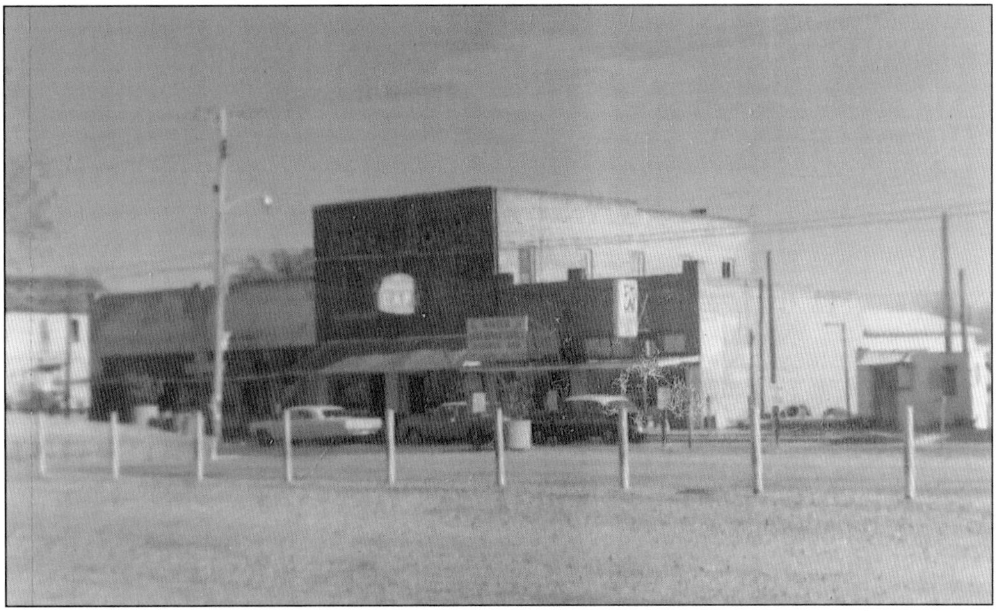

This view shows the entire group of stores that were located on "Back Street" (South Broadway) in Minden behind the 1905 Webster Parish Courthouse, which became Minden's City Hall in 1952. These stores were a strip mall of sorts for their era, and did a thriving business with all citizens of Minden, including African Americans. The little cluster of stores included a drug store, a cafe, a shoe repair shop, a general merchandise store, and a dress shop. Their destruction in 1969 marked the end of an era in Minden. (Courtesy of the B.T. Warren family.)

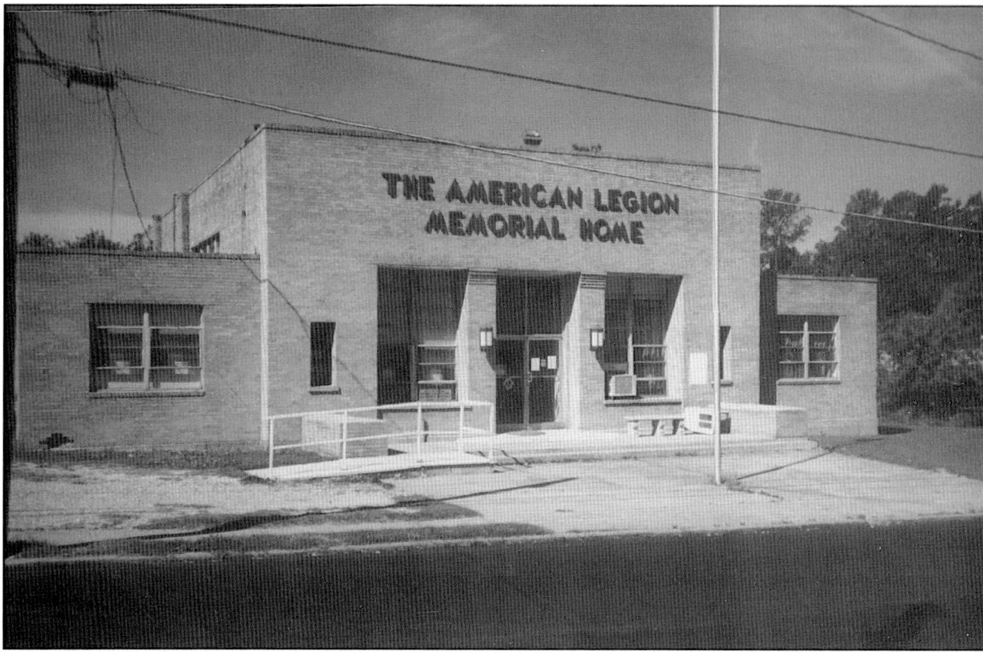

The American Legion Home was erected in 1950 on Pine Street in Minden. Prior to its construction, the Wiley-Pevy American Post met in various downtown buildings and several temporary locations. The post was founded in the early 1920s and named after the first two casualties from Minden in World War I. The building has also been used for various banquets and civic events, particularly before the construction of the Minden Civic Center. Today, in addition to the Legion Post, it is also home to the meetings of the Minden Downtown Lions Club and the Louisiana Office of Veterans' Affairs.

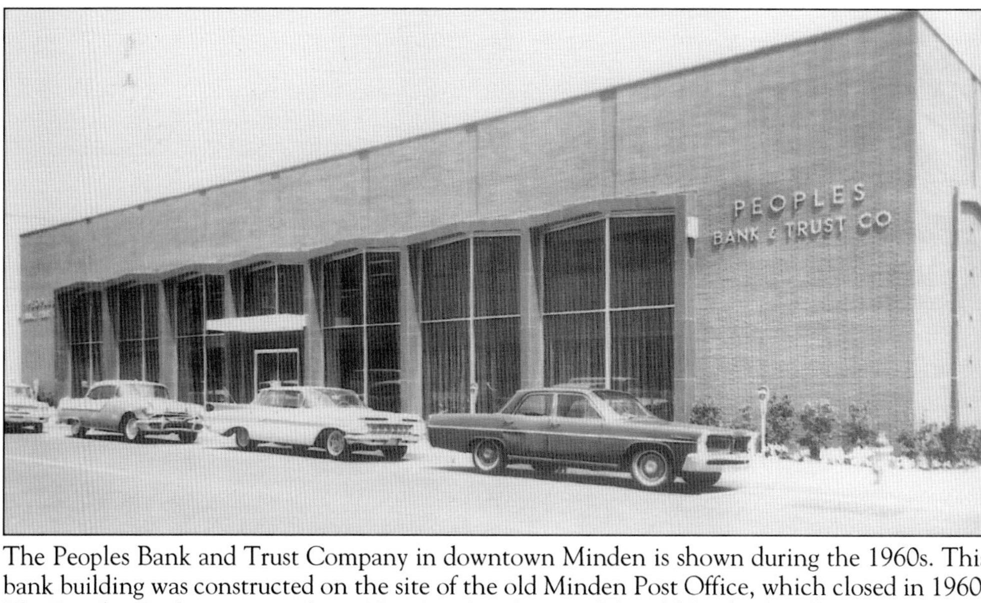

The Peoples Bank and Trust Company in downtown Minden is shown during the 1960s. This bank building was constructed on the site of the old Minden Post Office, which closed in 1960. The Peoples Bank was opened in 1931 after the closing of the old Bank of Webster. It operated in Minden for more than 60 years, before being acquired by Hibernia National Bank in the 1990s. Hibernia is still operating on this site today. (Courtesy of Major DePingre.)

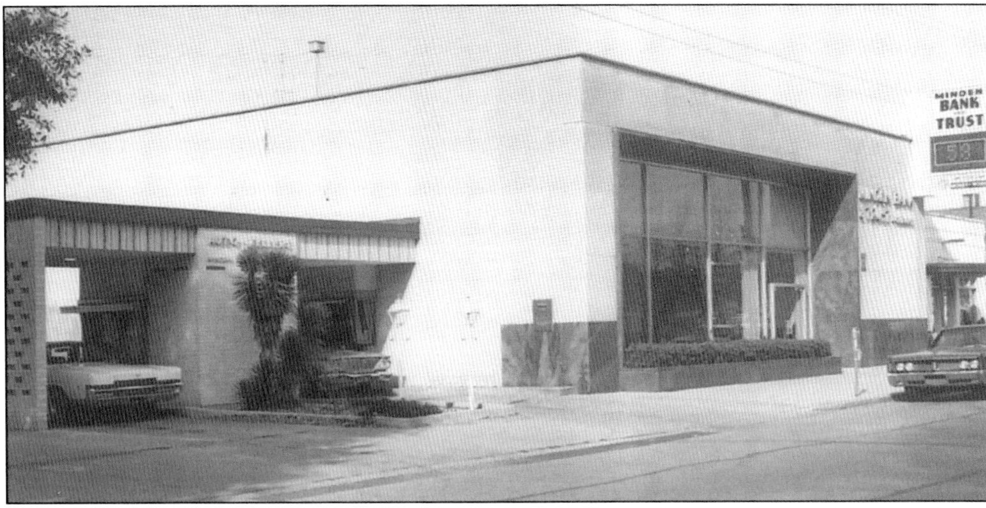

The other bank in Minden for most of the 20th century, the Minden Bank and Trust is shown in its location built in 1952. This bank opened in 1934 as the successor to the old Bank of Minden. Today the bank is located in a newer building constructed on this same site and adjacent property in the early 1980s. After the sale of Peoples Bank it was the last home-owned bank in Minden. However, effective June 2000, Minden Bank was acquired by Regions Bank & Trust, leaving Minden without a locally owned bank for the first time in more than a century. (Courtesy of Major DePingre.)

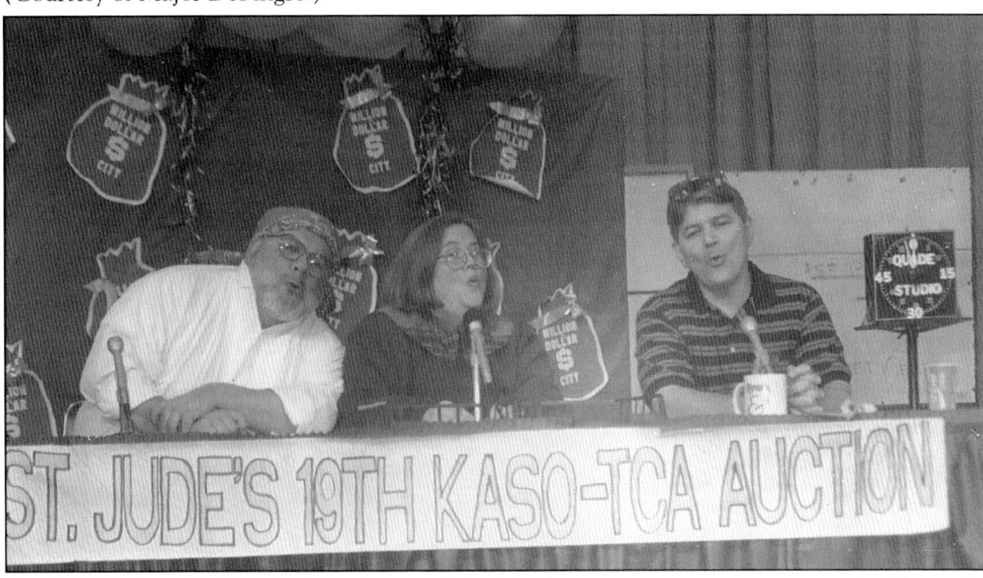

One of the most outstanding attributes of the Minden community is its generosity. Since the 1970s the local chapter of Friends of St. Jude's has conducted an auction each January. The auction originated as a radio affair sponsored by KASO radio, and later added the local cable company coverage to the auction. For several years, the residents of Minden through this auction and other fund-raising efforts have contributed more money, per capita, to St. Jude's Children Hospital than any other community in America. The entire town gets involved and participates in the fun of the event while opening their hearts and their checkbooks for the children of St. Jude's. Seen above "hamming" for the camera are Judge Harmon Drew Jr., Jean Talley Drew, and John Collins. (Courtesy of Minden *Press-Herald.*)

ACKNOWLEDGMENTS

The completion of this book would not have been possible without the efforts of my mother, Juanita Agan, who used her many contacts in all parts of Webster Parish to obtain most of the images of this book. I would like to acknowledge the help of all those who so willingly contributed the pictures used in this volume, and each donor is listed with the pictures they loaned. I would also like to thank the people of Webster Parish who created the interesting history of the parish, and encourage them to look on this book as only the tip of the iceberg, as there are many more photographs that can help complete our community's story.